Building finishes, fittings and domestic services

General editor: Colin Bassett, BSc, FCIOB, FFB

Publisher's note
The contents of this book were originally published in the author's larger four-volume work entitled *Construction Technology* (1973, 1974, 1976 and 1977), (second edition of all four volumes 1987). These chapters have been reproduced in a single volume reference book to meet the well-established need for such a volume.

Note regarding Building Regulations
The reader's attention is drawn to the fact that the Building Regulations, British Standards, Codes of Practice and similar documents are constantly under review and are therefore often revised or amended. It is therefore important that all the Building Regulations, British Standards, Codes of Practice and similar documents quoted in this book are checked by the reader to ensure that the current regulations or recommendations are known and used in practice. Changes in regulations and recommendations often change specific data but the basic principles embodied within them often remain unchanged.

Building finishes, fittings and domestic services

Second edition

R. Chudley M.C.I.O.B.
Chartered Builder

Illustrated by the author

Longman
Scientific &
Technical

Longman Scientific & Technical,
Longman Group UK Limited,
Longman House, Burnt Mill, Harlow,
Essex CM20 2JE, England
and Associated Companies throughout the world.

© Construction Press 1982
This edition © Longman Group UK Limited 1988

First published 1982 by Construction Press
Reprinted 1985
Second edition 1988
Second impression 1990
Third impression 1993

British Library Cataloguing in Publication Data
Chudley, R. (Roy)
    Building finishes, fittings and domestic
    services. — 2nd ed.
    1. Buildings. Construction
    I. Title
    690

ISBN 0-582-01975-3

Printed in Malaysia by TCP

Contents

Preface to the first edition

The compilation of this book has been carried out with the main objective of providing a reference book for the practical and practising builder. It may also be a useful reference work for building students of all levels engaged in assignment and project work. The contents have been arranged to cover basic non-structural elements and finishes of buildings above ground level together with simple domestic services installations. Complex services are not included since they require special study and therefore the reader is advised to consult reference books devoted to such services.

The contents of this book are based on typical construction technology concepts. Technology can be defined as the science of mechanical and industrial arts, as contrasted with fine arts. Similarly science can be defined as an ordered arrangement of facts under classes of headings, theoretical knowledge as distinguished from practical knowledge and knowledge of principles and rules. The information contained within this book is therefore based on the principles and techniques of construction and not on actual case studies of works in progress, however, if experience and practical knowledge are added to the technological concepts the result should provide buildings and construction techniques of a high and therefore acceptable standard.

The reader's attention is particularly drawm to the note at the beginning of the text regarding current Building Regulations.

R. Chudley
Guildford 1982

Acknowledgements

We are grateful to the following for permission to reproduce copyright material:

British Standards Institution for reference to British Standards Codes of Practice; Building Research Station for extracts from *Building Research Station Digests*; Her Majesty's Stationery Office for extracts from Acts, Regulations and Statutory Instruments.

Part I
Claddings

1
Simple framed building claddings

Claddings to buildings can be considered under two classifications:
1. Claddings fixed to a structural backing.
2. Claddings to framed structures.

Claddings fixed to a structural backing

Materials used in this form of cladding are generally considered to be small unit claddings and are applied for one of two reasons. If the structural wall is unable to provide an adequate barrier to the elements a covering of small unit claddings will generally raise the wall's resistance to an acceptable level. Alternatively small unit claddings can be used solely as a decorative feature, possibly to break up the monotony of a large plain area composed of a single material.

The materials used are tiles, slates, shingles, timber boarding, plastic boards and stone facings. The general method of fixing these small units is to secure them to timber battens fixed to the structure backing. Stone and similar facings, however, are usually secured by special mechanical fixings as described later when considering claddings to framed structures.

TILE HANGING
The tiles used in tile hanging can be ordinary plain roofing tiles or alternatively a tile of the same dimensions but having a patterned bottom edge solely for a decorative appearance. The tiles are hung and fixed to tiling battens although nibless tiles fixed directly to the backing wall are

sometimes used (see Fig. I.1). The battens should be impregnated to prevent fungi and insect attack so that their anticipated life is comparable to that of the tiles. Each tile should be twice nailed to its support batten with corrosion resistant nails of adequate length.

The general principles of tile hanging are similar to those of double lap roof tiling and the gauge is calculated in the same manner. The minimum lap recommended is 40 mm which would give a gauge of 112.5 mm using a standard 265 long tile.

A gauge dimension of 112.5 m is impracticable and therefore a gauge of 110 m would be usual. Typical details of top edge finishes, bottom edge finishes, corners and finishes at windows are shown in Figs. I.1 and I.2. It should be noted that if the structural backing is of timber framing a layer of impervious felt should be placed over the framing immediately underneath the battens to prevent any moisture which is blown in between the tiles from having adverse effects upon the structure. In this situation building paper is not considered to be a suitable substitute. The application of slates as a small unit hung cladding follows the principles outlined above for tile hanging.

TIMBER CLADDINGS

Timber claddings are usually in the form of moulded or shaped boards fixed to battens as either a horizontal or vertical cladding; typical examples are shown in Fig. I.3. Timber claddings will require regular maintenance to preserve their resistance to the elements. Softwoods are generally painted and will need repainting at intervals of three to five years according to the exposure. Hardwoods are sometimes treated with a preservative and left to bleach naturally; the preservative treatment needs to be carried out at two- to five-year intervals. Western red cedar is a very popular wood for timber cladding since it has a natural immunity to insect and fungi attack under normal conditions. It also has a pleasing natural red/brown colour which can be maintained if the timber is coated with a clear sealer such as polyurethane; however, it will bleach to a grey/white colour if exposed to the atmosphere. Plastic boards are a substitute for timber and are fixed in a similar manner.

Claddings to frame structures

The methods available to clad a frame structure are extensive and include panels of masonry constructed between the columns and beams, light infill panels of metal or timber, precast concrete panels and curtain walling which completely encloses the structure. A second-year course in construction technology confines itself

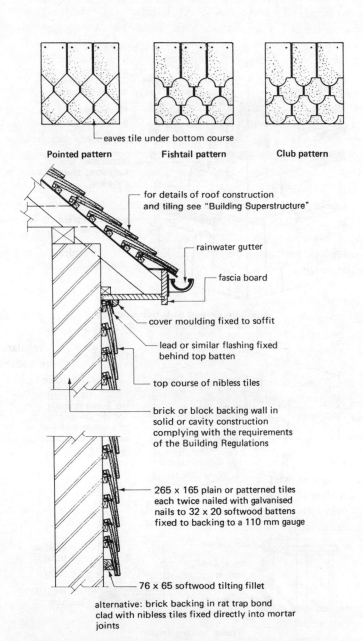

eaves tile under bottom course

Pointed pattern   **Fishtail pattern**   **Club pattern**

for details of roof construction
and tiling see "Building Superstructure"

rainwater gutter

fascia board

cover moulding fixed to soffit

lead or similar flashing fixed
behind top batten

top course of nibless tiles

brick or block backing wall in
solid or cavity construction
complying with the requirements
of the Building Regulations

265 x 165 plain or patterned tiles
each twice nailed with galvanised
nails to 32 x 20 softwood battens
fixed to backing to a 110 mm gauge

76 x 65 softwood tilting fillet

alternative: brick backing in rat trap bond
clad with nibless tiles fixed directly into mortar
joints

Fig. I.1 Vertical tile hanging — typical details 1

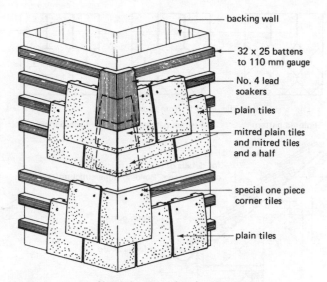

backing wall

32 x 25 battens
to 110 mm gauge

No. 4 lead
soakers

plain tiles

mitred plain tiles
and mitred tiles
and a half

special one piece
corner tiles

plain tiles

Alternative external angle treatments
(internal angles treatments similar)

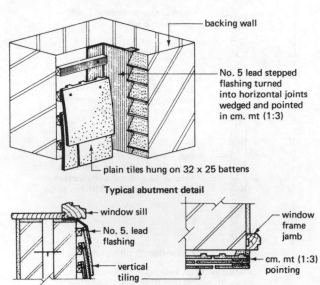

backing wall

No. 5 lead stepped
flashing turned
into horizontal joints
wedged and pointed
in cm. mt (1:3)

plain tiles hung on 32 x 25 battens

Typical abutment detail

window sill

No. 5. lead
flashing

vertical
tiling

window
frame
jamb

cm. mt (1:3)
pointing

Typical opening details

Fig. I.2 Vertical tile hanging — typical details 2

6

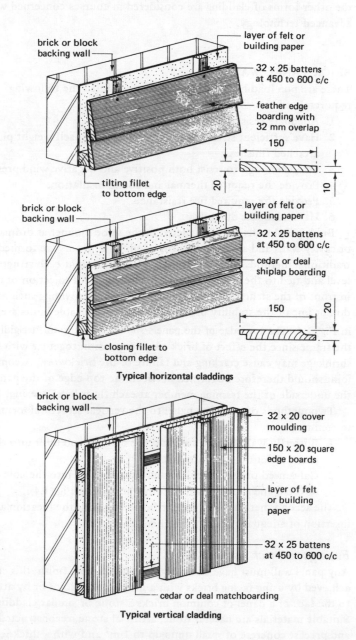

brick or block backing wall

layer of felt or building paper

32 x 25 battens at 450 to 600 c/c

feather edge boarding with 32 mm overlap

150

20

10

tilting fillet to bottom edge

brick or block backing wall

layer of felt or building paper

32 x 25 battens at 450 to 600 c/c

cedar or deal shiplap boarding

150

20

closing fillet to bottom edge

Typical horizontal claddings

brick or block backing wall

32 x 20 cover moulding

150 x 20 square edge boards

layer of felt or building paper

32 x 25 battens at 450 to 600 c/c

cedar or deal matchboarding

Typical vertical cladding

Fig. I.3   Timber wall claddings

to the study of panel walls and the facings which can be attached to them, the other forms of cladding are considered in courses concerned with advanced technology.

BRICK PANEL WALLS

These are non-load bearing walls which must fulfil the following requirements:

1. Adequate resistance to the elements.
2. Have sufficient strength to support their own self weight plus any attached finishes.
3. Strong enough to resist both positive and negative wind pressures.
4. Provide the required thermal and sound insulation.
5. Provide the required fire resistance.
6. Have adequate durability.

Brick panel walls are constructed in the same manner as ordinary solid or cavity walls and any openings for windows or doors are formed by traditional methods. The panels must be supported at each structural floor level and tied to the structure at the vertical edges. Projection of the panel in front of the structural members is permissible providing such overhangs do not impair the stability of the panel wall; acceptable limits are shown in Fig. I.4. The top edge of the panels should not be pinned rigidly to the frame since the effect of brick panel expansion together with frame shrinkage may cause cracking and failure of the brickwork. A compression joint should therefore be formed between the top edge of the panel and the underside of the framing member at each floor level (see Fig. I.4).

Two methods of tying the panel to the vertical structural members are in common use:

1. Butterfly wall tiles are cast into the column and built into the brick joints at four-course intervals.
2. Galvanised pressed steel dovetail slots are cast into the column and dovetail anchors are used to form the tie (see Fig. I.4).

The second method gives greater flexibility with the location and insertion of adequate ties but is higher in cost.

Facings to brick panel walls

Any panel wall must have an acceptable and durable finish; this can be achieved by using facing bricks with a neat pointed joint or by attaching to the face of a panel of common bricks a stone or similar cladding. Suitable materials are natural stone, artificial stone, reconstructed stone and precast concrete of small units up to 1 m^2 and with a thickness related to the density of the material. Dense materials such as slate and marble

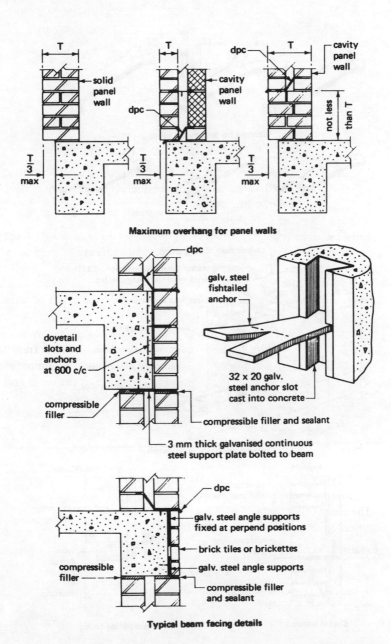

Maximum overhang for panel walls

dpc

galv. steel
fishtailed
anchor

dovetail
slots and
anchors
at 600 c/c

32 x 20 galv.
steel anchor slot
cast into concrete

compressible
filler

compressible filler and sealant

3 mm thick galvanised continuous
steel support plate bolted to beam

dpc

galv. steel angle supports
fixed at perpend positions

brick tiles or brickettes

compressible
filler

galv. steel angle supports

compressible filler
and sealant

Typical beam facing details

Fig. I.4   Brick panel walls

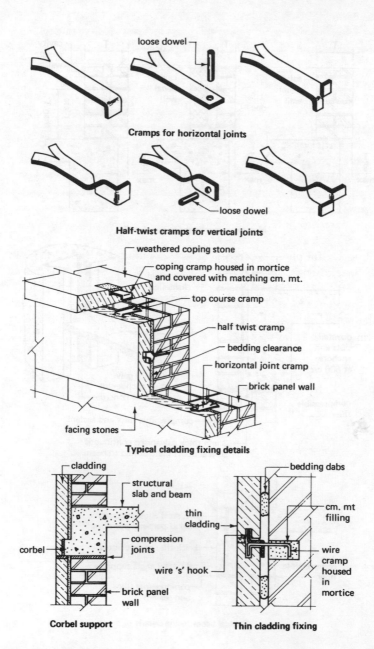

Cramps for horizontal joints

loose dowel

Half-twist cramps for vertical joints

loose dowel

weathered coping stone

coping cramp housed in mortice and covered with matching cm. mt.

top course cramp

half twist cramp

bedding clearance

horizontal joint cramp

brick panel wall

facing stones

Typical cladding fixing details

cladding

structural slab and beam

bedding dabs

thin cladding

cm. mt filling

corbel

compression joints

wire 's' hook

wire cramp housed in mortice

brick panel wall

Corbel support

Thin cladding fixing

Fig. I.5 Cladding fixings

10

need only be 40 mm thick, whereas the softer stones such as sandstone and limestone should be at least 75 mm thick.

Two major considerations must be taken into account when deciding on the method to be used to fix the facings to the brick backing:

1. Transferring the load to the structure.
2. Tying back the facing units.

The load of the facings can be transferred by using bonder stones or support corbels at each floor level, which should have a compression joint incorporated in the detail for the same reasons given above when considering brick panels (see Fig. I.5).

The tying back of the facings is carried out by various metal fixing devices called cramps which should be of a non-ferrous metal such as gunmetal, copper, phosphor bronze or stainless steel. To avoid the problem of corrosion caused by galvanic action between dissimilar metals a mixture of fixing materials should not be used. Typical examples of fixings and cramps for thick and thin facings are shown in Fig. I.5.

To provide for plumbing and alignment a bedding space of 12—15 mm should be left between the face of the brick panel and the back of the facing. Dense facings such as marble are usually bedded on a series of cement mortar dabs, whereas the more porous facings are usually placed against a solid bed which ensures that any saturation which occurs will be uniform over the entire face.

2
Claddings to framed structures

Claddings are a form of masking or infilling a structural frame and can be considered under the following headings:

1. Panel walls with or without attached facings — see Chapter 1.
2. Concrete and similar cladding panels.
3. Light infill panels.
4. Curtain walling which can be defined as a sheath cladding which encloses the entire structure and is usually studied in the second year of an advanced course of technology.

All forms of cladding must fulfil the following functions:

1. Be self supporting between the framing members.
2. Provide the necessary resistance to rain penetration.
3. Be capable of resisting both positive and negative wind pressures.
4. Provide the necessary resistance to wind penetration.
5. Give the required degree of thermal insulation.
6. Provide the required degree of sound insulation to suit the building type.
7. Give the required degree of fire resistance.
8. Provide sufficient openings for the admittance of natural daylight and ventilation.
9. Be constructed to a suitable size.

12

CONCRETE CLADDING PANELS

These are usually made of precast concrete with a textured face in a storey height or undersill panel format. The storey height panel is designed to span vertically from beam to beam and if constucted to a narrow module will give the illusion of a tall building. Undersill panels span horizontally from column to column and are used where a high wall/window ratio is required. Combinations of both formats are also possible.

Concrete cladding panels should be constructed of a dense concrete mix and suitably reinforced with bar reinforcement or steel welded fabric. The reinforcement should provide the necessary tensile resistance to the stresses induced in the final position and for the stresses set up during transportation and hoisting into position. Lifting lugs, positions or holes should be incorporated into the design to ensure that the panels are hoisted in the correct manner so that unwanted stresses are not induced. The usual specification for cover of concrete over reinforcement is 25 mm minimum. If thin panels are being used the use of galvanised or stainless steel reinforcement should be considered to reduce the risk of corrosion.

When designing or selecting a panel the following must be taken into account:

1. Column or beam spacing.
2. Lifting capacities of plant available.
3. Jointing method.
4. Exposure conditions.
5. Any special planning requirements as to finish or texture.

The greatest problem facing the designer and installer of concrete panels is one of jointing to allow for structural and thermal movements and at the same time provide an adequate long term joint — see Chapters 4 and 5. Typical examples of storey height and undersill panels are shown in Figs. I.6 and I.7.

Where a stone facing is required to a framed structure, possibly to comply with planning requirements, it may be advantageous to use a composite panel. These panels have the strength and reliability of precast concrete panel design and manufacture but the appearance of traditional stonework. This is achieved by casting a concrete backing to a suitably keyed natural or reconstructed stone facing and fixed to the frame by traditional masonry fixing cramps or by conventional fixings — see Fig. I.8.

Thermal insulation can be achieved when using precast concrete panels by creating a cavity as shown in Figs. I.6 and I.7. Alternatively the insulating material can be incorporated in a sandwich cladding panel as shown in Fig. I.15.

13

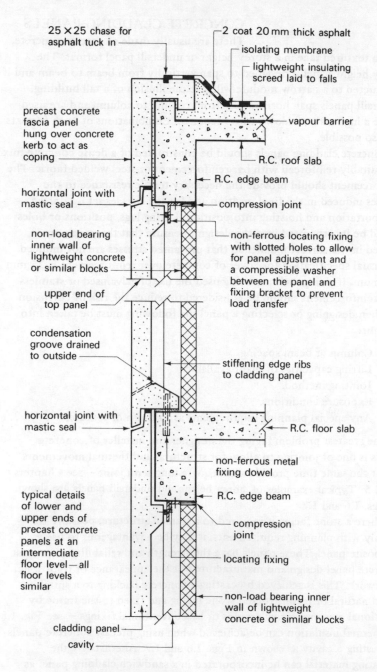

25 × 25 chase for asphalt tuck in

2 coat 20 mm thick asphalt

isolating membrane

lightweight insulating screed laid to falls

precast concrete fascia panel hung over concrete kerb to act as coping

vapour barrier

R.C. roof slab

R.C. edge beam

horizontal joint with mastic seal

compression joint

non-load bearing inner wall of lightweight concrete or similar blocks

non-ferrous locating fixing with slotted holes to allow for panel adjustment and a compressible washer between the panel and fixing bracket to prevent load transfer

upper end of top panel

condensation groove drained to outside

stiffening edge ribs to cladding panel

horizontal joint with mastic seal

R.C. floor slab

non-ferrous metal fixing dowel

typical details of lower and upper ends of precast concrete panels at an intermediate floor level—all floor levels similar

R.C. edge beam

compression joint

locating fixing

non-load bearing inner wall of lightweight concrete or similar blocks

cladding panel

cavity

Fig. I.6 Typical storey height concrete cladding panel

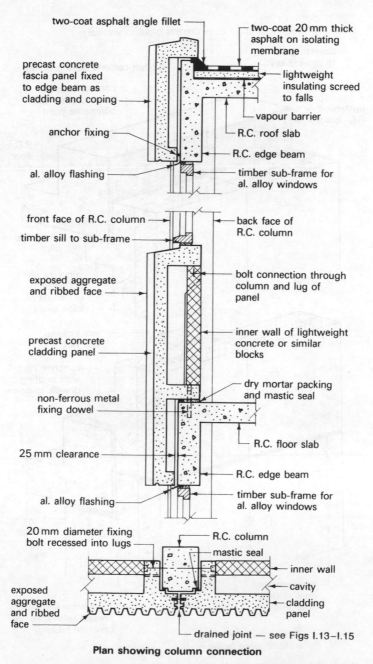

Fig. I.7 Typical undersill concrete cladding panel

two-coat asphalt angle fillet

two-coat 20 mm thick asphalt on isolating membrane

precast concrete fascia panel fixed to edge beam as cladding and coping

lightweight insulating screed to falls

vapour barrier

R.C. roof slab

anchor fixing

R.C. edge beam

al. alloy flashing

timber sub-frame for al. alloy windows

front face of R.C. column

back face of R.C. column

timber sill to sub-frame

exposed aggregate and ribbed face

bolt connection through column and lug of panel

inner wall of lightweight concrete or similar blocks

precast concrete cladding panel

dry mortar packing and mastic seal

non-ferrous metal fixing dowel

R.C. floor slab

25 mm clearance

R.C. edge beam

al. alloy flashing

timber sub-frame for al. alloy windows

20 mm diameter fixing bolt recessed into lugs

R.C. column

mastic seal

inner wall

exposed aggregate and ribbed face

cavity

cladding panel

drained joint — see Figs I.13—I.15

Plan showing column connection

15

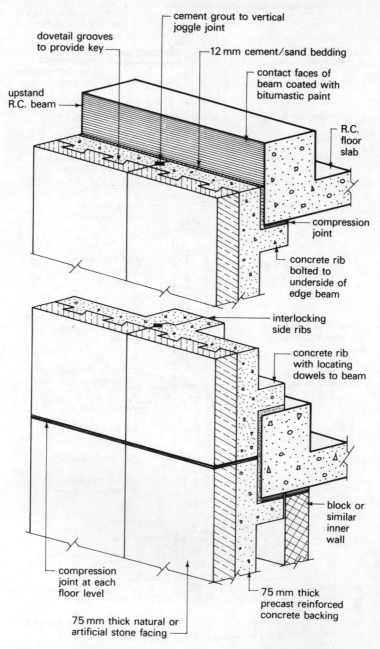

Fig. I.8 Typical storey height composite panel

dovetail grooves to provide key

cement grout to vertical joggle joint

upstand R.C. beam

12 mm cement/sand bedding

contact faces of beam coated with bitumastic paint

R.C. floor slab

compression joint

concrete rib bolted to underside of edge beam

interlocking side ribs

concrete rib with locating dowels to beam

block or similar inner wall

compression joint at each floor level

75 mm thick natural or artificial stone facing

75 mm thick precast reinforced concrete backing

Concrete cladding panels can be large and consequently heavy. To reduce the weight they are often designed to be relatively thin (50 to 75 mm) across the centre portion and stiffened around the edges with suitably reinforced ribs which usually occur on the back face but can be positioned on the front face as a feature which can also limit the amount of water which can enter the joint.

Another form of cladding material which is beginning to gain popularity and acceptance is glass fibre reinforced plastics (GRP) which consists of glass fibre reinforcement impregnated with resin, incorporating fillers, pigments and a suitable catalyst as a hardener. The resultant panels are lightweight, durable, non-corrosive, have good weather resistance, can be moulded to almost any profile and have good aesthetic properties. Students seeking further information are recommended to study the Building Research Establishment Digest 161.

3
Infill panels

The functions of an infill panel are as listed previously for cladding panels in general. Infill panels are lightweight and usually glazed to give good internal natural daylighting conditions. The panel layout can be so arranged to expose some or all of the structural members creating various optical impressions. For example, if horizontal panels are used, leaving only the beams exposed, an illusion of extra length and/or reduced height can be created — see Fig. I.9.

A wide variety of materials or combinations of materials can be employed such as timber, steel, aluminium and plastic. Single and double glazing techniques can be used to achieve the desired sound or thermal insulation. The glazing module should be such that a reasonable thickness of glass can be specified.

The design of the 'solid' panel is of great importance since this panel must provide the necessary resistance to fire, heat loss, sound penetration and interstitial condensation. Most of these panels are of composite or sandwich construction as shown in Figs. I.10 and I.11.

The jointing problem with infill panels occurs mainly at its junction with the structural frame and allowance for moisture or thermal movement is usually achieved by using a suitable mastic or sealant — see Chapter 5.

Most infill panels are supplied as a manufacturer's system, since purpose-made panels can be uneconomic, but whichever method is chosen the design aims remain constant; that is, to provide a panel which fulfils all the required functions and has a low long term maintenance factor. It should be noted that many of the essentially curtain walling systems are

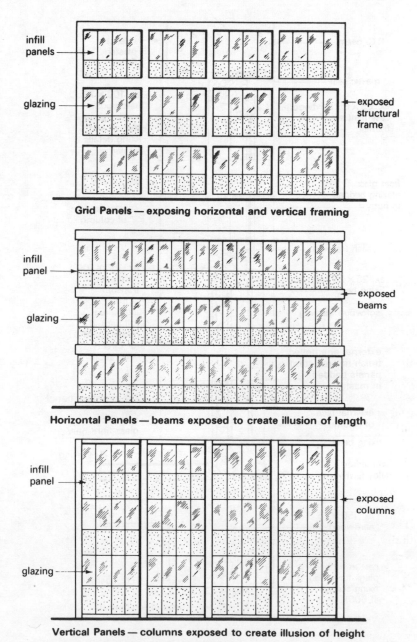

Fig. I.9 Typical infill panel arrangements

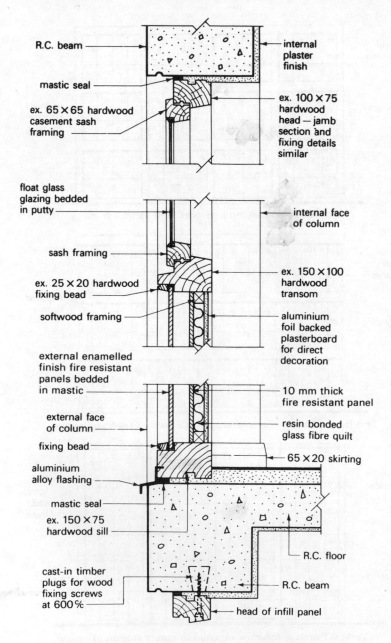

R.C. beam

internal plaster finish

mastic seal

ex. 65 × 65 hardwood casement sash framing

ex. 100 × 75 hardwood head — jamb section and fixing details similar

float glass glazing bedded in putty

internal face of column

sash framing

ex. 25 × 20 hardwood fixing bead

ex. 150 × 100 hardwood transom

softwood framing

aluminium foil backed plasterboard for direct decoration

external enamelled finish fire resistant panels bedded in mastic

10 mm thick fire resistant panel

external face of column

resin bonded glass fibre quilt

fixing bead

65 × 20 skirting

aluminium alloy flashing

mastic seal

ex. 150 × 75 hardwood sill

R.C. floor

cast-in timber plugs for wood fixing screws at 600 %

R.C. beam

head of infill panel

Fig. I.10 Typical timber infill panel details

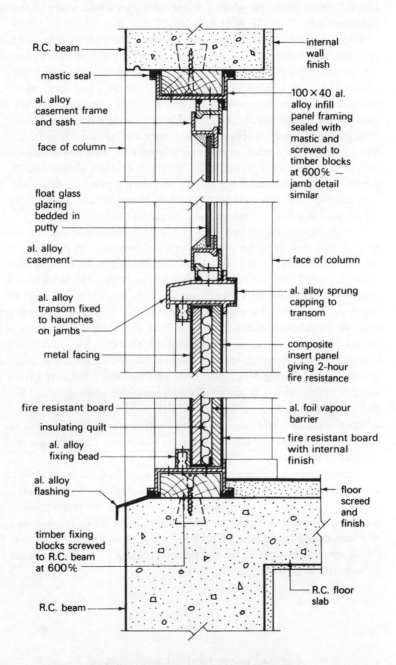

R.C. beam

mastic seal

al. alloy casement frame and sash

face of column →

float glass glazing bedded in putty

al. alloy casement

al. alloy transom fixed to haunches on jambs

metal facing

fire resistant board

insulating quilt

al. alloy fixing bead

al. alloy flashing

timber fixing blocks screwed to R.C. beam at 600%

R.C. beam

internal wall finish

100 × 40 al. alloy infill panel framing sealed with mastic and screwed to timber blocks at 600% — jamb detail similar

face of column

al. alloy sprung capping to transom

composite insert panel giving 2-hour fire resistance

al. foil vapour barrier

fire resistant board with internal finish

floor screed and finish

R.C. floor slab

Fig. I.11 Typical metal infill panel details

21

adaptable as infill panels which gives the designer a wide range of systems from which to select the most suitable.

One of the maintenance problems encountered with infill panels and probably to a lesser extent with the concrete claddings is the cleaning of the facade and in particular the glazing. All buildings collect dirt, the effects of which can vary with the material: concrete and masonry tend to accept dirt and weather naturally, whereas impervious materials such as glass do not accept dirt and can corrode or become less efficient.

If glass is allowed to become coated with dirt its visual appearance is less acceptable, its optical performance lessens since clarity of vision is reduced and the useful penetration of natural daylight diminishes. The number of times that cleaning will be necessary depends largely upon the area, ranging from three-monthly intervals in non-industrial areas to six-weekly intervals in areas with a high pollution factor.

Access for cleaning glazed areas can be external or internal. Windows at ground level present no access problems and present only the question of choice of method such as hand cloths or telescopic poles with squeegee heads. Low and medium rise structures can be reached by ladders or a mobile scaffold tower and usually present very few problems. High rise structures need careful consideration. External access to windows is gained by using a cradle suspended from roof level; this can be in the form of a temporary system consisting of counterweighted cantilevered beams from which the cradle is suspended. Permanent systems, which are incorporated as part of the building design, are more efficient and consist of a track on which a mobile trolley is mounted and from which davit arms can be projected beyond the roof edge to support the cradle. A single track fixed in front of the roof edge could also be considered; these are simple and reasonably efficient but the rail is always visible and can therefore mar the building's appearance.

Internal access for cleaning the external glass face can be achieved by using windows such as reversible sashes, horizontal and vertical sliding sashes, but the designer is restricted in his choice to the reach possible by the average person. It cannot be over emphasised that such windows can be a very dangerous hazard unless carefully designed so that all parts of the glazed area can be reached by the person cleaning the windows whilst he remains standing firmly on the floor.

4
Jointing

When incorporating precast concrete cladding panels in a framed structure the problem of making the joints waterproof is of paramount importance. Joints should be designed so that they fulfil the following requirements:

1. Exclude wind, rain and snow.
2. Allow for structural, thermal and moisture movement.
3. Good durability.
4. Easily maintained.
5. Maintain the thermal and sound insulation properties of the surrounding cladding.
6. Easily made or assembled.

Experience has shown that due to bad design, poor workmanship or lack of understanding of the function of a joint has led to water penetration through the joints between cladding panels. To overcome this problem it is essential that both the designer and the site operative fully appreciate the design principles and the need for accurate installation. Suitable joints can be classified under two headings:

1. Filled joints.
2. Drained joints.

Filled joints are generally satisfactory if the cladding panel module is small since if incorporated in large module panels filled joints can crack and allow water to penetrate. This failure is due either to the filling materials being incapable of accommodating movement or a breakdown of adhesion between the filling material and the panel. Research has shown that if the above failures are possible the most effective alternative is the drained joint.

Filled joints: these joints are not easy to construct and rely mainly upon mortars, sealants, mastics or preformed gaskets to provide the barrier against the infiltration of wind and rain. They are limited in their performance by the amount that the sealing material(s) can accommodate movement and to a certain extent their weathering properties such as their resistance to ultra-violet rays. The disadvantages of filled joints can be enumerated thus:

1. Difficulty in making and placing the joints accurately particularly with combinations of materials.
2. Providing for structural, thermal and moisture movement.
3. Only suitable for small module claddings.

For typical detail see Fig. I.12.

Drained joints: these joints have been designed and developed to overcome the disadvantages of the filled joint by:

1. Designing the joint to have a drainage zone.
2. Providing an air-tight seal at the rear of the joint.

Drained joints have two components which must be considered, namely the vertical joint and the horizontal joint.

Vertical joints: consist basically of a deep narrow gap between adjacent panels where the rear of the joint is adequately sealed to prevent the passage of air and moisture. The width of the joint does not significantly affect the amount of water reaching the rear seal since:

1. Most of the water entering the joint (approximately 80%) will do so by following over the face of the panel, the remainder (approximately 20%) will enter the joint directly and most of this water entering the joint will drain down within the first 50 mm of the joint depth. Usually the deciding factor for determining the joint width is the type of mastic or sealant being used and its ability to accommodate movement.
2. Checks on the amount of water entering the drainage zone such as ribs to joint edges, exposed aggregate external surfaces and the use of baffles.

Baffles are loose strips of material such as neoprene, butyl rubber or plasticised PVC which are unaffected by direct sunlight and act as a first line of defence to water penetration. The baffles are inserted, after the panels have been positioned and fixed, either by pulling them through prepared grooves or by direct insertion into the locating grooves from the face or back of panel according to the joint design. Care must be taken when inserting baffles by the pulling method since they invariably stretch during insertion and they must be allowed to return to their original length before trimming off the surplus to ensure adequate cover at the intersection of the vertical and horizontal joint.

The adequate sealing at the back of the joint is of utmost importance since some water will usually penetrate past the open drainage zone or the baffle, and any air movement through the joint seal will also assist the passage of water or moisture. Drained joints which have only a back seal or a baffle and seal can have a cold bridge effect on the internal face giving rise to local condensation: therefore consideration must be given to maintaining the continuity of the thermal insulation value of the cladding — see typical details in Figs. I.12 and I.13.

Horizontal joints: these are usually in the form of a rebated lap joint, the upper panel being lapped over the top edge of the lower panel. As with the vertical joints, the provision of an adequate back seal to prevent air movement through the joint is of paramount importance. The seal must also perform the function of a compression joint, therefore the sealing strip is of a compressible material such as bituminised foamed polyurethane or a preformed cellular rubber strip.

The profile of the joint is such that any water entering the gap by flowing from the panel face or by being blown in by the wind is encouraged to drain back on to the face of the lower panel. The depth of joint overlap is usually determined by the degree of exposure and ranges from 50 mm for normal exposure to 100 mm for severe exposure — see Fig. I.14 for typical details. It must be noted that the effective overlap of a horizontal joint is measured from the bottom edge of the baffle in the vertical joint to the seal and not from the rebated edge of the lower panel — see Fig. I.15.

Intersection of joints: this is an important feature of drained joint design and detail since it is necessary to shed any water draining down the vertical joint on to the face of the lower panels where the vertical and horizontal joints intersect because the joints are designed to cater only for the entry of water from any one panel connection at a time. The usual method is to use a flashing starting at the back of the panel, dressed over and stuck to the upper edge of the lower panel as shown in Fig. I.15. The choice of material for the flashing must be carefully considered since it must accept the load of the upper panel and any movements made whilst the panel is

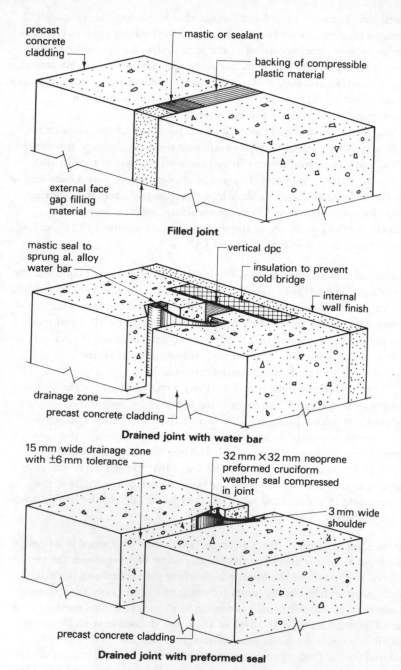

Fig. I.12 Typical filled and drained joints

26

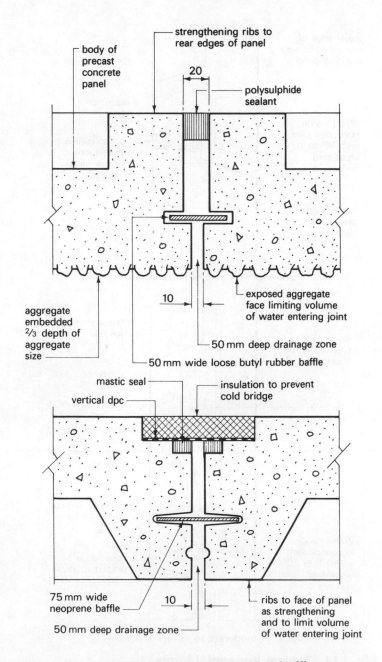

Fig. I.13 **Typical drained joints using baffles**

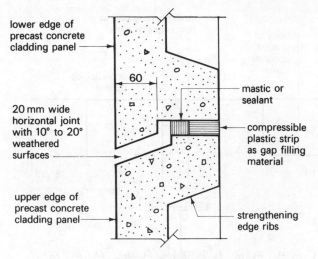

lower edge of precast concrete cladding panel

60

20 mm wide horizontal joint with 10° to 20° weathered surfaces

upper edge of precast concrete cladding panel

mastic or sealant

compressible plastic strip as gap filling material

strengthening edge ribs

Joint for low to moderate exposure

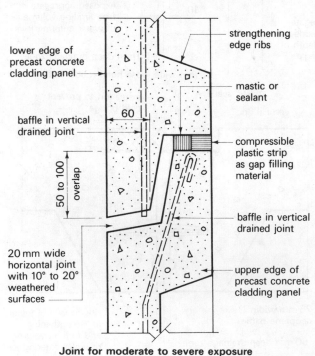

lower edge of precast concrete cladding panel

baffle in vertical drained joint

60

50 to 100 overlap

20 mm wide horizontal joint with 10° to 20° weathered surfaces

strengthening edge ribs

mastic or sealant

compressible plastic strip as gap filling material

baffle in vertical drained joint

upper edge of precast concrete cladding panel

Joint for moderate to severe exposure

Fig. I.14 Typical horizontal joints

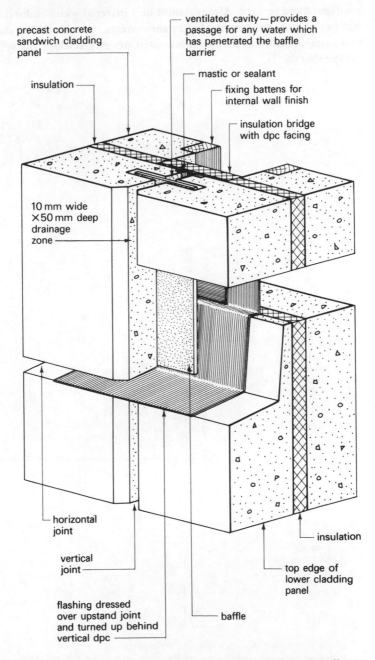

precast concrete sandwich cladding panel

insulation

ventilated cavity — provides a passage for any water which has penetrated the baffle barrier

mastic or sealant

fixing battens for internal wall finish

insulation bridge with dpc facing

10 mm wide ×50 mm deep drainage zone

horizontal joint

vertical joint

flashing dressed over upstand joint and turned up behind vertical dpc

baffle

insulation

top edge of lower cladding panel

Fig. I.15 Typical drained joint intersection detail

positioned and secured. Also it should be a material which is durable but will not give rise to staining of the panel surface. Experience has shown that suitable materials are bitumen coated woven glasscloth and synthetic rubber sheet.

5
Mastics and sealants

Materials which are to be used for sealing joints whether in the context of claddings or for sealing the gap between a simple frame and the reveals has to fulfil the following requirements:

1. Provide a weathertight seal.
2. Accommodate movement due to thermal expansion, wind loadings, structural movement and/or moisture movement.
3. Accommodate and mask tolerance variations.
4. Stable; that is, to remain in position without slumping.
5. Should not give rise to the staining of adjacent materials.

Mastics and sealants have a limited life ranging from 10 to 25 years, which in most cases is less than the design life of the structure, therefore all joints must be designed in such a way that the seals can be renewed with reasonable ease, efficiency and cost. The common form of sealing material, called putty, is unsuitable for many applications since it hardens soon after application and cannot therefore accept the movements which can be expected in claddings and similar situations. It was this inability to accommodate movement that led to the development of mastics and sealants.

Mastics: materials which are applied in a plastic state and form a surface skin over the core which remains pliable for a number of years.

Sealants: capable of accommodating greater movement than mastics, are more durable but dearer in both material and installation costs. They are applied in a plastic state and are converted by chemical reactions into an elastomer or synthetic rubber.

A wide variety of mastics and sealants are available to the designer and builder giving a variety of properties and applications. A text of this nature does not lend itself to a complete analysis of all the types available but only to a comparison of the most common grades.

Butyl mastics: a basic mastic with the addition of butyl rubber or related polymers making it suitable for glazing. They have a durability of up to 10 years and can accommodate both negative and positive movements up to 5% using a maximum joint width of 20 mm and a minimum joint depth of 6—10 mm.

Oil-bound mastics: the most widely used mastic, made with non-drying oils and has similar properties to the butyl mastics but in some cases a better durability of up to 15 years. Joint width 25 mm maximum although some special grades can be up to 50 mm, but in all cases the minimum joint depth is 12 mm.

Two-part polysulphide sealant: the best known elastomer sealant having an excellent durability of 25 years or more with a movement accommodation of approximately 15%. It is supplied as two components, a polysulphide base and a curing agent, which are mixed on site shortly before use, the mixture having a pot life of approximately 4 hours. The two parts will chemically react to form a synthetic rubber and should be used with a maximum joint width of 25 mm and a minimum joint depth of 6 mm when used in conjunction with metal or glass and a 10 mm minimum joint depth when used in connection with concrete. Two part polysulphide sealants should conform to the recommendations of BS 4254.

One-part polysulphide sealant: does not require premixing on site before application and is converted into a synthetic rubber by absorbing moisture from the atmosphere. The joint sizing is similar to that described for a two-part polysulphide but the final movement accommodation is less at approximately plus or minus 12½%. The curing process is slow, 1—2 months, and during this period the movement accommodation is very low. One-part polysulphides are generally specified for pointing and where early or excessive movements are unlikely to occur.

Silicone rubber sealant: a one-part sealing compound which converts to an elastomer by absorbing moisture from the atmosphere and has similar properties to the one-part polysulphide. It is available as a pure white or as a translucent material which makes it suitable for the sealing of internal tiling.

Mastics and sealants can be applied in a variety of ways such as gun or knife applications. The most common method is by hand-held gun using disposable cartridges fitted into the body of the applicator. Most guns can be fitted with various nozzles to produce a neat bead of the required shape and size. Mastics are also available for knife application, the material being supplied in tins or kegs up to 25 kg capacity.

The joint should be carefully prepared to receive the mastic or sealant by ensuring that the contact surfaces are free from all dirt, grease and oil. The contact surfaces must be perfectly dry and in some instances they may have to be primed before applying the jointing compound.

It should be noted that as an alternative to using mastics and sealants for jointing, pre-formed gaskets of various designs and shapes are available — see Fig. I.12. These can have better durability than mastics and sealants but the design and manufacture of the joint profile requires a high degree of accuracy if a successful joint is to be obtained.

6
Factory buildings – walls

The walls of factory buildings have to fulfil the same functions as any enclosing wall to a building, namely:

1. Protection from the elements.
2. Provision of the required sound and thermal insulation.
3. Provision of the required degree of fire resistance.
4. Provide access to and exit from the interior.
5. Provide natural daylighting to the interior.
6. Give reasonable security protection to the premises.
7. Resist anticipated wind pressures.
8. Reasonable durability to keep long term maintenance costs down to an acceptable level.

Most contemporary factory buildings are constructed as framed structures using a three dimensional frame or a system of portal frames, which means that the enclosing walls can be considered as non-loading bearing claddings supporting their own dead weight plus any wind loading. The wall can be designed as a complete envelope masking entirely the structural framework using brick walling, precast concrete panels, curtain walling techniques or lightweight wall claddings or alternatively an infill panel technique could be used making a feature of the structural members.

The choice will depend on such factors as appearance, local planning requirements, short and long term costs and personal preference. Unless the factory is small, containing both works and offices within the same building and hence presenting the company's image to the would-be clients, appearance is very often considered to be of secondary importance.

Students should have already studied the topic of brick panel walls and their attached facings in the context of framed buildings (see Chapter 1). The use of precast concrete cladding panels and lightweight infill panels have already been covered in Chapters 2 and 3 of this text. Many manufacturers of portal frame buildings offer a complete service of design, fabrication, supply and erection of the complete structure including the roof and wall coverings and students are advised to study the data sheets issued by these companies. It is proposed therefore to deal only with the lightweight wall claddings, in this chapter, which can be applied to the type of factory building under consideration.

LIGHTWEIGHT WALL CLADDINGS

In common with other cladding methods for framed buildings, lightweight wall claddings do not require high compressive strength since they only have to support their own dead load and any imposed wind loading, which will become more critical as the height and/or exposure increases. The subject of wind pressures is dealt with in greater detail in the next chapter. Lightweight claddings are usually manufactured from impervious materials which means that the run off of rain water can be high particularly under storm conditions when the discharge per minute could reach 2 litres per square metre of wall area exposed to the rain.

A wide variety of materials can be used as a cladding medium, most being profiled to a corrugated or trough form since the shaping will increase the strength of the material over its flat sheet form. Flat sheet materials are available but are rarely applied to large buildings because of the higher strength obtained from a profiled sheet of similar thickness. Special contoured sheets have been devised by many manufacturers to give the designer a wide range of choice in the context of aesthetic appeal. Claddings of various sandwich construction are also available to provide reasonable degrees of thermal insulation, sound insulation and to combat the condensation hazard which can occur with lightweight claddings of any nature.

The sheets are fixed in a similar manner to that studied in the second year of a typical construction technology course for sheet roof coverings. The support purlins are replaced in walls by a similar member called a sheeting rail which is fixed by cleats to the vertical structural frame members. The major difference occurs with the position of the fixings which in wall claddings are usually specified as being positioned in the trough of the profile as opposed to the crest when fixing roof coverings. This change in fixing detail is to ensure that the wall cladding is pulled tightly up to the sheeting rail or lining tray.

Plastic protective caps for the heads of fixings are available, generally of a colour and texture which will blend with the wall cladding. A full range of fittings and trims are usually obtainable for most materials and profiles to accommodate openings, returns, top edge and bottom edge closing. Typical cladding details are shown in Figs. I.16 and I.17.

Common materials used for lightweight wall claddings are:

1. *Fibre cement* — non-combustible material in corrugated and troughed sheets which are generally satisfactory when exposed to the weather but are susceptible to impact damage. Average life is about 20 years which can be increased considerably by paint protection. Unpainted sheets loose their surface finish at the exposed surface by carbonation and become ingrained with dirt. To achieve reasonable thermal insulation standards a lining material will be required, which is normally sandwiched between the cladding and an inner lining tray.

2. *Coated steel sheets* — non-combustible material with a wide range of profiles produced by various manufacturers. The steel sheet forms the core of the cladding providing its strength and this is covered with various forms of coatings to give weather protection, texture and colour. A typical specification would be a galvanised steel sheet core covered on both sides with a layer of asbestos felt to increase resistance to fire, a layer of bitumen-impregnated felt to act as a barrier to the passage of moisture to the core and on the face surface a coloured and textured coating of plastic. Fixing and the availability of fittings is as described above for asbestos cement.

3. *Aluminium alloy sheets* — non-combustible material in corrugated and troughed profiles which are usually made to the recommendations of CP 143 Pt 1 and BS 4868 respectively. Other profiles are also available as manufacturers' standards. Durability will depend upon the alloy used but this can be increased by paint applications; if unpainted, regular cleaning may be necessary if its natural bright appearance is to be maintained. Fixing, fittings and the availability of linings is as given for other cladding materials.

4. *Polyvinyl chloride sheets* — generally supplied in a corrugated profile with an embedded wire reinforcement to provide a cladding with a surface spread of flame classification of class 1 in accordance with BS 476: Part 7. The durability of this form of cladding is somewhat lower than those previously considered and the colours available are limited. The usual range of fittings and trims are available.

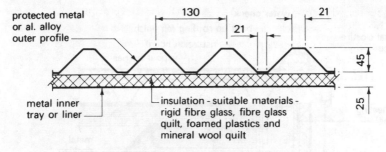

protected metal
or al. alloy
outer profile

130

21

21

45

25

metal inner
tray or liner

insulation - suitable materials -
rigid fibre glass, fibre glass
quilt, foamed plastics and
mineral wool quilt

Typical cladding profile

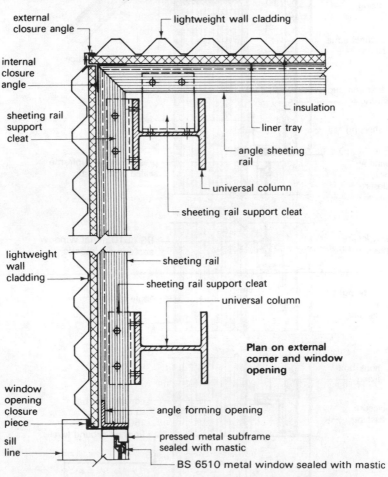

external
closure angle

lightweight wall cladding

internal
closure
angle

sheeting rail
support
cleat

insulation

liner tray

angle sheeting
rail

universal column

sheeting rail support cleat

lightweight
wall
cladding

sheeting rail

sheeting rail support cleat

universal column

**Plan on external
corner and window
opening**

window
opening
closure
piece

angle forming opening

sill
line

pressed metal subframe
sealed with mastic

BS 6510 metal window sealed with mastic

Fig. I.16 Lightweight wall cladding — typical details 1

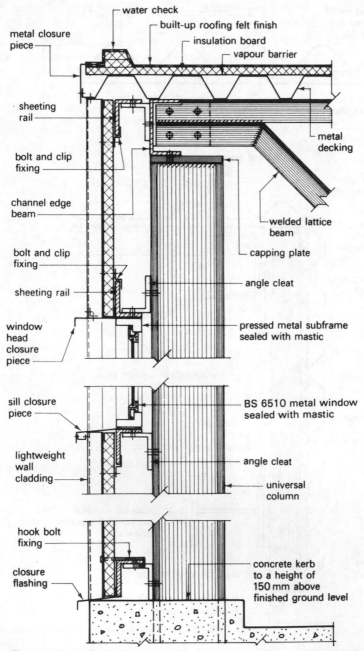

Fig. I.17 Lightweight wall cladding — typical details 2

water check

metal closure piece

built-up roofing felt finish

insulation board

vapour barrier

sheeting rail

bolt and clip fixing

channel edge beam

bolt and clip fixing

sheeting rail

window head closure piece

metal decking

welded lattice beam

capping plate

angle cleat

pressed metal subframe sealed with mastic

sill closure piece

lightweight wall cladding

BS 6510 metal window sealed with mastic

angle cleat

universal column

hook bolt fixing

closure flashing

concrete kerb to a height of 150 mm above finished ground level

The importance of adequate design, detail and fixing of all forms of lightweight cladding cannot be overstressed since the primary objective of these claddings is to provide a lightweight envelope to the building giving basic weather protection and internal comfort at a reasonable cost. Claddings which will fulfil these objectives are very susceptible to wind damage unless properly secured to the structural frame.

7
Curtain walling

Curtain walls are a form of external light-weight cladding attached to a framed structure forming a complete envelope or sheath around the structural frame. They are non-load-bearing claddings which have to support only their own deadweight and any imposed wind loadings which are transferred to the structural frame through connectors which are usually positioned at floor levels. The basic conception of most curtain walls is a series of vertical mullions spanning from floor to floor interconnected by horizontal transoms forming openings into which can be fixed panels of glass or infill panels of opaque materials. Most curtain walls are constructed by using a patent or proprietary system produced by metal window manufacturers.

The primary objectives of using curtain walling systems are:

1. Provide an enclosure to the structure which will give the necessary protection against the elements.
2. Make use of dry construction methods.
3. Impose onto the structural frame the minimum load in the form of claddings.
4. Exploit an architectural feature.

To fulfil its primary functions a curtain wall must meet the following requirements:

1. Resistance to the elements — the materials used in curtain walls are usually impervious and therefore in themselves present no problem but by virtue of the way in which they are fabricated a large number

of joints occur. These joints must be made as impervious as the surrounding materials or designed as a drained joint. The jointing materials must also allow for any local thermal, structural or moisture movement and generally consist of mastics, sealants and/or preformed gaskets of synthetic rubber or PVC.

2. Assist in maintaining the designed internal temperatures — since curtain walls usually include a large percentage of glass the overall resistance to the transfer of heat is low and therefore preventive measures may have to be incorporated into the design. Another problem with large glazed areas is solar heat gain since glass will allow the short wave radiations from the sun to pass through and consequently warm up the surfaces of internal walls, equipment and furniture. These surfaces will in turn radiate this acquired heat in the form of long wave radiations which cannot pass back through the glazing thus creating an internal heat build-up. Louvres fixed within a curtain walling system will have little effect upon this heat build-up but they will reduce solar glare. A system of non-transparent external louvres will slightly reduce the heat gain by absorbing heat and radiating it back to the external air. The usual methods employed to solve the problem of internal heat gain are:

   (a) Deep recessed windows which could be used in conjunction with external vertical fins.
   (b) Balanced internal heating and ventilation systems.
   (c) Use of special solar control glass such as reflective glasses which during manufacture are modified by depositing on the surface of the glass a metallic or dielectric reflective layer. The efficiency of this form of glazing can be increased if the class is tilted by $5°$ to $15°$ to increase the angle of incidence.

3. Adequate strength — although curtain walls are classified as non-load-bearing they must be able to carry their own weight and resist both positive and negative wind loadings. The magnitude of this latter loading will depend upon three basic factors:

   (a) Height of building;
   (b) Degree of exposure;
   (c) Location of building.

   The strength of curtain walling relies mainly upon the stiffness of the vertical component or mullion together with its anchorage or fixing to the structural frame. Glazing beads and the use of compressible materials also add to the resistance of possible wind damage of the glazed and infill panel areas by enabling these units to move independently of the curtain wall framing.

4. Provide required degree of fire resistance — this is probably one of the greatest restrictions encountered when using curtain walling techniques because of the large proportion of unprotected areas as defined in Approved Document B supporting Building Regulation B4 — external fire spread (see Part IV). By using suitable materials or combinations of materials the opaque infill panels can normally achieve the required fire resistance to enable them to be classified as protected areas.

5. Easy to assemble and fix — the principal member of a curtain walling system is usually the mullion which can be a solid or box section which is fixed to the structural frame at floor levels by means of adjustable anchorages or connectors. The infill framing and panels may be obtained as a series of individual components or as a single prefabricated unit. The main problems are ease of handling, amount of site assembly required and mode of access to the fixing position.

6. Provide required degree of sound insulation — sound originating from within the structure may be transmitted vertically through the curtain walling members. The chief source of this form of structure-borne sound is machinery and this may be reduced by isolating the offending machines by mounting them on resilient pads and/or using resilient connectors in the joints between mullion lengths. Airborne sound can be troublesome with curtain walling systems since the lightweight cladding has little mass to offer in the form of a sound barrier, the weakest point being the glazed areas. A reduction in the amount of sound transmitted can be achieved by:
   (a) Reducing the areas of glazing.
   (b) Using sealed windows of increased glass thickness.
   (c) Double glazing in the form of inner and outer panes of glass with an air space of 150 to 200 mm between them.

7. Provide for thermal and structural movements — since curtain walling is situated on an external face of the structure it will be more exposed than the structural frame and will therefore be subject to greater amounts of temperature change resulting in high thermal movement. The main frame may also be subjected to greater settlement than the claddings attached to its outer face. These differential movements mean that the curtain walling systems should be so designed, fabricated and fixed that the attached cladding can move independently of the structure. The usual methods of providing for this required movement are to have slotted bolt connections and, to allow for movement within the curtain walling itself, to have spigot connections and/or mastic sealed joints. Figures I.18 and I.19 show typical curtain walling examples to illustrate these principles.

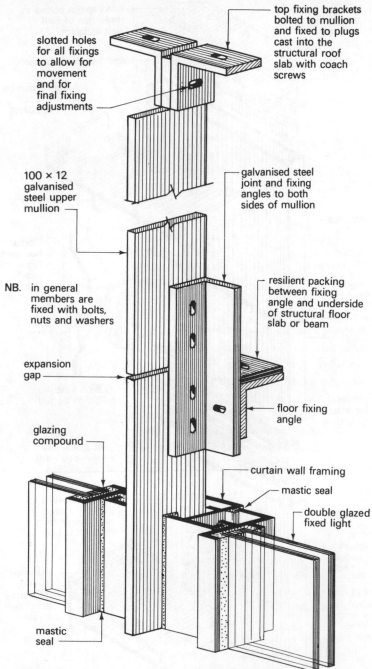

top fixing brackets bolted to mullion and fixed to plugs cast into the structural roof slab with coach screws

slotted holes for all fixings to allow for movement and for final fixing adjustments

100 × 12 galvanised steel upper mullion

galvanised steel joint and fixing angles to both sides of mullion

NB. in general members are fixed with bolts, nuts and washers

resilient packing between fixing angle and underside of structural floor slab or beam

expansion gap

floor fixing angle

glazing compound

curtain wall framing

mastic seal

double glazed fixed light

mastic seal

Fig. I.18 Typical curtain walling details 1

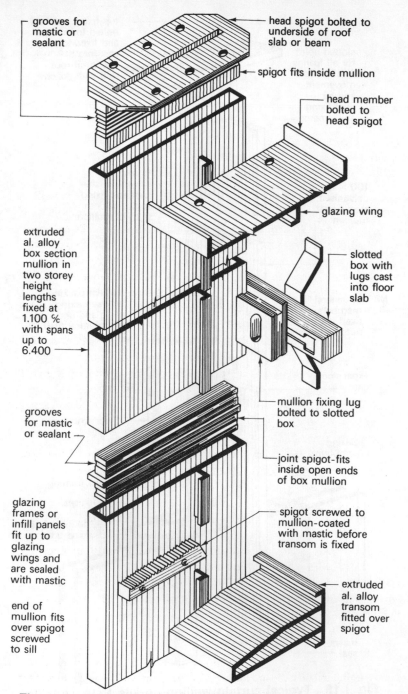

grooves for mastic or sealant

head spigot bolted to underside of roof slab or beam

spigot fits inside mullion

head member bolted to head spigot

glazing wing

slotted box with lugs cast into floor slab

extruded al. alloy box section mullion in two storey height lengths fixed at 1.100 % with spans up to 6.400

mullion fixing lug bolted to slotted box

grooves for mastic or sealant

joint spigot-fits inside open ends of box mullion

glazing frames or infill panels fit up to glazing wings and are sealed with mastic

spigot screwed to mullion-coated with mastic before transom is fixed

extruded al. alloy transom fitted over spigot

end of mullion fits over spigot screwed to sill

Fig. I.19 Typical curtain walling details 2

44

Infill Panels

The panels used to form the opaque areas in a curtain walling system should have the following properties:

1. Lightweight.
2. Rigid.
3. Impermeable.
4. Suitable fire resistance.
5. Suitable resistance to heat transfer.
6. Good durability requiring little or no maintenance.

No one material has all the above listed properties and therefore infill panels are usually manufactured in the form of a sandwich or combination panel. One of the major problems encountered with any form of external sandwich panel is interstitial condensation which is usually overcome by including a vapour barrier of suitable material situated near to the inner face of the panel. A vapour barrier can be defined as a membrane with a vapour resistivity greater than 100 MN/g. Suitable materials include adequately lapped sheeting such as aluminium foil, waterproof building papers, polythene sheet and applied materials such as two coats of bitumen paint or two coats of chlorinated rubber paint. Care must be taken when positioning vapour barriers to ensure that an interaction is not set up between adjacent materials such as the alkali attack of aluminium if placed next to concrete or asbestos cement.

The choice of external facing for these infill cladding materials is very important because of their direct exposure to the elements. Plastic and plastic coated materials are obvious choices provided they meet the minimum requirements set out in Approved Document B. One of the most popular materials for the external facing of infill panels is vitreous enamelled steel or aluminium sheets. In the preparation process a thin coating of glass is fused onto the metal surface at a temperature of between $800°$ and $860°C$ resulting in an extremely hard, impervious, acid and corrosion resistant panel which will withstand severe abrasive action, also the finish will not be subject to crazing or cracking resulting in an attractive finish with the strength of the base metal. When used in combination with other materials a thin lightweight infill panel giving 'U' values in the order of $1.14 \text{ W/m}^2 \text{ K}$ can be created. Typical infill panel examples are shown in Fig. I.20.

Glazing

The primary function of any material fixed into an opening in the external façade of a building is to provide a weather seal. Glass also provides general daylight illumination of the interior of the

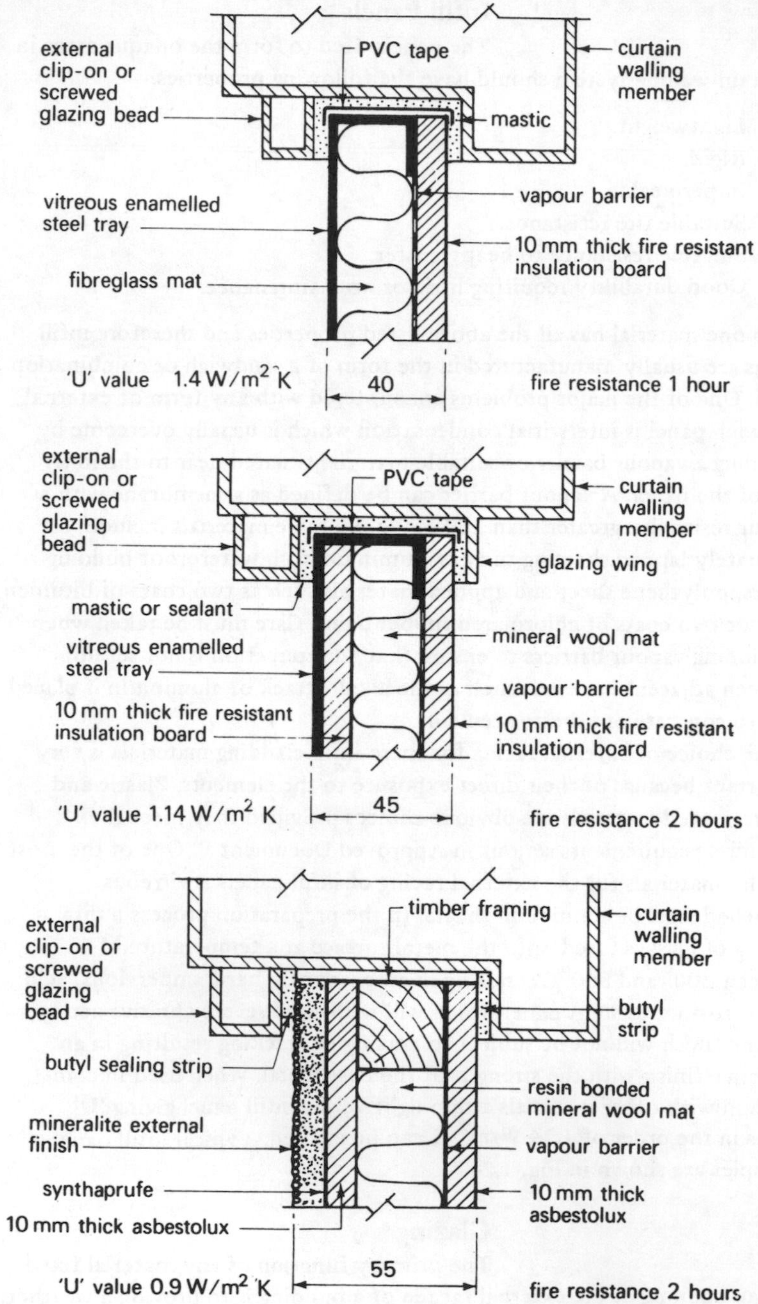
external clip-on or screwed glazing bead
PVC tape
curtain walling member
mastic
vitreous enamelled steel tray
vapour barrier
10 mm thick fire resistant insulation board
fibreglass mat
'U' value 1.4 W/m² K
40
fire resistance 1 hour
external clip-on or screwed glazing bead
PVC tape
curtain walling member
glazing wing
mastic or sealant
vitreous enamelled steel tray
mineral wool mat
vapour barrier
10 mm thick fire resistant insulation board
10 mm thick fire resistant insulation board
'U' value 1.14 W/m² K
45
fire resistance 2 hours
timber framing
external clip-on or screwed glazing bead
curtain walling member
butyl strip
butyl sealing strip
resin bonded mineral wool mat
mineralite external finish
vapour barrier
synthaprufe
10 mm thick asbestolux
10 mm thick asbestolux
55
'U' value 0.9 W/m² K
fire resistance 2 hours

Fig. I.20 Typical curtain walling infill panel details

building, provides daylight for carrying out specific tasks and at the same time it can provide a view out or visual contact with the outside world. It is not really necessary to have the internal space of a building illuminated by natural daylight since this can be adequately covered by a well-designed and installed artificial lighting system but in psychological and energy conservation terms it is usually considered desirable to have a reasonable proportion of glazed areas.

The nature of work to be carried out and the position of the working plane will largely determine whether daylight from glazed areas alone can provide sufficient illumination for specific work tasks. Many of these tasks are carried out on a horizontal surface which is best illuminated by vertical light; therefore careful design of window size, window position and possible daylight factors need to be assessed if glazed areas are to provide the main source of work task illumination. The need for visual contact with the outside world like the need for daylight illumination of the interior is largely a case of psychological well-being rather than dire necessity but to provide an acceptable view out the areas of glazing need to be planned bearing in mind the size, orientation and view obtained. The problems of solar heat gain, solar glare, thermal and sound insulation have already been considered at the beginning of this chapter and therefore no further comment seems necessary under this heading. The major problem remaining when using glass in the façades of high rise structures and in particular for curtain walling is providing a means of access for cleaning and maintenance.

The cleaning of windows in this context can be a dangerous and costly process but such glazed areas do need cleaning for the following reasons:

1. Prevention of dirt accumulation resulting in a distortion of the original visual appearance.
2. Maintaining the designed daylight transmission.
3. Maintaining the clarity of vision out.
4. Prevention of deterioration of the glazing materials due to chemical and/or dirt attack.

The usual method of cleaning windows is by washing with water using swabs, chamois leather, scrims and squeegee cleaners, all of which are hand held requiring close access to the glass to be cleaned. Cleaning the internal surfaces does not normally present a problem but unless pivot or tilt and turn windows are used the cleaning of the outside surface will require a means of external access. In the low to medium rise structures access can be by means of trestles, step ladders or straight ladders; the latter being possible up to 11.000 after which they become dangerous because of flexing and the lack of overall control. Tower scaffolds are seldom used for window cleaning because of the cost and time involved in assembly but lightweight quickly erected scaffold systems could be considered for heights up to 6.000.

Access for external cleaning of curtain wall façades in high rise structures is generally by the use of suspended cradles which can be of a temporary nature, or alternatively they can be of a permanent system designed and constructed as an integral part of the structure. The simplest form is to install a universal beam section at roof level positioned about 450 mm in front of the general façade line and continuous around the perimeter of the roof. A conventional cradle is attached by means of castors located on the bottom flange of the ring or edge beam. Control is by means of ropes from the cradle which must be lowered to ground level for access purposes.

A better form is where the transversing track is concealed by placing a pair of rails to a 750 mm gauge to which is fixed a trolley having projecting beams or davits which can be retracted and/or luffed, the latter being particularly useful for negotiating projections in the general façade. The trolley may be manually operated from the cradle for transversing or it may be an electric-powered trolley giving vertical movement of between 5 and 15 m per minute or horizontal movement of 5 to 12 m per minute. This form of trolley is usually considered essential for heights over 45.000. In all cases the roof must have been structurally designed to accept the load of the apparatus.

If the height of suspension is over 30.000 it is a statutory requirement that some form of cable restraint is incorporated in the design to overcome the problem of unacceptable cradle movement due to the action of wind around the structure. Winds moving up the face of the building will cause the cradle to swing at right angles to the face giving rise to possible impact damage to the face of the structure as well as placing the operatives in a hazardous situation.

Crosswinds can cause the cradle to move horizontally along the face of the building with equally disastrous results. Methods of cradle and cable restraint available are the use of suction grips, eyebolts fixed to the façade through which the suspension ropes can be threaded, suspension ropes suitably tensioned at ground level, electrical cutouts at intervals of 15.000 which will prevent further cradle movement until a special plug through which the hoist line passes has been inserted and using the mullions as a guide for rollers which are either in contact with the mullion face to prevent lateral movement or by castors located behind a mullion flange to prevent outward movement.

Part II

Finishes and fittings

8
Doors, door frames and linings

Doors

A door is a screen used to seal an opening into a building or between rooms within a building. It can be made of timber, glass, metal or plastic or any combination of these materials. Doors can be designed to swing from one edge, slide, slide and fold or roll to close an opening. The doors to be considered in this book are those made of timber and those made of timber and glass which are hung so that they swing from one edge. All doors may be classified by their position in a building, by their function or by their method of construction.

External doors

These are used to close the access to the interior of a building and provide a measure of security. They need to be weather resistant since in general they are exposed to the elements, this resistance is provided by the thickness, stability and durability of the construction and materials used together with protective coatings of paint or polish. The external walls of a building are designed to give the interior of a building a degree of thermal and sound insulation, doors in such walls should therefore be constructed, as far as practicable, to maintain the insulation properties of the external enclosure.

The standard sizes for external timber doors are 1981 mm high x 762 or 838 mm wide x 45 mm thick which is a metric conversion of the old Imperial door sizes. Metric doors are produced so that, together with the frame, they fit into a modular coordinated opening size and are usually supplied as door sets with the door already attached or hung in the frame.

Internal doors

These are used to close the access through internal walls, partitions and to the inside of cupboards. As with external doors the aim of the design should be to maintain the properties of the wall in which they are housed. Generally internal doors are thinner than their external counterparts since weather protection is no longer a requirement. Standard sizes are similar to external doors but with a wider range of widths to cater for narrow cupboard openings.

PURPOSE MADE DOORS

The design and construction of these doors is usually based on BS 459 for standard doors but are made to non-standard sizes, shapes or designs. Most door manufacturers produce a range of non-standard doors which are often ornate and are used mainly for the front elevation doors of domestic buildings. Purpose made doors are also used in buildings such as banks, civic buildings, shops, theatres and hotels to blend with or emphasise the external façade design or internal decor (see Fig. II.1).

METHODS OF CONSTRUCTION

The British Standard Code of Practice 151 for wood doors and frames covers all aspects of door and frame construction. A British Standard for special door formats is also published:

BS 459 Part 3: Fire-check doors.
     Part 4: Matchboarded doors.
CP 151: all wood doors and frames.

Standard doors are used extensively since they are mass produced to known requirements, are readily available from stock and are cheaper than purpose made doors.

Panelled and glazed wood doors

The Code of Practice gives a wide variety of types all of which are based upon the one, two, three or four panel format. They are constructed of timber which should be in accordance with the recommendations of BS 1186 with plywood or glass panels. External doors with panels of plywood should be constructed using an external quality plywood (see Fig. II.2).

52

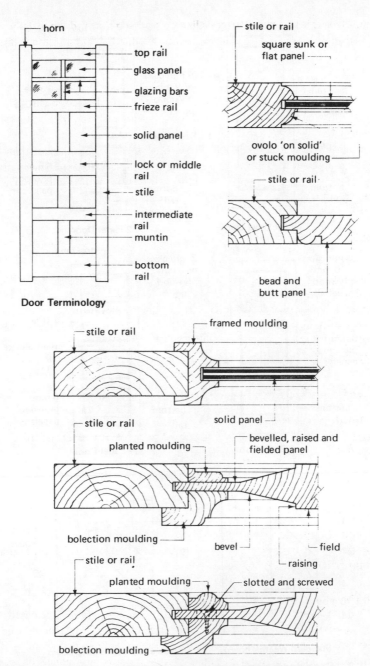

horn

top rail

glass panel

glazing bars

frieze rail

solid panel

lock or middle rail

stile

intermediate rail

muntin

bottom rail

Door Terminology

stile or rail

square sunk or flat panel

ovolo 'on solid' or stuck moulding

stile or rail

bead and butt panel

stile or rail

framed moulding

solid panel

stile or rail

planted moulding

bevelled, raised and fielded panel

bolection moulding

bevel

field

raising

stile or rail

planted moulding

slotted and screwed

bolection moulding

Fig. II.1 Purpose made doors and mouldings

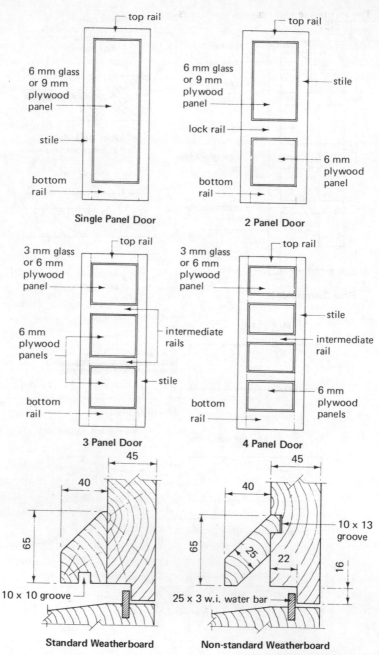

Fig. II.2 Standard panelled doors and weatherboards

The joints used in framing the doors can be a dowelled joint or a mortise and tenon joint. The dowelled joint is considered superior to the mortise and tenon joint and is cheaper when used in the mass production of standard doors. Bottom and lock rails have three dowels, top rails have two dowels and intermediate rails have a single dowel connection (see Fig. II.3). The plywood panels are framed into grooves with closely fitting sides with a movement allowance within the depth of the groove of 2 mm. The mouldings at the rail intersections are scribed, whereas the loose glazing beads are mitred. Weatherboards for use on external doors can be supplied to fit onto the bottom rail of the door which can also be rebated to close over a water bar (see Fig. II.2).

Flush doors

This type of door is very popular with both the designer and the occupier—it has a plain face which is easy to clean and decorate, it is also free of the mouldings which collect dust. Flush doors can be faced with hardboard, plywood or a plastic laminate and by using a thin sheet veneer of good quality timber the appearance of high class joinery can be created.

The Code of Practice specifies the requirements for flush doors but leaves the method of construction to the manufacturer which gives him complete freedom in his design; therefore the forms of flush door construction are many and varied but basically they can be considered as either skeleton core doors or solid core doors. The former consists of an outer frame with small section intermediate members over which is fixed the facing material. The facing has a tendency to deflect between the core members and this can be very noticeable on the surface especially if the facing is coated with gloss paint. Solid core doors are designed to overcome this problem and at the same time improve the sound insulation properties of flush doors. Solid doors of suitably faced block or lamin board are available for internal and external use. Another method of construction is to infill the voids created by a skeleton core with a lightweight material such as foamed plastic which will give support to the facings but will not add appreciably to the weight of the door.

The facings of flush doors are very vulnerable to damage at the edges, therefore a lipping of solid material should be fixed to at least the vertical edges (good class doors have lippings on all four edges).

Small glazed observation panels can be incorporated in flush doors when the glass panel is secured by loose fixing beads (see Figs. II.4 and II.5).

Fire-check flush doors

These doors provide an effective barrier to the passage of fire for the time designated by their type but to achieve this they must be used in

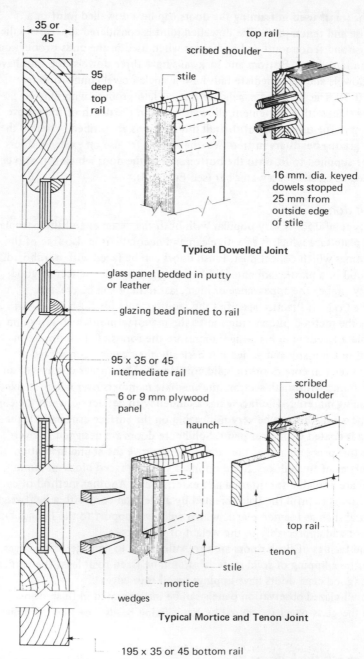

35 or 45

95 deep top rail

top rail

scribed shoulder

stile

16 mm. dia. keyed dowels stopped 25 mm from outside edge of stile

Typical Dowelled Joint

glass panel bedded in putty or leather

glazing bead pinned to rail

95 x 35 or 45 intermediate rail

6 or 9 mm plywood panel

scribed shoulder

haunch

top rail

tenon

stile

mortice

wedges

Typical Mortice and Tenon Joint

195 x 35 or 45 bottom rail

Fig. II.3 Panelled door details

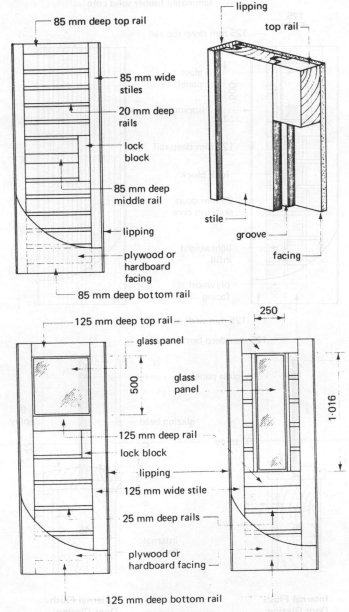

85 mm deep top rail

lipping

top rail

85 mm wide stiles

20 mm deep rails

lock block

85 mm deep middle rail

lipping

plywood or hardboard facing

85 mm deep bottom rail

stile

groove

facing

250

125 mm deep top rail

glass panel

500

glass panel

125 mm deep rail

lock block

lipping

125 mm wide stile

25 mm deep rails

plywood or hardboard facing

125 mm deep bottom rail

1·016

Fig. II.4   Skeleton core flush doors

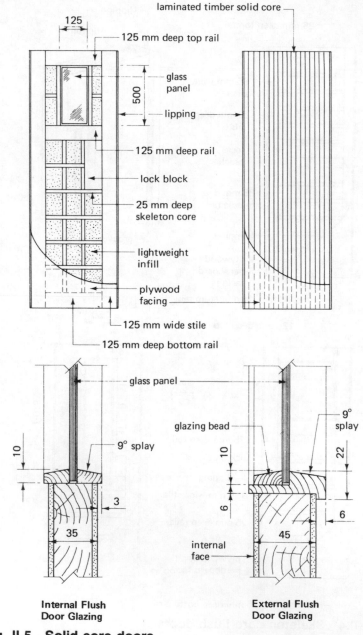

125

125 mm deep top rail

laminated timber solid core

glass
panel

500

lipping

125 mm deep rail

lock block

25 mm deep
skeleton core

lightweight
infill

plywood
facing

125 mm wide stile

125 mm deep bottom rail

glass panel

9° splay

10

3

35

**Internal Flush
Door Glazing**

glazing bead

9°
splay

10

22

6

6

45

internal
face

**External Flush
Door Glazing**

Fig. II.5 Solid core doors

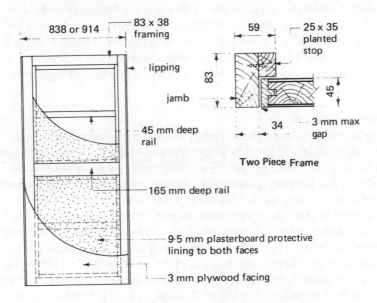

Half-hour Type Fire-check Door and Frame

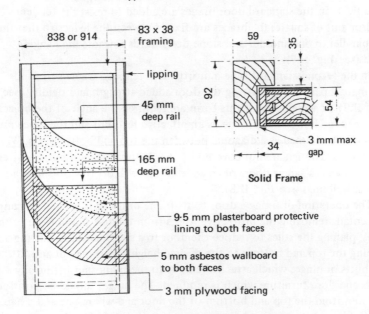

One Hour Type Fire-check Door and Frame

Fig. II.6   Fire-check doors and frames

conjunction with the correct frame. Two types are designated in BS 459. namely half-hour and one-hour resistance. This resistance is obtained by placing beneath the plywood facing a suitable protective lining material or materials. Half-hour type doors are hung using one pair of hinges whereas one-hour type doors require one and a half pairs of hinges (see Fig. II.6).

Matchboarded doors

These doors can be used as external or internal doors and as a standard door takes one of two forms, a ledged and braced door or a framed ledged and braced door, the latter being a stronger and more attractive version.

The face of the door is made from tongue and grooved boarding which has edge chamfers to one or both faces; these form a vee joint between consecutive boards. Three horizontal members called 'ledges' clamp the boards together and in this form a non-standard door called a ledged and battened door has been made. It is simple and cheap to construct but has the disadvantage of being able to drop at the closing edge thus pulling the door out of square—the only resistance offered is that of the nails holding the boards to the ledges. The use of this type of door is limited to buildings such as sheds, outhouses and to small units like trapdoors (see Fig. II.7). In the standard door braces are added to resist the tendency to drop out of square; the braces are fixed between the ledges so that they are parallel to one another and slope downwards towards the hanging edge (see Fig. II.7).

In the second standard type a mortise and tenoned frame surrounds the matchboarded panel giving the door added strength and rigidity (see Fig. II.7). If wide doors of this form are required the angle of the braces becomes too low to be of value as an effective restraint and the brace must therefore be framed as a diagonal between the top and bottom rails. Wide doors of this design are not covered by the British Standard but are often used in pairs as garage doors or as wide entrance doors to workshops and similar buildings (see Fig. II.8).

The operation of fixing a door to its frame or lining is termed hanging and entails removing the protective horns from the top and bottom of the stiles; planing the stiles to reduce the door to a suitable width; cutting and planing the top and bottom to the desired height; marking out and fitting the butts or hinges which attach the door to the frame and fitting any locks and door furniture which is required. The hinges should be positioned 225 mm from the top and bottom of the door and where one and a half pairs of hinges are specified for heavy doors the third hinge is positioned midway between the bottom and top hinges.

A door irrespective of the soundness of its construction will deteriorate if improperly treated during transportation, storage and after hanging. It

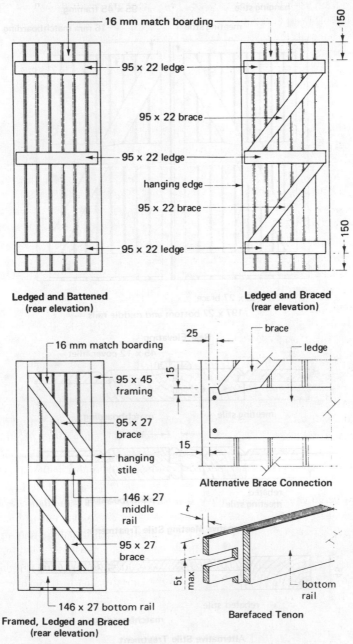

Ledged and Battened
(rear elevation)

16 mm match boarding

95 × 22 ledge

95 × 22 brace

95 × 22 ledge

hanging edge

95 × 22 brace

95 × 22 ledge

Ledged and Braced
(rear elevation)

150

brace

150

16 mm match boarding

95 × 45 framing

95 × 27 brace

hanging stile

146 × 27 middle rail

95 × 27 brace

146 × 27 bottom rail

Framed, Ledged and Braced
(rear elevation)

25

15

15

brace

ledge

Alternative Brace Connection

t

5t max

bottom rail

Barefaced Tenon

Fig. II.7 Matchboarded doors

61

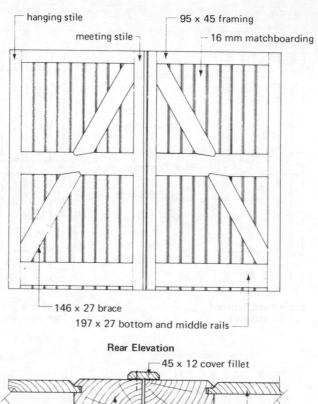

hanging stile

meeting stile

95 x 45 framing

16 mm matchboarding

146 x 27 brace

197 x 27 bottom and middle rails

Rear Elevation

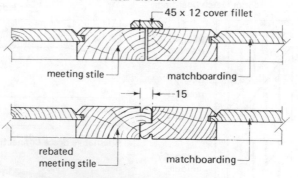

45 x 12 cover fillet

meeting stile

matchboarding

15

rebated
meeting stile

matchboarding

Alternative Meeting Stile Treatments

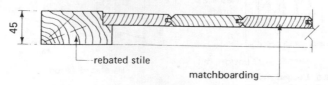

45

rebated stile

matchboarding

Alternative Stile Treatment

Fig. II.8 Matchboarded double doors

should receive a wood priming coat of paint before or immediately after delivery, be stored in the dry and in a flat position so that it does not twist—it should also receive the finishing coats of paint as soon as practicable after hanging.

Frames and linings

A door frame or lining is attached to the opening in which a door is to be fitted, it provides a surround for the door and is the member to which a door is fixed or hung. Door sets consisting of a storey heigh. frame with a solid or glazed panel over the door head are also available; these come supplied with the door ready hung on lift off hinges (see Fig. II.10).

TIMBER DOOR FRAMES

These are made from rectangular section timber in which a rebate is formed or to which a planted door stop is fixed to provide the housing for the door. Generally a door frame is approximately twice as wide as its thickness plus the stop. Frames are used for most external doors, for heavy doors and for doors situated in thin non-load bearing partitions.

A timber door frame consists of three or four members—namely the head, two posts or jambs and a sill or threshold. The members can be joined together by wedged mortise and tenon joints, combed joints or mortise and tenon joints pinned with a metal star shaped dowel or a round timber dowel. All joints should have either a coating of adhesive or a coating of a lead based paint (see Fig. II.9).

Door frames which do not have a sill are fitted with mild steel dowels driven into the base of the jambs and cast into the floor slab or alternatively grouted into pre-formed pockets as a means of securing the feet of the frame to the floor. If the frame is in an exposed position it is advisable to sit the feet of the jambs on a damp-proof pad such as lead or bituminous felt, to prevent moisture soaking into the frame and creating the conditions for fungi attack.

Door frames fitted with a sill are designed for one of two conditions:

1. Doors opening out.
2. Doors opening in.

In both cases the sill must be designed to prevent the entry of rain and wind under the bottom edge of the door. Doors opening out close onto a rebate in the sill whereas doors opening in have a rebated bottom rail and close over a water bar set into the sill (see Fig. II.9).

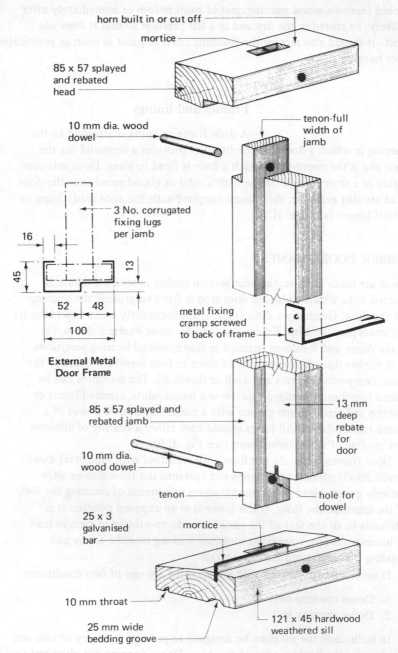

horn built in or cut off

mortice

85 x 57 splayed
and rebated
head

10 mm dia. wood
dowel

tenon-full
width of
jamb

3 No. corrugated
fixing lugs
per jamb

16

45

13

52   48

100

**External Metal
Door Frame**

metal fixing
cramp screwed
to back of frame

85 x 57 splayed and
rebated jamb

13 mm
deep
rebate
for
door

10 mm dia.
wood dowel

tenon

hole for
dowel

25 x 3
galvanised
bar

mortice

10 mm throat

121 x 45 hardwood
weathered sill

25 mm wide
bedding groove

Fig. II.9   Door frames

64

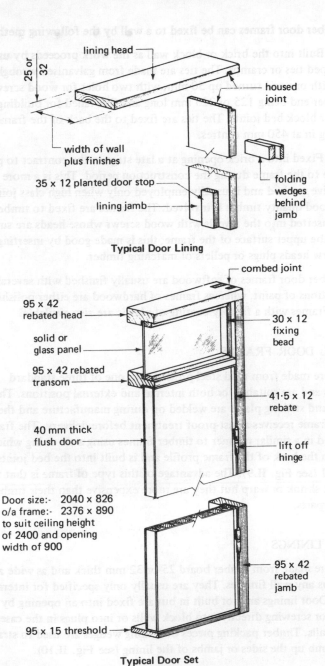

25 or 32

lining head

housed joint

width of wall plus finishes

35 x 12 planted door stop

folding wedges behind jamb

lining jamb

Typical Door Lining

combed joint

95 x 42 rebated head

30 x 12 fixing bead

solid or glass panel

95 x 42 rebated transom

41·5 x 12 rebate

40 mm thick flush door

lift off hinge

Door size:- 2040 x 826
o/a frame:- 2376 x 890
to suit ceiling height
of 2400 and opening
width of 900

95 x 42 rebated jamb

95 x 15 threshold

Typical Door Set

Fig. II.10 Door linings and door sets

Timber door frames can be fixed to a wall by the following methods:

(a) Built into the brick or block wall as the work proceeds by using 'L' shaped ties or cramps. The ties are made from galvanised wrought steel with one end turned up 50 mm, with two holes for wood screws, the other end being 125 or 225 mm long and fish-tailed for building into brick or block bed joints. The ties are fixed to the back of the frame for building in at 450 mm centres.

(b) Fixed into a brick opening at a late stage in the contract to prevent damage to the frame during the construction period. This is a more expensive method and is usually employed only when high class joinery using good quality timber is involved. The frames are fixed to timber plugs inserted into the reveals with wood screws whose heads are sunk below the upper surface of the frame; this is made good by inserting over the screw heads plugs or pellets of matching timber.

Timber door frames of softwood are usually finished with several applications of paint, whereas frames of hardwood are either polished or oiled. Frames with a factory coating of plastic are also available.

METAL DOOR FRAMES

These are made from mild steel pressed into one of three standard profiles and are suitable for both internal and external positions. The hinges and striking plates are welded on during manufacture and the whole frame receives a rust-proof treatment before delivery. The frames are fixed in a similar manner to timber frames using a tie or lug which fits into the back of the frame profile and is built into the bed joints of the wall (see Fig. II.9). The advantage of this type of frame is that they will not shrink or warp but they are more expensive than their timber counterparts.

DOOR LININGS

These are made from timber board 25 or 32 mm thick and as wide as the wall plus any wall finishes. They are usually only specified for internal doors. Door linings are not built in but are fixed into an opening by nailing or screwing directly into block walls or into plugs in the case of brick walls. Timber packing pieces or folding wedges are used to straighten and plumb up the sides or jambs of the lining (see Fig. II.10).

9

Windows, glass and glazing

The primary function of a window is to provide a means for admission of natural daylight to the interior of a building. A window can also serve as a means of providing the necessary ventilation of dwellings, as required under Building Regulation F1, by including into the window design opening lights.

Windows, like doors, can be made from a variety of materials or a combination of these materials such as timber, metal and plastic. They can also be designed to operate in various ways by arranging for the sashes to slide, pivot or swing, by being hung to one of the frame members. This latter arrangement is known as a casement window and it is this form which is studied in this volume.

BUILDINGS REGULATIONS

Approved Document F deals with the ventilation of habitable rooms and kitchens in dwellings. A habitable room is defined as a room used for dwelling purposes but not a kitchen. A habitable room must have ventilation openings unless it is adequately ventilated by mechanical means.

A ventilation opening includes any permanent or closable means of ventilation which opens directly to the external air. Included in this category are openable parts of windows, louvres, air bricks, window trickle ventilators and doors which open directly to the external air. The three general objectives of providing a means of ventilation are; to extract moisture from rooms where it is produced in significant quantities such as kitchens and bathrooms; to provide for occasional rapid ventilation where moisture presence is likely to produce condensation and to achieve a background ventilation which is adequate without affecting the comfort of the room.

Approved Document F gives the following for dwellings:

1. Habitable rooms – provision of ventilation opening(s) with a total area of at least one-twentieth of the floor area of the room or rooms it serves and with some part of the ventilation opening(s) at least 1750 mm above the floor level. Background ventilation to be provided by ventilation opening(s) having a total area of not less than 4000 mm^2 by a means which is controllable, secure and sited to avoid draughts.
2. Kitchens – provision of rapid ventilation by intermittent operation of mechanical extract ventilation rated at not less than 60 litres per second or if incorporated in a cooker hood to be rated at not less than 30 litres per second. Background ventilation provision to be as for habitable rooms or alternatively continuous mechanical ventilation rated at a nominal one air-change per hour can be used.
3. Bathrooms – ventilation requirement can be satisfied by using intermittent mechanical extract ventilation rated at not less than 15 litres per second.
4. Sanitary accommodation – ventilation requirement can be satisfied by using intermittent mechanical extract ventilation, giving at least three air-changes per hour with a fifteen minute minimum overrun.

Traditional casement windows

Figure II: 11 shows a typical arrangement and details of this type of window. A wide range of designs can be produced by using various combinations of the members, the only limiting factor being the size of glass pane relevant to is thickness.

The general arrangement of the framing is important, heads and sills always extend across the full width of the frame and in many cases have projecting horns for building into the wall. The jambs and mullions span between the head and sill; these are joined to them by a wedged or pinned mortise and tenon joint. This arrangement gives maximum strength since the vertical members will act as struts–it will also give a simple assembly process.

The traditional casement window frame has deep rebates to accommodate the full thickness of the sash, which is the term used for the framing of the opening ventilator. If fixed glazing or lights are required it is necessary to have a sash frame surround to the glass since the depth of rebate in the window frame is too great for direct glazing to the frame.

STANDARD WOOD CASEMENT WINDOWS

BS 644, Part 1, gives details of the quality, construction and design of a wide range of wood casement windows. The frames, sashes and ventlights are made from standard sections of softwood timbers arranged to give a variety in design and size. The sashes and ventlights are designed so that their edges

68

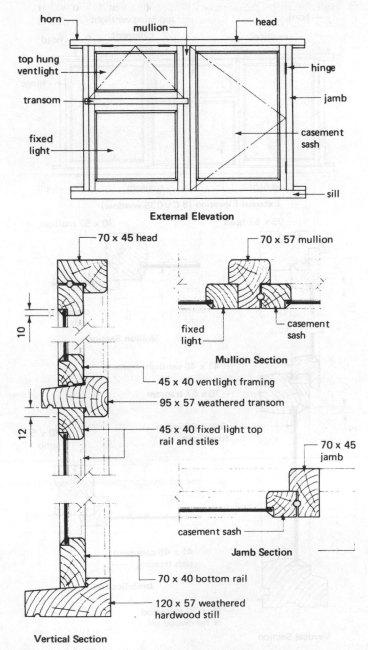

horn — mullion — head

top hung ventlight — hinge

transom — jamb

fixed light — casement sash

sill

External Elevation

70 x 45 head

70 x 57 mullion

fixed light — casement sash

Mullion Section

10

45 x 40 ventlight framing

95 x 57 weathered transom

12

45 x 40 fixed light top rail and stiles

70 x 45 jamb

casement sash

Jamb Section

70 x 40 bottom rail

120 x 57 weathered hardwood still

Vertical Section

Fig. II.11 Traditional timber casement window

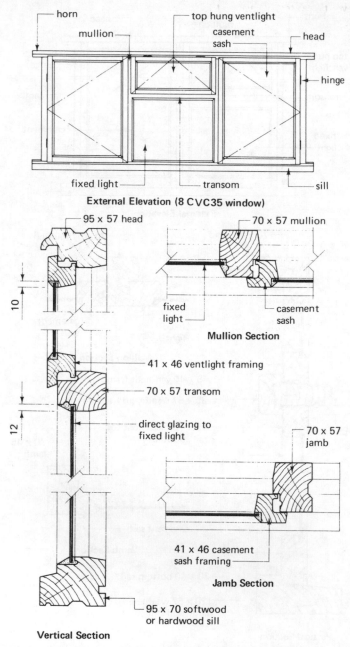

horn

mullion

top hung ventlight

casement sash

head

hinge

fixed light

transom

sill

External Elevation (8 CVC35 window)

95 x 57 head

70 x 57 mullion

10

fixed light

casement sash

Mullion Section

41 x 46 ventlight framing

70 x 57 transom

12

direct glazing to fixed light

70 x 57 jamb

41 x 46 casement sash framing

Jamb Section

95 x 70 softwood or hardwood sill

Vertical Section

Fig. II.12 Typical modified BS casement window

rebate over the external face of the frame to form a double barrier to the entry of wind and rain. The general construction is similar to that described for traditional casement windows and the fixing of the frame into walls follows that described for door frames.

Most joinery manufacturers produced a range of modified standard casement windows following the basic principles set out in BS 644 but with improved head, sill and sash sections. The range produced is based on a module for basic spaces of 300 mm giving the following lengths (in mm):

600; 900; 1 200; 1 800; 2 400.

Frame heights follow the same pattern with the exception of one half module (in mm):

600; 900; 1 050; 1 200; 1 500.

Window types are identified by a notation of figures and letters, for example, 4CV30 where:

4 = four width modules = 4 × 300 mm = 1 200 mm.
C = casement.
V = ventlight.
30 = three height modules = 3 × 300 mm = 900 mm.

For typical details see Fig. II.12.

STEEL CASEMENT WINDOWS

These windows are produced to conform with the recommendations of BS 6510 which gives details of construction, sections, sizes, composites and hardware. The standard range covers fixed lights, hung casements, pivot casements and doors. The lengths, in the main, conform to the basic space first preference of 300 mm giving the following range (in mm):

500; 600; 800; 900; 1 200; 1 500; 1 800.

Frame heights are based upon basic spaces for the preferred head and sill heights for public sector housing giving the following sizes (in mm):

200; 500; 700; 900; 1 100; 1 300; 1 500.

Steel windows, like wood windows, are identified by a notation of numbers and letters:

Prefix number: × 100 = basic space length.

Code letters: F = fixed light.
                              C = side hung casement opening out.

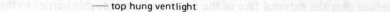
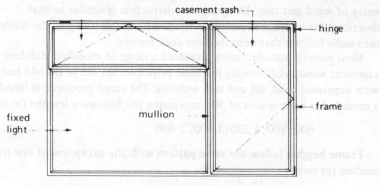

top hung ventlight

casement sash

hinge

frame

fixed light

mullion

External Elevation (18 FCT 11 RH window)

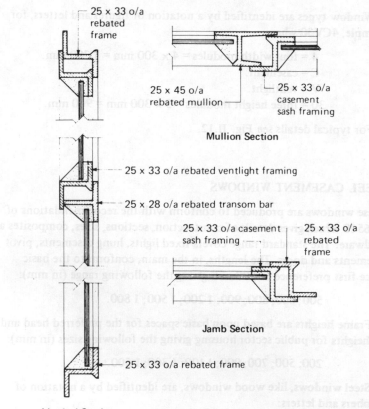

25 x 33 o/a rebated frame

25 x 45 o/a rebated mullion

25 x 33 o/a casement sash framing

Mullion Section

25 x 33 o/a rebated ventlight framing

25 x 28 o/a rebated transom bar

25 x 33 o/a casement sash framing

25 x 33 o/a rebated frame

Jamb Section

25 x 33 o/a rebated frame

Vertical Section

Fig. II.13 Typical steel window details

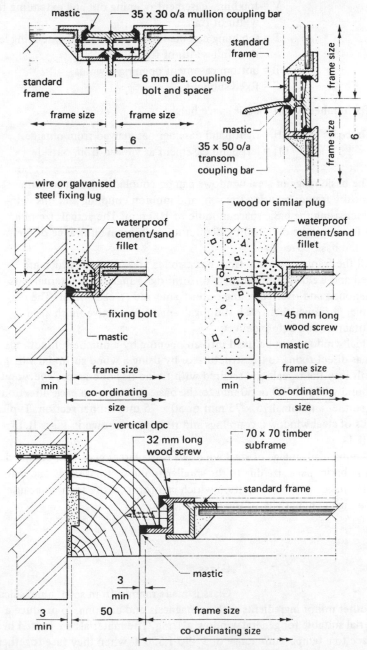

mastic

35 x 30 o/a mullion coupling bar

standard frame

standard frame

6 mm dia. coupling bolt and spacer

frame size

frame size

frame size

frame size

6

6

mastic

35 x 50 o/a transom coupling bar

wire or galvanised steel fixing lug

waterproof cement/sand fillet

fixing bolt

mastic

3 min

frame size

co-ordinating size

wood or similar plug

waterproof cement/sand fillet

45 mm long wood screw

mastic

3 min

frame size

co-ordinating size

vertical dpc

32 mm long wood screw

70 x 70 timber subframe

standard frame

mastic

3 min

3 min

50

frame size

co-ordinating size

Fig. II.14 Steel window couplings and fixings

V = top hung casement opening out and extending full width of frame.

T = top hung casement opening out and extending less than full width of frame.

B = bottom casement opening inwards.

S = fixed sublight.

Suffix number: x 100 = basic space height.

Suffix code: RH = right-hand casement as viewed from outside.

LH = left-hand casement as viewed from outside.

The basic range of steel windows can be coupled together to form composite frames by using transom and mullion coupling sections without increasing the basic space module of 100 mm. The actual size of a steel frame can be obtained by deducting the margin allowance of 6 mm from the basic space size.

All the frames are made from basic rolled steel sections which are mitred and welded at the corners to form right-angles; the internal bars are tenoned and rivetted to the outer frame and to each other. The completed frame receives a hot dip galvanised protective finish after manufacture and before delivery.

Steel windows can be fixed into an opening by a number of methods such as direct fixing to the structure or by using a wood surround which is built into the reveals and secured with fixing ties or cramps. The wood surround will add 100 or 50 mm to the basic space size in each direction using either a nominal 75 x 75 mm or 50 x 75 mm timber section. Typical details of steel windows, couplings and fixings are shown in Figs. II.13 and II.14.

The main advantage of steel windows is the larger glass area obtained for any basic space size due to the smaller frame sections used. The main disadvantage is the condensation which can form on the frames because of the high conductivity of the metal members.

Glass

Glass is made mainly from soda, lime, silica and other minor ingredients such as magnesia and alumina, to produce a material suitable for general window glazing. The materials are heated in a furnace to a temperature range of 1 490-1 550°C when they fuse together in a molten state—they are then formed into sheets by a process of drawing, floating or rolling.

DRAWN CLEAR SHEET GLASS

There are two principal methods of producing drawn clear sheet glass: the first is by vertical drawing from a pool of molten glass which when 1 m or so above the pool level is rigid enough to be engaged by a series of asbestos faced rollers that continue to draw the ribbon of glass up a tower some 10 m high, after which the ribbon is cut into sheets and washed in a dilute acid to remove surface deposits. In the second method the glass is initially drawn in the vertical plane but it is turned over a roller so that it is drawn in the horizontal direction for some 60 m and passes into an annealing furnace, at the cold end of which it is cut into sheets.

Clear sheet glass is a transparent glass with 85% light transmission, with a fire finished surface, but because the two surfaces are never perfectly flat or parallel there is always some distortion of vision and reflection. BS 952 recommends three qualities for sheet glass:

1. Ordinary glazing quality (OQ) to be used for general glazing purposes.
2. Selected glazing quality (SGQ) for glazing work requiring a sheet glass above the ordinary glazing quality.
3. Special selected quality (SSQ) for high grade work where a superfine sheet glass is required such as cabinets.

Generally six thicknesses are produced ranging from 2-6 mm thick, the 2 mm thickness not being recommended for general glazing.

FLOAT GLASS

This is a transparent glass giving 85% light transmission and is a truly flat glass with undistorted vision. It is formed by floating a continuous ribbon of molten glass over a bath of liquid metal at a controlled rate and temperature. A general glazing quality and a selected quality are produced in six thicknesses ranging from 3-12 mm thick.

ROLLED AND ROUGH CAST GLASS

This is a term applied to a flat glass produced by a rolling process. Generally the glass produced in this manner is translucent which transmits light with varying degrees of diffusion so that vision is not clear. A wired transparent glass with 80% light transmission is, however, produced generally in one thickness of 6 mm. The glass is made translucent by rolling on to one face a texture or pattern which will give 70-85% light transmission. Rough cast glass has an irregular texture to one side; wired rough cast glass comes in two forms, Georgian wired, which has a 12 mm square mesh electrically welded wire reinforcement, or hexagonally wired which is reinforced with hexagonal wire of approximately 20 mm mesh.

Rough cast glass is produced in 5, 6 and 10 mm thicknesses and is made for safety and fire resistant glazing purposes.

Glazing

The securing of glass in prepared openings such as in doors, windows and partitions is termed glazing. The actual calculations for glass sizing are beyond the scope of this book but it is logical that as the area of glass pane increases so must its thickness also increase; similarly position, wind load and building usage must be taken into account.

GLAZING WITHOUT BEADS

This is a suitable method for general domestic window and door panes, the glass is bedded in a compound and secured with sprigs, pegs or clips and fronted with a weathered surface putty. Putty is a glazing compound which will require a protective coating of paint as soon as practicable after glazing. Two kinds of putty are in general use:

1. **Linseed oil putty**: for use with primed wood members and is made from linseed oil and whiting, usually to the recommendations of BS 544.
2. **Metal casement putty**: for use with metal or non-absorbent wood members and is made from refined vegetable drying oils and finely ground chalk.

The glass pane should be cut to allow a minimum clearance of 2 mm all round for both wood and metal frames. Sufficient putty is applied to the rebate to give at least 2 mm of back putty when the glass is pressed into the rebate, any surplus putty being stripped off level or at an angle above the rebate. The glass should be secured with sprigs or clips at not more than 440 mm centres and finished off on the front edge with a weathered putty fillet so that the top edge of the fillet is at or just below the sight line (see Fig. II.15).

GLAZING WITH BEADS

For domestic work glazing with beads is generally applied to good class joinery. The beads should be secured with either panel pins or screws—for hardwoods it is usual to use cups and screws. The glass is bedded in a compound or a suitable glazing felt mainly to prevent damage by vibration to the glass. Beads are usually mitred at the corners to give continuity of any moulding. Beads for metal windows are usually supplied with the surround or frame and fixing of glass should follow the manufacturer's instructions (see Fig. II.15).

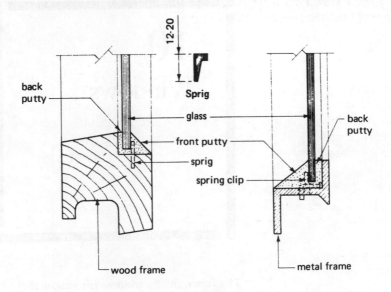

12-20

Sprig

back putty

glass

front putty

sprig

spring clip

back putty

wood frame

metal frame

Glazing Without Beads

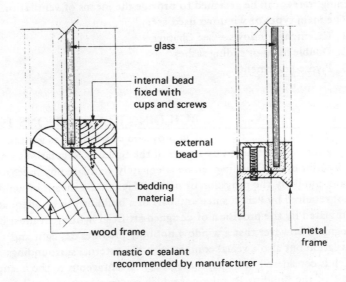

glass

internal bead fixed with cups and screws

external bead

bedding material

wood frame

metal frame

mastic or sealant recommended by manufacturer

Glazing With Beads

Fig. II.15 Glazing details

10
Windows

The function of a window is to allow the entry of light and air into the interior of the building. A window is essentially a frame of timber or metal set in an opening to which separate opening frames can be attached to provide the means of ventilation.

The main types of windows used are:

1. Casement windows — see Chapter 9.
2. Double hung or sliding sashes.
3. Pivoted casements.

BUILDING REGULATIONS 1985

The provision of windows as a means of ventilation is not required by Part F of the Building Regulations since the interior of any building can be adequately ventilated by mechanical means. Similarly the provision of natural daylight by means of windows is not required by Part F since any part of a building can be adequately illuminated by the provision of designed artificial lighting. It must be recognised however that a window not only provides daylight and ventilation but also a visual contact with the external surroundings, which is considered to be psychologically advantageous to the occupants. Part F of the Building Regulations which covers means of ventilation applies only to dwellings, rooms containing sanitary conveniences, bathrooms and buildings containing dwellings.

Building Regulation F1 requires that an adequate supply of air is provided for persons in the building. Approved Document F gives

recommendations of ways of achieving this objective. The basic
recommendations are:

1. Total area of ventilating opening(s) shall be not less than one-twentieth
   of the floor area of the room(s) it serves and one-fiftieth of the floor area
   for common spaces in buildings containing dwellings.
2. In habitable rooms some part of the ventilation opening(s) should be at
   least 1750 mm above floor level.
3. A door opening directly to the external air can be classed as a ventilation
   opening.
4. Background ventilation is to be provided by ventilation opening(s)
   having a total area of not less than 4000 mm² by a means which is
   controllable, secure are sited to avoid undue draughts.

If a form mechanical ventilation is to be used Approved Document F
recommends the following:

1. Kitchens – intermittent rapid ventilation of not less than 60 litres per
   second or if incorporated in a cooker hood not less than 30 litres per
   second, both with suitable background ventilation.
2. Bathrooms – intermittent minimum extraction rate of 15 litres per
   second.
3. Sanitary accommodation – intermittent minimum extraction rate of three
   air-changes per hour with a fifteen minute minimum overrun.
4. Common spaces – minimum extraction rate of air-change per hour.

Approved Document F also gives guidance as to the ventilation of a
habitable room facing a wall which is within 15.000 m of the ventilation
opening. Recommendations for both open and closed courts are given
(see Fig. II.16).

It should be noted that apart from providing ventilation and natural daylight
windows also contribute to heat loss from within the building. Therefore in the
context of conservation of fuel and power the maximum aggregate area of
windows and rooflights and/or the maximum calculated rate of heat loss are
controlled by Part L of the Building Regulations. The requirements under Part
L cover all types of buildings and are not, unlike Part F, concerned essentially
with dwellings – see Chapter 23 on page 199.

Bay windows

Any window which projects in front of the
main wall line is considered to be a bay window; various names are, however,
given to various plan layouts (see Fig. II.17). Bay windows can be constructed
of timber, and/or metal and designed with casement or sliding sashes; the
main difference in detail is the corner post, which can be made from the solid,
jointed or masked in the case of timber and tubular for metal windows
(see Fig. II.17).

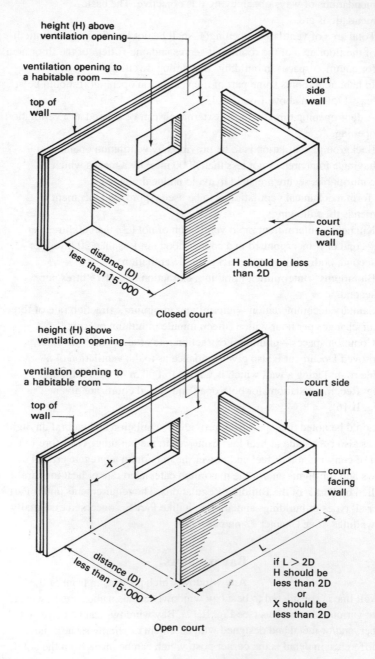

height (H) above
ventilation opening

ventilation opening to
a habitable room

top of
wall

court
side
wall

court
facing
wall

distance (D)
less than 15·000

H should be less
than 2D

Closed court

height (H) above
ventilation opening

ventilation opening to
a habitable room

top of
wall

court side
wall

X

court
facing
wall

distance (D)
less than 15·000

L

if L > 2D
H should be
less than 2D
or
X should be
less than 2D

Open court

Fig. II.16 Ventilation openings facing courts

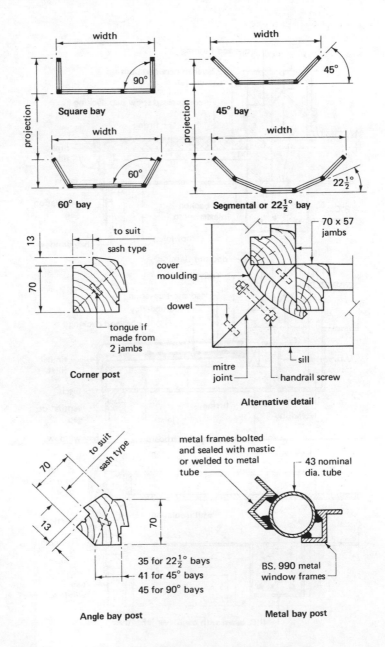

Fig. II.17 Bay window types and corner posts

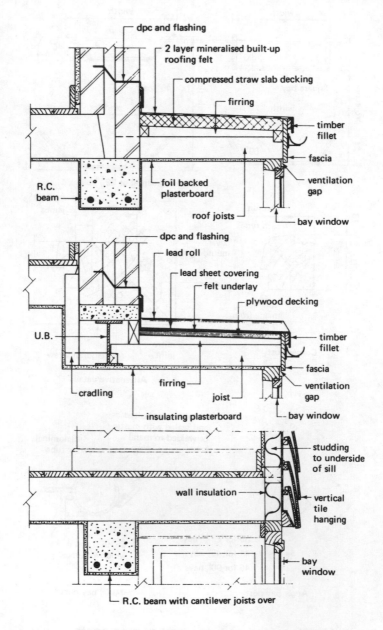

dpc and flashing
2 layer mineralised built-up roofing felt
compressed straw slab decking
firring
timber fillet
fascia
ventilation gap
R.C. beam
foil backed plasterboard
roof joists
bay window

dpc and flashing
lead roll
lead sheet covering
felt underlay
plywood decking
timber fillet
fascia
ventilation gap
U.B.
cradling
firring
joist
insulating plasterboard
bay window

studding to underside of sill
wall insulation
vertical tile hanging
bay window
R.C. beam with cantilever joists over

Fig. II.18   Bay window roofs and 2-storey bays

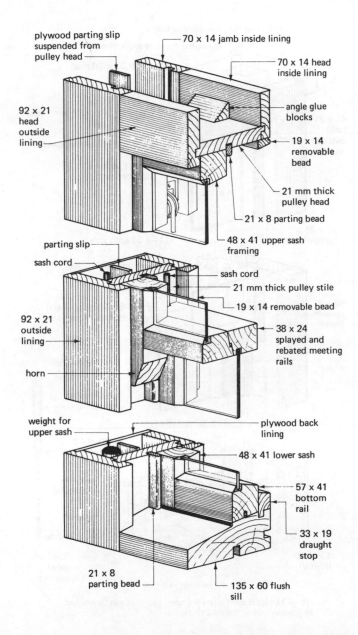

plywood parting slip suspended from pulley head

70 x 14 jamb inside lining

70 x 14 head inside lining

92 x 21 head outside lining

angle glue blocks

19 x 14 removable bead

21 mm thick pulley head

21 x 8 parting bead

48 x 41 upper sash framing

parting slip

sash cord

sash cord

21 mm thick pulley stile

19 x 14 removable bead

92 x 21 outside lining

38 x 24 splayed and rebated meeting rails

horn

weight for upper sash

plywood back lining

48 x 41 lower sash

57 x 41 bottom rail

33 x 19 draught stop

21 x 8 parting bead

135 x 60 flush sill

Fig. II.19   Double hung weight-balanced sash windows

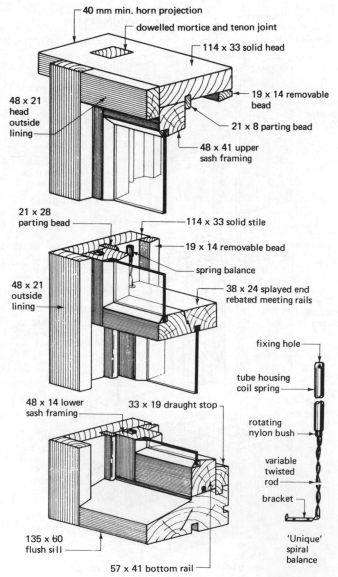

40 mm min. horn projection

dowelled mortice and tenon joint

114 x 33 solid head

48 x 21 head outside lining

19 x 14 removable bead

21 x 8 parting bead

48 x 41 upper sash framing

21 x 28 parting bead

114 x 33 solid stile

19 x 14 removable bead

spring balance

48 x 21 outside lining

38 x 24 splayed end rebated meeting rails

fixing hole

tube housing coil spring

rotating nylon bush

variable twisted rod

bracket

48 x 14 lower sash framing

33 x 19 draught stop

135 x 60 flush sill

57 x 41 bottom rail

'Unique' spiral balance

NB if 114 x 60 solid stiles are used balances can be housed in grooves within the stile thickness

Fig. II.20   Double hung spring-balanced sash windows

The bay window can be applied to one floor only or continued over several storeys. Any roof treatment can be used to cover in the projection and weather seal it to the main wall (see Fig. II.18). No minimum head-room heights for bay windows or habitable rooms is given in the Building Regulations but 2.000 in bay windows and 2.300 in rooms would be considered reasonable. A bay window which occurs only on upper storeys is generally called an oriel window.

Double hung sash windows

These windows are sometimes called vertical sliding sash windows and consist of two sashes sliding vertically over one another. They are costly to construct but are considered to be more stable than side hung sashes and have a better control over the size of ventilation opening thus reducing the possibility of draughts.

In timber two methods of suspension are possible:

1. Weight balanced type.
2. Spring balanced type.

The former is the older method in which the counter balance weights suspended by cords are housed in a boxed framed jamb or mullion and have been generally superseded by the metal spring balance which uses a solid frame and needs less maintenance (see Figs. II.19 and II.20).

Double hung sashes in metal are supported and controlled by spring balances or by friction devices but the basic principles remain the same.

Pivot windows

The basic construction of the frame and sash is similar to that of a standard casement frame and sash. The sash can be arranged to pivot horizontally or vertically on friction pivots housed in the jambs or in the cill and head. These windows give good adjustment for ventilation purposes and in the main both faces of the glazing can be cleaned from the inside of the building.

11

Rooflights in pitched roofs

Rooflights can be included in the design of a pitched roof to provide daylight and ventilation to rooms within the roof space or to supplement the daylight from windows in the walls of medium and large span single storey buildings.

In domestic work a rooflight generally takes one of two forms — the dormer window or skylight. A dormer window has a vertical sash and therefore projects from the main roof, the cheeks or sides can be clad with a sheet material such as lead or tile hanging and the roof can be pitched or flat of traditional construction (see Fig. II.21).

A skylight is fixed in a trimmed opening and follows approximately the pitch of the roof. It can be constructed as an opening or dead light (see Fig. II.22). In common with all rooflights in pitched roofs, making the junctions water and weathertight present the greatest problems, and careful attention must be given to the detail and workmanship involved in the construction of dormer windows and rooflights.

Roofs of the type used on medium span industrial buildings with coverings such as corrugated fibre cement sheeting supported by purlins and steel roof trusses require a different treatment. The amount of useful daylight entering the interior of such a building from windows fixed in the external walls will depend upon:

1. The size of windows.
2. The height of window above the floor level.
3. The span of building.

Generally the maximum distance useful daylight will penetrate is approximately 10.000 m, over this distance artificial lights or roof lights

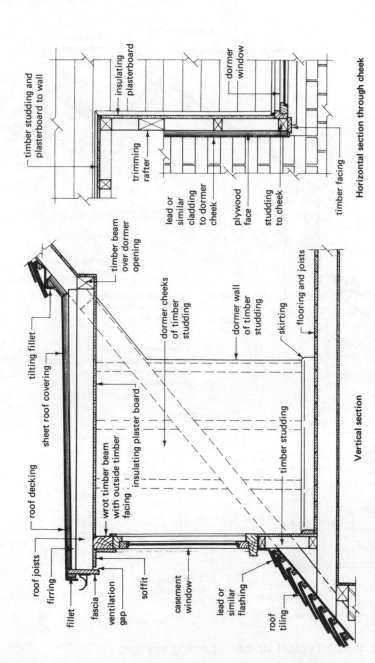

timber studding and plasterboard to wall

insulating plasterboard

dormer window

trimming rafter

lead or similar cladding to dormer cheek

plywood face

studding to cheek

timber facing

Horizontal section through cheek

tilting fillet

sheet roof covering

timber beam over dormer opening

dormer cheeks of timber studding

dormer wall of timber studding

skirting

flooring and joists

roof decking

wrot timber beam with outside timber facing

insulating plaster board

timber studding

roof joists

firring

fillet

fascia

ventilation gap

soffit

casement window

lead or similar flashing

roof tiling

Vertical section

Fig. II.21 Typical flat roof dormer window details

87

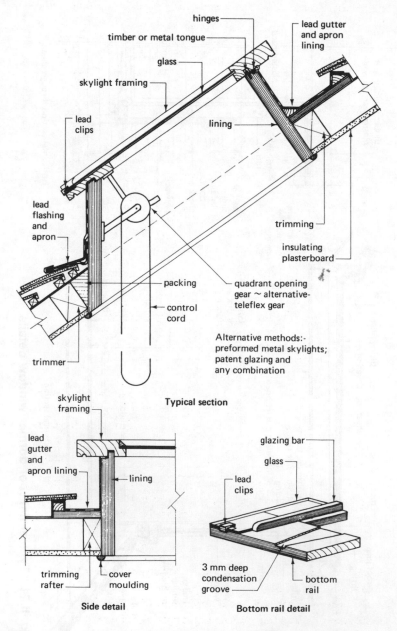

hinges

timber or metal tongue

glass

lead gutter
and apron
lining

skylight framing

lead
clips

lining

lead
flashing
and
apron

trimming

insulating
plasterboard

packing

quadrant opening
gear ~ alternative-
teleflex gear

control
cord

trimmer

Alternative methods:-
preformed metal skylights;
patent glazing and
any combination

skylight
framing

Typical section

lead
gutter
and
apron lining

lining

glazing bar

glass

lead
clips

trimming
rafter

cover
moulding

3 mm deep
condensation
groove

bottom
rail

Side detail

Bottom rail detail

Fig. II.22 Typical timber opening skylight

will be required during the daylight period. Three methods are available for the provision of roof lights in profiled sheeted roofs.

Special rooflight units of fibre cement consisting of an upstand kerb surmounted by either a fixed or opening glazed sash can be fixed instead of a standard profiled sheet. These units are useful where the design calls for a series of small isolated glazed rooflights to supplement the natural daylight. An alternative is to use translucent profiled sheets which are of the same size and profile as the main roof covering. In selecting the type of sheet to be used the requirements of Part B of the Building Regulations must be considered. Approved Document B (A3) deals specifically with the fire risks of roof coverings and refers to the designations defined in BS 476: Part 3. These designations consist of two letters, the first letter represents the time of penetration when subjected to external fire and the second letter is the distance of spread of flame along the external surface. Each group of designations has four letters and in both cases the letter A has the highest resistance. Specimens used in the BS 476 test are either tested for use on a flat surface or a sloping surface and therefore the material designation is preceded by either EXT. F or EXT. S.

Most of the translucent profiled sheets have a high light transmission, are light in weight and can be fixed in the same manner as the general roof covering. It is advisable to weather seal all lapping edges of profiled rooflights with asbestos tape or mastic to accommodate the variations in thickness and expansion rate of the adjacent materials. Typical examples are:

Polyester glass fibre sheets: made from polyester resins reinforced with glass fibre and nylon to the recommendations of BS 4154. These sheets can be of natural colour or tinted and are made to suit most corrugated asbestos cement and metal profiles. Typical designations are EXT. S.AA for self-extinguishing sheets and EXT. S.AB for general-purpose sheets.

Wire reinforced PVC sheets: made from unplasticised PVC reinforced with a fine wire mesh to give a high resistance to shattering by impact. Designation is EXT. S.AA and they can therefore be used for all roofing applications. Profiles are generally limited to Class 1 and 2 defined in BS 690:Part 3.

PVC sheets: made from heavy gauge clear unplasticised rigid PVC to the recommendations of BS 4203 are classified as self-extinguishing when tested in accordance with method 508A of BS 2782 and may be used on the roof of a building provided that part of the roof is at least 6.000 m from any boundary. If that part of the roof is less than

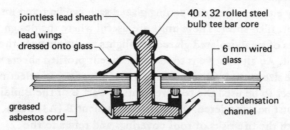

jointless lead sheath

lead wings
dressed onto glass

40 x 32 rolled steel
bulb tee bar core

6 mm wired
glass

greased
asbestos cord

condensation
channel

Crittall-Hope lead-clothed steel bar

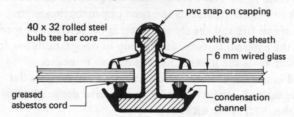

40 x 32 rolled steel
bulb tee bar core

pvc snap on capping

white pvc sheath

6 mm wired glass

greased
asbestos cord

condensation
channel

Crittall-Hope polyclad bar

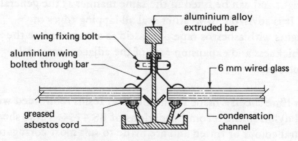

aluminium alloy
extruded bar

wing fixing bolt

aluminium wing
bolted through bar

6 mm wired glass

greased
asbestos cord

condensation
channel

British Challenge aluminium bar

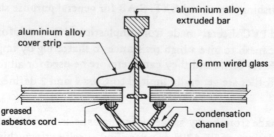

aluminium alloy
extruded bar

aluminium alloy
cover strip

6 mm wired glass

greased
asbestos cord

condensation
channel

Heywood Williams 'Aluminex' bar

Fig. II.23 Typical patent glazing bar sections

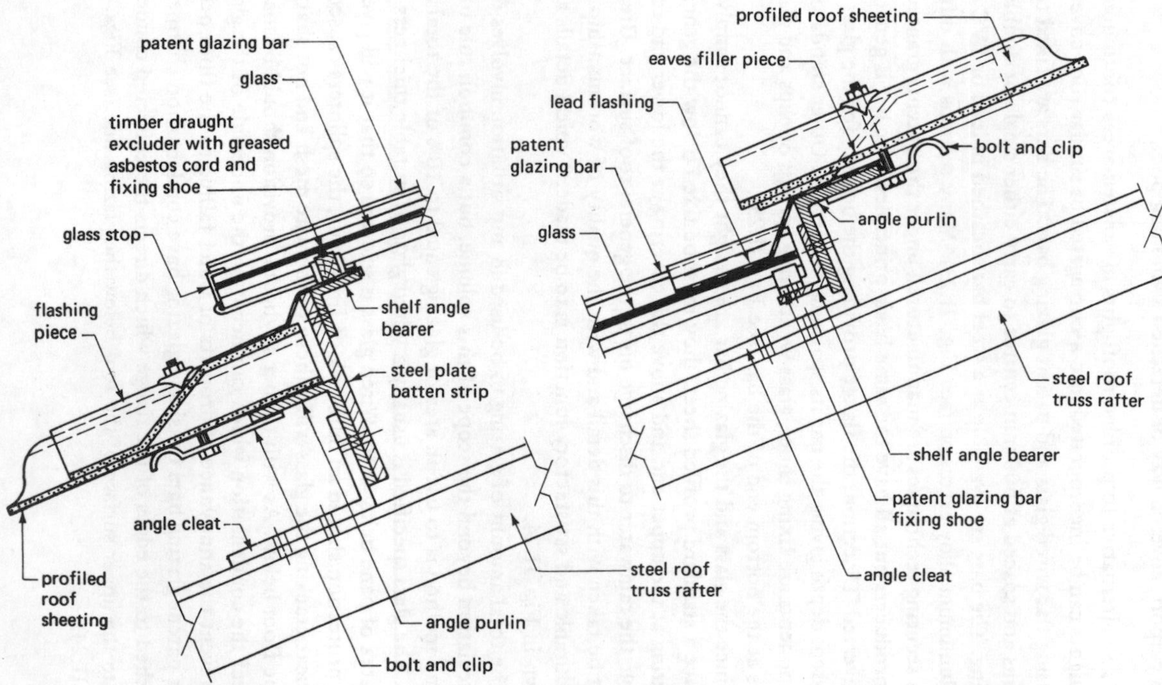
patent glazing bar
glass
timber draught excluder with greased asbestos cord and fixing shoe
glass stop
flashing piece
shelf angle bearer
steel plate batten strip
angle cleat
profiled roof sheeting
angle purlin
bolt and clip
steel roof truss rafter
profiled roof sheeting
eaves filler piece
lead flashing
patent glazing bar
bolt and clip
angle purlin
glass
steel roof truss rafter
shelf angle bearer
patent glazing bar fixing shoe
angle cleat

Fig. II.24 Patent glazing and profiled roof covering connection details

6.000 m from any boundary and covers a garage, conservatory or out-house with a floor area of less than 40 m^2 PVC sheets can be used without restriction. Table 6.3 of Approved Document B defines the use of these sheets for the roof covering of a canopy over a balcony, veranda, open carport, covered way or detached swimming pool.

As an alternative to profiled rooflights in isolated areas continuous rooflights can be incorporated into a corrugated or similar roof covering by using flat wired glass and patent glazing bars. The bars are fixed to the purlins and spaced at 600 mm centres to carry either single or double glazing. The bars are available as a steel bar sheathed in lead or PVC or as an aluminium alloy extrusion (see Fig. II.23). Many sections with different glass securing techniques are manufactured under the patents granted to the producers but all have the same basic principles. The bar is generally an inverted 'T' section, the flange providing the bearing for the glass and the stem depth giving the bar its spanning properties. Other standard components are fixing shoes, glass weathering springs or clips and glass stops at the bottom end of the bar (see Fig. II.23).

Since the glass and the glazing bar are straight they cannot simply replace a standard profiled sheet, they must be fixed below the general covering at the upper end and above the covering at the lower end to enable the rainwater to discharge on to the general roof surface. Great care must be taken with this detail and with the quality of workmanship on site if a durable and satisfactory junction is to be made. Typical details are shown in Fig. II.24.

The total amount of glazing to be used in any situation involves design appreciation beyond the scope of this volume, but a common rule of thumb method is to use an area of glazing equal to 10% of the total roof area. The glass specified is usually a wired glass of suitable thickness for the area of pane being used. Wired glass is selected so that it will give the best protection should an outbreak of fire occur; the splinters caused by the heat cracking the glass will adhere to the wire mesh and not shatter on to the floor below. As with timber skylights, provision should be made to collect the condensation which can occur on the underside of the glazing to prevent the annoyance of droplets of water falling to the floor below. Most patent glazing bars for single glazing have condensation channels attached to the edges of the flange which directs the collected condensa-tion to the upper surface of the roof below the glazing line (see Figs. II.23 and II.24).

12
Finishes, fittings and decorating – partitions

Internal walls which divide the interior of a building into areas of accommodation and circulation are called partitions and these can be classified as load bearing or non-load bearing partitions.

Load bearing partitions

These are designed and constructed to receive superimposed loadings and transmit these loads to a foundation. Generally load bearing partitions are constructed of bricks or blocks bonded to the external walls. Openings are formed in the same manner as for external walls; a lintel spans the opening carrying the load above to the reveals on either side of the opening. Fixings can usually be made direct into block walls, whereas walls of bricks require to be drilled and plugged to receive nails or screws. Apart from receiving direct fixings block partitions are lighter, cheaper, quicker to build and have better thermal insulation properties than brick walls but their sound insulation values are slightly lower. For these reasons blockwork is usually specified for load bearing partitions in domestic work. Load bearing partitions are, because of their method of construction, considered to be permanently positioned.

Non-load bearing partitions

These partitions, like load bearing partitions, must be designed and constructed to carry their own weight and any

93

fittings or fixings which may be attached to them, but they must not under any circumstances be used to carry or assist in the transmission of structural loadings. They must be designed to provide a suitable division between internal spaces and be able to resist impact loadings on their faces, also any vibrations set up by doors being closed or slammed.

Bricks or blocks can be used for the construction of non-load bearing partitions being built directly off the floor and pinned (or wedged) to the underside of the ceiling or joists with slate or tile slips and mortar. If the partition is built off a suspended timber floor a larger joist section or two joists side by side must be used to carry the load of the partition to the floor support walls. Openings are constructed as for load bearing walls or alternatively a storey height frame could be used.

Timber stud partitions with suitable facings are lighter than brick or block partitions but are less efficient as sound or thermal insulators. They are easy to construct and provide a good fixing background and because of their lightness are suitable for building off a suspended timber floor. The basic principle is to construct a simple framed grid of timber to which a dry lining such as plywood, plasterboard or hardboard can be attached. The lining material will determine the spacing of the uprights or studs to save undue wastage in cutting the boards to terminate on the centre line of a stud. To achieve a good finish it is advisable to use studs which have equal thicknesses since the thin lining materials will follow any irregularity of the face of the studwork. Openings are formed by framing a head between two studs and fixing a lining or door frame into the opening in the stud partition; typical details are shown in Fig. II.25.

Plasterboard bonded on either side of a strong paper cellure core to form rigid panels are suitable as non-load bearing partitions. These are fixed to wall and ceiling battens and supported on a timber sole plate. Timber blocks are inserted into the core to provide the fixing medium for door frames or linings and skirtings (see Fig. II.26). This form of partition is available with facings suitable for direct decoration, plaster coat finish or with a plastic face as a self finish.

Compressed strawboard panels provide another alternative method for non-load bearing partitions. The storey height panels are secured to a sole plate and a head plate by skew or tosh nailing through the leading edge. The 3 mm joint between consecutive panels is made with an adhesive supplied by the manufacturer. Openings are formed by using storey height frames fixed with 100 mm screws direct into the edge of the panel. The joints are covered with a strip of hessian scrim and the whole partition is given a skim coat of board plaster finish (see Fig. II.26).

Partially prefabricated partitions, such as the plasterboard and straw-board described above, can be erected on site without undue mess. Being mainly a dry construction they reduce the drying time required with the

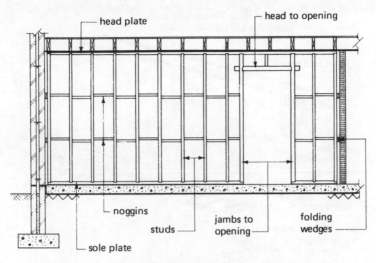

head plate

head to opening

noggins

studs

jambs to opening

folding wedges

sole plate

Typical Arrangement

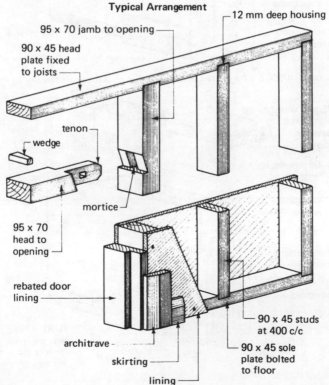

12 mm deep housing

95 x 70 jamb to opening

90 x 45 head plate fixed to joists

tenon

wedge

mortice

95 x 70 head to opening

rebated door lining

architrave

skirting

lining

90 x 45 studs at 400 c/c

90 x 45 sole plate bolted to floor

Fig. II.25 Typical timber stud partition

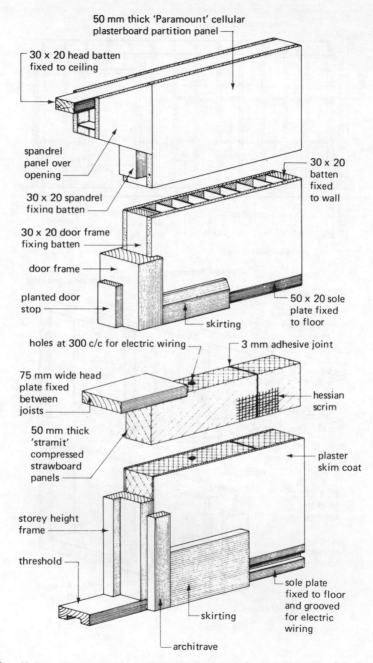

50 mm thick 'Paramount' cellular plasterboard partition panel

30 x 20 head batten fixed to ceiling

spandrel panel over opening

30 x 20 spandrel fixing batten

30 x 20 batten fixed to wall

30 x 20 door frame fixing batten

door frame

planted door stop

50 x 20 sole plate fixed to floor

skirting

holes at 300 c/c for electric wiring

3 mm adhesive joint

75 mm wide head plate fixed between joists

hessian scrim

50 mm thick 'stramit' compressed strawboard panels

plaster skim coat

storey height frame

threshold

sole plate fixed to floor and grooved for electric wiring

skirting

architrave

Fig. II.26 Typical preformed partions

traditional brick and block walls. They also have the advantage, like timber stud partitions, of being capable of removal or repositioning without causing serious damage to the structure or without causing serious problems to a contractor.

13
Finishes – floor, wall and ceiling

FLOOR FINISHES

The type of floor finish to be applied to a floor will depend upon a number of factors such as type of base, room usage, degree of comfort required, maintenance problems, cost, appearance, safety and individual preference.

Floor finishes can be considered under three main headings:

1. *In situ* **floor finishes**: the finishes which are mixed on site, laid in a fluid state, allowed to dry and set to form a hard jointless surface.
2. **Applied floor finishes**: those finishes which are supplied in tile or sheet form and are laid on to a suitably prepared base.
3. **Timber floor finishes**: these are boards, sheets and blocks of timber laid on or attached to a suitable structural frame or base.

In situ floor finishes

MASTIC ASPHALT

This is a naturally occurring bituminous material obtained from asphalt lakes like those in Trinidad or it can also be derived from crude oil residues. Trinidad lake asphalt is used as a matrix or cement to a suitably graded mineral aggregate to form mastic asphalt as a material suitable for floor finishing. When laid mastic asphalt is impervious to water and is ideal for situations such as sculleries and wash rooms. It also forms a very good surface on which to apply thin tile and sheet finishes (for example,

PVC) and will at the same time fulfil the function of a damp-proof membrane.

Mastic asphalt is a thermoplastic material and has to be melted before it can be applied to form a jointless floor finish. Hot mastic asphalt is applied by means of a float at a temperature of between 180 and 210°C in a single 13 mm coat as a base for applied finishes or in a 16 mm single coat for a self finish. Any sound and rigid subfloor is suitable but a layer of ordinary black sheathing felt should be included between the subfloor and mastic asphalt to overcome the problems caused by differential movement. The finish obtained is smooth and hard but the colour range is limited to dark colours such as red, brown and black. A matt surface can be produced by giving the top surface a dusting of sand or powdered stone.

PITCH MASTIC

Pitch mastic is a similar material to mastic asphalt but is produced from a mixture of calcareous and/or siliceous aggregates bonded with coal tar pitch. It is laid to a similar thickness and in a similar manner to mastic asphalt with a polished or matt finish. Pitch mastic floors are resistant to water but have a better resistance to oil and fats than mastic asphalt and are therefore suitable for sculleries, washrooms and kitchens.

GRANOLITHIC

This is a mixture of Portland cement and granite chippings which can be applied to a 'green' concrete subfloor or to a cured concrete subfloor. Green concrete is a term used to describe newly laid concrete which is not more than three hours old. A typical mix for granolithic is 1 part cement : 1 part sand : 2 parts granite chippings (5-10 mm free from dust) by volume. The finish obtained is very hard wearing, noisy and cold to touch; it is used mainly in situations where easy maintenance and durability are paramount such as a common entrance hall to a block of flats.

If granolithic is being applied to a green concrete subfloor as a topping it is applied in a single layer approximately 20 mm thick in bay sizes not exceeding 28 m^2 and trowelled to a smooth surface. This method will result in a monolithic floor and finish construction.

The surface of mature concrete will need to be prepared by hacking the entire area and brushing well to remove all the laitance before laying a single layer of granolithic which should be at least 40 mm thick. The finish should be laid, on a wet cement slurry coating to improve the bond, in bay sizes not exceeding 14 m^2.

MAGNESIUM OXYCHLORIDE

This is a composition flooring which is sometimes used as a substitute for asphalt since it has similar wearing and appearance properties. It is mixed on site using a solution of magnesium chloride with burned magnesite and fillers such as wood flour, sawdust, powdered asbestos or limestone. It is essential that the ingredients are thoroughly mixed in a dry state before the correct amount of solution is added. The mixed material is laid in one or two layers giving a total thickness of approximately 20 mm. The sub-floor must be absolutely dry otherwise the finish will lift and crack, therefore a damp-proof membrane in the subfloor is essential.

Applied floor finishes

Many of the applied floor finishes are thin flexible materials and should be laid on a subfloor with a smooth finish. This is often achieved by laying a cement/sand bed or screed with a steel float finish to the concrete subfloor. The usual screed mix is 1:3 cement/ sand and great care must be taken to ensure that a good bond is obtained with the subfloor. If the screed is laid on green concrete a thickness of 12 mm is usually specified whereas screeds laid on mature concrete require a thickness of 40 mm. A mature concrete subfloor must be clean, free from dust and dampened with water to reduce the suction before applying the bonding agent to receive the screed. To reduce the possibility of drying shrinkage cracks screeds should not be laid in bays exceeding 15 m^2 in area.

FLEXIBLE PVC TILES AND SHEET

Flexible PVC is a popular hardwearing floor finish produced by a mixture of polyvinyl chloride resin, pigments and mineral fillers. It is produced as 300 x 300 mm square tiles or in sheet form up to 2 400 mm wide with a range of thicknesses from 1·5-3 mm. The floor tiles and sheet are fixed with an adhesive recommended by the manufacturer and produce a surface suitable for most situations. PVC tiles, like all other small unit coverings, should be laid from the centre of the area towards the edges, so that if the area is not an exact tile module an even border of cut tiles is obtained.

THERMOPLASTIC TILES

These are sometimes called asphalt tiles and are produced from coumarone indene resins, fillers and pigments; the earlier use of asphalt binders limited the range of colours available. These tiles are hardwearing, moisture resistant and are suitable for most situations, being produced generally as a 225 mm square tile either 3 or 4·5 mm thick. To make them pliable they are usually heated before being fixed with a bituminous adhesive.

RUBBER TILES AND SHEET

Solid rubber tiles or sheet is produced from natural or synthetic rubber compounded with fillers to give colour and texture, the rubber content being not less than 35%. The covering is hardwearing, quiet and water resistant and suitable for bathrooms and washrooms. Thicknesses range from 3-6·5 mm with square tile sizes ranging from 150-1 200 mm; sheet widths range from 900-1 800 mm. Fixing is by rubber based adhesives, as recommended by the manufacturer, to a smooth surface.

LINOLEUM

Linoleum is produced in sheet or tile form from a mixture of drying oils, resins, fillers and pigments which is pressed on to a hessian or bitumen saturated felt paper backing. Good quality linoleum has the pattern inlaid or continuing through the thickness whereas the cheaper quality has only a printed surface pattern. Linoleum gives a quiet, resilient and hardwearing surface suitable for most domestic floors. Thicknesses vary from 2-6·5 mm for a standard sheet width of 1 800 mm; tiles are usually 300 mm square with the same range of thicknesses. Fixing of linoleum tiles and sheet is by adhesive to any dry smooth surface, although the adhesive is sometimes omitted with the thicker sheets.

CARPET

The chief materials used in the production of carpets are nylon, acrylics and wool or mixtures of these materials. There is a vast range of styles, types, patterns, colours, qualities and sizes available for general domestic use in dry situations since the resistance of carpets to dampness is generally poor. To obtain maximum life carpets should be laid over an underlay of felt or latex and secured by adhesives, nailing around the perimeter or being stretched over and attached to special edge fixing strips. Carpet is supplied in narrow or wide rolls, carpet squares (600 x 600 x 25 mm thick) are also available for covering floors without the use of adhesives; these rely on the interlocking of the edge fibres to form a continuous covering.

CORK TILES AND CARPET

Cork tiles are cut from baked blocks of granulated cork where the natural resins act as the binder. The tiles are generally 300 mm square with thicknesses of 5 mm upwards according to the wearing quality required and are supplied in three natural shades. They are hardwearing, quiet and resilient but unless treated with a surface sealant they may collect dirt and grit. Fixing is by using an adhesive recommended by the manufacturer, with the addition of nine steel pins around the edge to prevent curling.

Cork carpet is a similar material but it is made pliable by bonding the cork granules with linseed oil and resins on to a jute canvas backing. It is laid in the same manner as described above for linoleum and should be treated with a surface sealant to resist dirt and grit penetration.

QUARRY TILES

The term 'quarry' is derived from the Italian word *quadro* meaning square and does not mean that the tiles are cut or won from an open excavation or quarry. They are made from ordinary or unrefined clays worked into a plastic form, pressed into shape and hard burnt. Being hardwearing and with a good resistance to water they are suitable for kitchens and entrance halls but they tend to be noisy and cold. Quarry tiles are produced as square tiles in sizes ranging from 100 x 100 x 20 mm to 225 x 225 x 32 mm thick.

Three methods of laying quarry tiles are recommended to allow for differential movement due to drying shrinkage or thermal movement of the screed. The first method is to bed the tiles in a 10-15 mm thick bed of cement mortar over a separating layer of sheet material such as polythene, which could perform the dual function of damp-proof membrane and separating layer. To avoid the use of a separating layer the 'thick bed' method can be used. With this method the concrete subfloor should be dampened to reduce suction and then covered with a semi-dry 1 : 4 cement/sand mix to a thickness of approximately 40 mm. The top surface of the compacted semi-dry 'thick bed' should be treated with a 1 : 1 cement/sand grout before tapping the tiles in to the grout with a wood beater. Alternatively a dry cement may be trowelled into the 'thick bed' surface before bedding in the tiles. Special cement based adhesives are also available for bedding tiles to a screed and these should be used in accordance with the manufacturer's instructions to provide a thin bed fixing.

Clay tiles may expand probably due to physical adsorption of water and chemical hydration and for this reason an expansion joint of compressible material should be incorporated around the perimeter of the floor (see Fig. II.27). In no circumstances should the length or width of a quarry tile floor exceed 7 500 mm without an expansion joint. The joints between quarry tiles are usually grouted with a 1 : 1 cement/sand grout and then, after cleaning, the floor should be protected with sand or saw-dust for four or five days. There is a wide variety of tread patterns available to provide a non-slip surface, also a wide range of fittings are available to form skirtings and edge coves (see Fig. II.27).

PLAIN CLAY FLOOR TILES

These are similar to quarry tiles but are produced from refined natural clays which are pressed after grinding and tempering into the desired shape before being fired at a high temperature. Plain clay floor tiles, being denser than quarry tiles, are made as smaller and thinner units ranging from 75 x 75 mm to 150 x 150 mm, all sizes being 13 mm thick.

Laying, finishes and fittings available are all as described for quarry tiles.

Timber floor finishes

Timber is a very popular floor finish with both designer and user because of its natural appearance, resilience and warmth. It is available as a board, strip, sheet or block finish and if attached to joists, as in the case of a suspended timber floor, it also acts as the structural decking.

TIMBER BOARDS

Softwood timber floor boards are joined together by tongued and grooved joints along their edges and are fixed by nailing to the support joists or fillets attached to a solid floor. The boards are butt jointed in their length, the joints being positioned centrally over the supports and staggered so that butt joints do not occur in the same position in consecutive lengths. The support spacing will be governed by the spanning properties of the board (which is controlled by its thickness) and supports placed at 400 mm centres are usual for boards of 19 and 22 mm thick. The tongue is positioned slightly off centre and the boards should be laid with the narrow shoulder on the underside to give maximum wear. It is essential that the boards are well cramped together before being fixed to form a tight joint and that they are laid in a position where they will not be affected by dampness. Timber is a hygroscopic material and will therefore swell and shrink as its moisture content varies—ideally this should be maintained at around 12%.

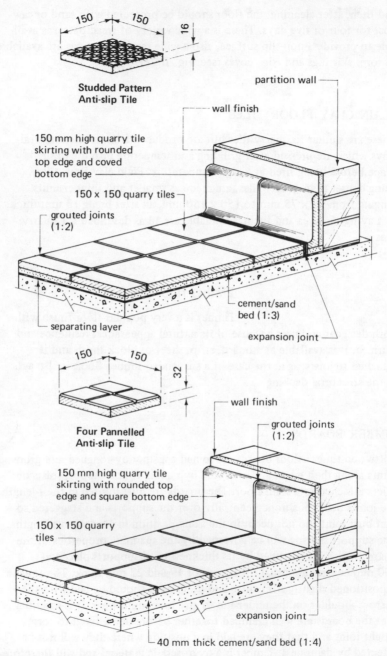

150
150
16

**Studded Pattern
Anti-slip Tile**

partition wall

wall finish

150 mm high quarry tile
skirting with rounded
top edge and coved
bottom edge

150 x 150 quarry tiles

grouted joints
(1:2)

cement/sand
bed (1:3)

separating layer

expansion joint

150
150
32

**Four Pannelled
Anti-slip Tile**

wall finish

grouted joints
(1:2)

150 mm high quarry tile
skirting with rounded top
edge and square bottom edge

150 x 150 quarry
tiles

expansion joint

40 mm thick cement/sand bed (1:4)

Fig. II.27 Typical quarry tile floors

TIMBER STRIP

These are narrow boards being under 100 mm wide to reduce the amount
of shrinkage and consequent opening of the joints. Timber strip can be
supplied in softwood or hardwood and is considered to be a superior
floor finish to boards. Jointing and laying is as described for boards,
except that hardwood strip is very often laid one strip at a time and
secret nailed (see Fig. II.28).

TIMBER SHEET FLOOR FINISH

Chipboard is manufactured from wood chips or shavings bonded together
with thermosetting synthetic resins, and forms rigid sheets 12·5 and
19 mm thick which is suitable as a floor finish. The sheets are fixed by
nailing or screwing to support joists or fillets and should have a plywood
reinforcement in the form of a loose tongue to all adjoining edges which
need to be grooved to receive the tongue. If the sheet is used as an exposed
finish a coating of sealer should be used. Alternatively chipboard can be
used as a decking to which a thin tile or carpet finish can be applied.

    Tongued and grooved boards of 600 mm width are also available as a
floor decking material which do not need to be jointed over a joist.

WOOD BLOCKS

These are small blocks of timber usually of hardwood which are designed
to be laid in set patterns. Lengths range from 150-300 mm with widths up
to 89 mm; the width being proportional to the length to enable the
various patterns to be created. Block thicknesses range from 20-30 mm
thick and the final thickness after sanding and polishing being about
5-10 mm thinner.

    The blocks are jointed along their edges with a tongued and grooved
joint and have a rebate, chamfer or dovetail along the bottom longitudinal
edges to take up any surplus adhesive used for fixing. Two methods can
be used for fixing wood blocks: the first uses hot bitumen and the second
a cold latex bitumen emulsion. If hot bitumen is used the upper surface
of the subfloor is first primed with black varnish to improve adhesion,
and then, before laying, the bottom face of the block is dipped into the
hot bitumen. The cold adhesive does not require a priming coat to the
subfloor. Blocks, like tiled floors, should be laid from the centre of the
floor towards the perimeter, which is generally terminated with a margin
border. To allow for moisture movement a cork expansion strip should be
placed around the entire edge of the block floor (see Fig. II.28).

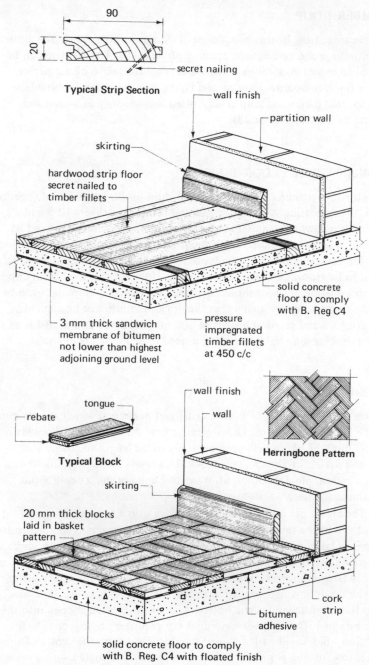

90

20

secret nailing

Typical Strip Section

wall finish

partition wall

skirting

hardwood strip floor
secret nailed to
timber fillets

solid concrete
floor to comply
with B. Reg C4

3 mm thick sandwich
membrane of bitumen
not lower than highest
adjoining ground level

pressure
impregnated
timber fillets
at 450 c/c

tongue

rebate

Typical Block

wall finish

wall

Herringbone Pattern

skirting

20 mm thick blocks
laid in basket
pattern

cork
strip

bitumen
adhesive

solid concrete floor to comply
with B. Reg. C4 with floated finish

Fig. II.28 Typical timber floor finishes

PARQUET

This is a superior form of wood block flooring made from specially selected hardwoods chosen mainly for their decorative appearance. Parquet blocks are generally smaller and thinner than hardwood blocks and are usually fixed to a timber subfloor which is level and smooth. Fixing can be by adhesives or secret nailed, alternatively they can be supplied as a patterned panel fixed to a suitable backing sheet in panel sizes from 300-600 mm square.

Wall finishes

External brickwork with an exposed face of facing bricks is a self finish and requires no further treatment. External walls of common bricks or blocks can be treated to give an acceptable appearance by the application of paint, an applied wall finish such as rendering or be clad with boards or tiles. Internal walls or partitions can be built with a fair face of natural materials such as bricks or stone but generally it is cheaper to use a material such as blocks with an applied finish like plaster, dry lining or glazed tiles.

External rendering

This is a form of plastering using a mixture of cement and sand, or cement, lime and sand, applied to the face of a building to give extra protection against the penetration of moisture or to provide a desired texture. It can also be used in the dual capacity of providing protection and appearance.

The rendering must have the properties of durability, moisture resistance and an acceptable appearance. The factors to be taken into account in achieving the above requirements are mix design, bond to the backing material, texture of surface, degree of exposure of the building and the standard of workmanship in applying the rendering.

Cement and sand mixes will produce a strong moisture resistant rendering but one which is subject to cracking due to high drying shrinkage. These mixes are used mainly on members which may be vulnerable to impact damage such as columns. Cement, lime and sand mixes have a lower drying shrinkage but are more absorbent than cement and sand mixes; they will, however, dry out rapidly after periods of rain and are therefore the mix recommended for general use.

The two factors which govern the proportions to be used in a mix are:

1. Background to which the rendering is to be applied.
2. Degree of exposure of the building.

The two common volume mix ratios are:

(a) $1 : \frac{1}{2} : 4\text{-}4\frac{1}{2}$ cement : lime : sand which is used for dense, strong backgrounds of moderate to severe exposure and for application to metal lathing or expanded metal backgrounds.

(b) $1 : 1 : 5\text{-}6$ cement : lime : sand which is for general use.

If the rendering is to be applied in a cold, damp situation the cement content of the mix ratio should be increased by 1. The final coat is usually a weaker mix than the undercoats, for example, when using an undercoat mix $1 : 1 : 6$ the final coat mix ratio should be $1 : 2 : 9$, this will reduce the amount of shrinkage in the final coat. The number of coats required will depend upon the surface condition of the background and the degree of exposure. Generally a two coat application is acceptable, except where the background is very irregular or the building is in a position of severe exposure when a three coat application would be specified. The thickness of any one coat should not exceed 15 mm and each subsequent coat thickness is reduced by approximately 3 mm to give a final coat thickness of 6-10 mm.

Various textured surfaces can be obtained on renderings by surface treatments such as scraping the surface with combs, saw blades or similar tools to remove a surface skin of mortar. These operations are carried out some three to four hours after the initial application of the rendering and before the final set takes place.

Alternative treatments are:

1. **Roughcast:** a wet plaster mix of 1 part cement : $\frac{1}{2}$ part lime : $1\frac{1}{2}$ parts shingle : 3 parts sand which is thrown on to a porous coat of rendering to give an even distribution.
2. **Pebbledash:** selected aggregate such as pea shingle is dashed or thrown on to a rendering background before it has set and is tamped into the surface with a wood float to obtain a good bond.
3. **Spattered finishes:** these are finishes applied by a machine (which can be hand operated), guns or sprays using special mixes prepared by the machine manufacturers.

Plastering

Plastering like brickwork is one of the old established crafts in this country having been introduced by the Romans. The plaster used was a lime plaster which generally has been superseded by gypsum plasters. The disadvantages of lime plastering are:

1. Drying shrinkage which causes cracking.

2. Slow drying out process which can take several weeks causing delays for the following trades.
3. Need to apply lime plaster in several coats, usually termed render, float and set, to reduce the amount of shrinkage.

Any plaster finish must fulfil the functions of camouflaging irregularities in the backing wall, provide a smooth continuous surface which is suitable for direct decoration and be sufficiently hard to resist damage by impact upon its surface; gypsum plasters fulfil these requirements.

Gypsum is a crystalline combination of calcium sulphate and water. Deposits of suitable raw material are found in several parts of England and after crushing and screening the gypsum is heated to dehydrate the material. The amount of water remaining at the end of this process defines its class under BS 1191. If powdered gypsum is heated to about 170°C it loses about three-quarters of its combined water and is called hemi-hydrate gypsum plaster but is probably better known as 'plaster of Paris'. If a retarder is added to the hemi-hydrate plaster a new class of finishing plaster is formed to which the addition of expanded perlite and other additives will form a one-coat or universal plaster, a renovating grade plaster or a spray plaster for application by a spray machine.

Part I of BS 1911 lists two classes of plaster:

Class A: hemi-hydrate plaster of Paris.
Class B: retarded hemi-hydrate finishing plasters.

Part 2 of BS 1191 covers pre-mixed lightweight plasters which are defined as plasters consisting of suitable lightweight aggregates and retarded hemi-hydrate gypsum plasters complying with BS 1191, Part 1, Class B.

Class A or plaster of Paris is a hemi-hydrate plaster having approximately 25% of its original combined water left and has a very rapid setting time of about ten minutes. It can be used neat or mixed with a little sand and is suitable for use as a filler, moulding and repair work.

Class B is a hemi-hydrate plaster to which an animal protein such as keratin has been added during manufacture to retard the setting time.

Class A and B plasters are supplied in non-returnable multi-walled paper sacks of 50 kg capacity and care must be taken not to tear the sacks before the plaster is used. The absorption of moisture by gypsum plasters shortens the normal setting time of approximately one and a half hours which may reduce the strength of the set plaster. It follows therefore that all plasters should be stored in dry conditions preferably on timber palettes.

Gypsum plasters are not suitable for use in temperatures exceeding 43°C and should not be applied to frozen backgrounds. However, plasters can be applied under frosty conditions providing the surfaces are adequately protected from freezing after application. The dry bagged plaster in store is unaffected by low temperatures.

The plaster should be mixed in a clean plastic or rubber bucket using clean water only. Cleanliness is imperative since any set plaster left in the mixing bucket from a previous mixing will shorten the setting time which may reduce the strength of the plaster when set.

Premixed plasters are primarily Class B plasters incorporating light-weight aggregates such as expanded perlite and exfoliated vermiculite. Perlite is a glassy volcanic rock combining in its chemical composition a small percentage of water. When subjected to a high temperature the water turns into steam thus expanding the natural perlite to many times its original volume. Vermiculite is a form of mica with many ultra thin layers between which are minute amounts of water, which expand or exfoliate the natural material to many times its original volume when subjected to high temperatures by the water turning into steam and forcing the layers of flakes apart. The density of a lightweight plaster is about one-third that of a comparable sanded plaster and it has a thermal value of about three times that of sanded plasters, resulting in a reduction of heat loss, less condensation and a reduction in the risk of pattern staining. They also have superior adhesion properties to all backgrounds including smooth dry clean concrete.

The choice of plaster mix, type and number of coats will depend upon the background or surface to which the plaster is to be applied. Roughness and suction properties are two of the major considerations. The roughness can affect the keying of the plaster to its background, special keyed bricks are available for this purpose; or alternatively the joints can be raked out to a depth of 15—20 mm as the wall is being built. *In situ* concrete can be cast using sawn formwork giving a rough texture hence forming a suitable key. Generally all lightweight concrete blocks provide a suitable key for the direct application of plasters. Bonding agents in the form of resin emulsions are available for smooth surfaces — these must be applied in strict accordance with the manufacturer's instructions to achieve satisfactory results.

The suction properties of the background can affect the drying rate of the plaster by absorbing the moisture of the mix: too much suction can result in the plaster failing to set properly—thus losing its adhesion to its background; too little suction can give rise to drying shrinkage cracks due to the retention of excess water in the plaster.

The actual mix chosen will depend upon the class of plaster used and the properties of the background material. Cement backing to plasters usually have a volume mix of 1 : 1 : 6 cement : lime : sand, whereas finishing plaster coats can be applied neat or with up to 25% slaked lime putty by volume,

Undercoat plasters are applied by means of a wooden float or rule worked between dots or runs of plaster to give a true and level surface. The runs or rules and dots are of the same mix as the cement backing coat and are positioned over the background at suitable intervals to an accurate level so that the main application of plaster can be worked around the guide points. The upper surface of the undercoat plaster should be scored or scratched to provide a suitable key for the finishing coat. The thin finishing coat of plaster is applied to a depth of approximately 3 mm and finished with a steel float to give a smooth surface.

Dry lining techniques

External walls or internal walls and partitions can be dry lined with a variety of materials which can be self finished, ready for direct decoration or have a surface suitable for a single final coat of board finish plaster. The main advantages of dry lining techniques are speed, reduction in the amount of water used in the construction of buildings thus reducing the drying out period and in some cases increased thermal insulation.

Suitable materials are hardboard, plywood, chipboard and plasterboard. Hardboard, plywood and chipboard are fixed to timber battens attached to the wall at centres to suit the spanning properties and module size of the board. Finishing can be a direct application of paint, varnish or wallpaper but masking the fixings and joints may present problems. As an alternative the joints can be made a feature of the design by the use of edge chamfers or by using moulded cover fillets.

Plasterboard consists of an aerated gypsum core encased in and bonded to specially prepared bonded paper liners. The grey coloured liner is intended for a skim coat of plaster and the ivory coloured liner is for direct decoration. Plasterboard can also be obtained with a veneer of polished aluminium foil to one side to act as a reflective insulator when the board is fixed adjacent to a cavity. Four types of board are produced: wallboard, baseboard, lath and plank, all of which can be used for the dry lining of walls.

Wallboard is manufactured to metric coordinated widths of 600, 900 and 1 200 mm with coordinated lengths from 1 800-3 000 mm and thicknesses of 9·5 and 12·7 mm. The board can be obtained with a tapered edge for a seamless joint, a square edge for cover fillet treatment or with a chamfered edge for a vee-joint feature.

Baseboard is produced with square edges as a suitable base for a single coat of board finish plaster. One standard width is manufactured with a thickness of 9·5 mm, lengths are 1 200, 1 219 and 1 372 mm. Before the plaster coat is applied the joints should be covered with a jute scrim 100 mm wide (see Fig. II.29).

Plasterboard lath is a narrow plasterboard with rounded edges which removes the need for a jute scrim over the joints. The standard width is 406 mm with similar lengths to baseboard and thicknesses of 9·5 and 12·7 mm.

The fixing of dry linings is usually by nails to timber battens suitably spaced, plumbed and levelled to overcome any irregularities in the background. Fixing battens are placed vertically between the horizontal battens fixed at the junctions of the ceiling and floor with the wall. It is advisable to treat all fixing battens with an insecticide and a fungicide to lessen the risk of beetle infestation and fungal attack. The spacing of the battens will be governed by the spanning properties of the lining material, fixing battens at 450 mm centres are required for 9·5 mm thick plasterboards and at 600 mm centres for 12·7 mm thick plasterboards; so placed that they coincide with the board joints.

Plasterboard can also be fixed to a solid background by the use of 'dots' or 'dabs'. The dots consist of a 75 x 50 mm thin pad of bitumen impregnated fibreboard secured to the background with board finish plaster. Dots are placed at 1 000 mm centres vertically and 1 800 mm centres horizontally and levelled in all directions over the entire wall surface. Using these initial dots as datum points, intermediate dots are placed so that they coincide with the board joints. Once the dots have set (about one hour being usual), thick dabs of board finish plaster are applied vertically between the dots so that they stand proud of the dots. The plasterboard is then placed in position and tapped firmly until it is in contact with the dots, a double headed nail is used to temporarily secure the boards to the dots whilst the dabs are setting, after which the nails are removed and the joints made good. It is recommended that tapered edge boards are always used for this method of fixing.

Glazed wall tiles

Two processes are used in the manufacture of these hard glazed tiles. Firstly, the body or 'biscuit' tile is made from materials such as china clay, ball clay, flint and limestone which are mixed by careful processes into a fine powder before being heavily pressed into the required shape and size. The tile is then fired at a temperature of up to 1 150°C. The second process is the glazing which is applied in the form of a mixed liquid consisting of fine particles of glaze and water. The coated tiles are then fired for a second time at a temperature of approximately 1 050°C when the glazing coating fuses to the surface of the tile. Gloss, matt and eggshell finishes are available together with a wide choice of colours, designs and patterns.

A range of fittings with rounded edges and mitres are produced to blend with the standard 150 x 150 mm square tiles, 5 or 6 mm thick, also a similar range of fittings are made for the 108 x 108 mm, 4 or 6 mm thick, square tiles. The appearance and easily cleaned surface of glazed tiles makes them suitable for the complete or partial tiling of bathrooms and the provision of splashbacks for sinks and basins.

Tiles are fixed with a suitable adhesive which can be of a thin bed of mastic adhesive or a bed of a cement based adhesive; the former requires a flat surface such as a mortar screed. Ceramic or glazed tiles are considered to be practically inert, therefore careful selection of the right adhesive to suit the backing and final condition is essential. Manufacturer's instructions or the recommendations of BS 5385 should always be carefully followed.

Glazed tiles can be cut easily using the same method employed for glass. The tile is scored on its upper face with a glass cutter, this is followed by tapping the back of the tile behind the scored line over a rigid and sharp angle such as a flat straight-edge.

CEILING FINISHES

Ceilings can be finished by any of the dry lining techniques previously described for walls. The usual method is a plasterboard base with a skim coat of plaster. The plasterboards are secured to the underside of the floor or ceiling joists with galvanised plasterboard nails to reduce the risk of corrosion to the fixings. If square edged plasterboards are used as the base a jute scrim over the joints is essential. The most vulnerable point in a ceiling to cracking is at the junction between the ceiling and wall, this junction should be strengthened with a jute scrim around the internal angle (see Fig. II.29), or alternatively

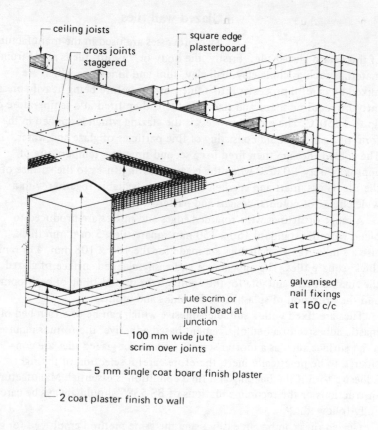

ceiling joists

cross joints
staggered

square edge
plasterboard

galvanised
nail fixings
at 150 c/c

jute scrim or
metal bead at
junction

100 mm wide jute
scrim over joints

5 mm single coat board finish plaster

2 coat plaster finish to wall

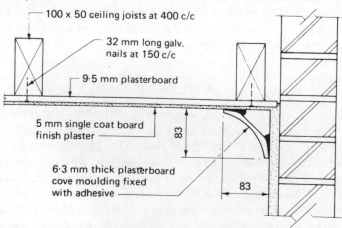

100 x 50 ceiling joists at 400 c/c

32 mm long galv.
nails at 150 c/c

9·5 mm plasterboard

5 mm single coat board
finish plaster

83

83

6·3 mm thick plasterboard
cove moulding fixed
with adhesive

Fig. II.29 Plasterboard ceilings

the junction can be masked with a decorative plasterboard or polystyrene cove moulding.

The cove moulding is made in a similar manner to plasterboard and is intended for direct decoration. Plasterboard cove moulding is jointed at internal and external angles with a mitred joint and with a butt joint in the running length. Any clean, dry and rigid background is suitable for the attachment of plasterboard cove which can be fixed in one of two ways. It can be secured by using a special water mixed adhesive applied to the contact edges of the moulding which is pressed into position; any surplus adhesive should be removed from the edges before it sets. Alternatively the cove moulding can be fixed with galvanised steel or brass screws to plugs or battens—fixings to the wall are spaced at 300 mm centres and to the ceiling at 600 mm centres. A typical plasterboard cove detail is shown in Fig. II.29.

Many forms of ceiling tiles are available for application to a joisted ceiling or solid ceiling with a sheet or solid background. Fixing to joists should be by concealed or secret nailing through the tongued and grooved joint. If the background is solid such as a concrete slab then dabs of a recommended adhesive are used to secure the tiles. Materials available include expanded polystyrene, mineral fibre, fibreboard and glass fibre with a rigid vinyl face.

Other forms of finish which may be applied to ceilings are sprayed plasters which can be of a thick or thin coat variety. Spray plasters are usually of a proprietary mixture applied by spraying apparatus directly on to the soffit giving a coarse texture which can be trowelled smooth if required. Various patterned ceiling papers are produced to give a textured finish. These papers are applied directly to the soffit or over a stout lining paper. Some ceiling papers are designed to be a self finish but others require one or more coats of emulsion paint.

14
Internal fixings and shelves

Internal fixings consist of trims in the form of skirtings, dado rails, frieze or picture rails, architraves and cornices; whereas fittings would include such things as cupboards and shelves.

SKIRTINGS

A skirting is a horizontal member fixed around the skirt or base of a wall primarily to mask the junction between a wall finish and a floor. It can be an integral part of the floor finish such as quarry tile or PVC skirtings or it can be made from timber, metal or plastic. Timber is the most common material used and is fixed by nails direct to the background but if it is a dense material that will not accept nails, plugs or special fixing bricks can be built into the wall. External angles in skirtings are formed by mitres but internal angles are usually scribed (see Fig. II.30).

ARCHITRAVES

These are mouldings cut and fixed around door and window openings to mask the joint between the wall finish and the frame. Like skirtings the usual material is timber but metal and plastic mouldings are available. Architraves are fixed with nails to the frame or lining and to the wall in a similar manner to skirtings if the architrave section is large (see Fig. II.30).

DADO RAILS

These are horizontal mouldings fixed in a position to prevent the walls

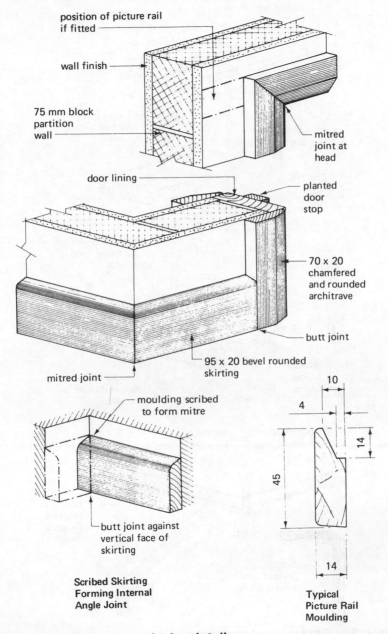

position of picture rail
if fitted

wall finish

75 mm block
partition
wall

mitred
joint at
head

door lining

planted
door
stop

70 x 20
chamfered
and rounded
architrave

butt joint

95 x 20 bevel rounded
skirting

mitred joint

moulding scribed
to form mitre

10

4

14

45

butt joint against
vertical face of
skirting

14

Scribed Skirting
Forming Internal
Angle Joint

Typical
Picture Rail
Moulding

Fig. II.30 Typical wood trim details

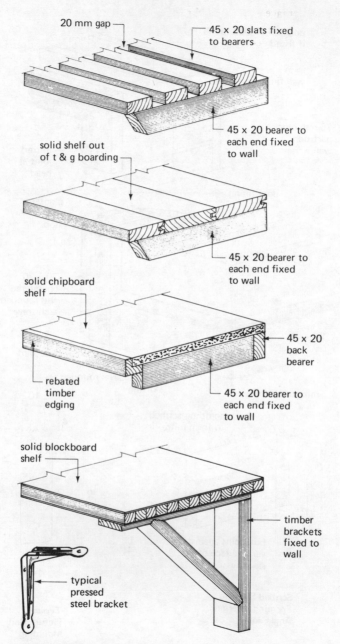

20 mm gap

45 x 20 slats fixed
to bearers

45 x 20 bearer to
each end fixed
to wall

solid shelf out
of t & g boarding

45 x 20 bearer to
each end fixed
to wall

solid chipboard
shelf

45 x 20
back
bearer

rebated
timber
edging

45 x 20 bearer to
each end fixed
to wall

solid blockboard
shelf

timber
brackets
fixed to
wall

typical
pressed
steel bracket

Fig. II.31   Shelves and supports

from being damaged by the backs of chairs pushed against them. They are very seldom used today since modern chair design renders them unnecessary. If used they are fixed by nails directly to the wall or to plugs inserted in the wall.

PICTURE RAILS

These are moulded rails fixed horizontally around the walls of a room from which pictures may be suspended and are usually positioned in line with the top edges of the door architrave. They can be of timber or metal and like the dado rail are very seldom used in modern domestic buildings. They would be fixed by nails in the same manner as dado rails and skirtings; a typical picture rail moulding is shown in Fig. II.30.

CORNICES

Cornices are timber or plaster ornate mouldings used to mask the junction between the wall and ceiling. These are very seldom used today having been superseded by the cove mouldings.

CUPBOARD FITTINGS

These are usually supplied as a complete fitting and only require positioning on site; they can be free standing or plugged and screwed to the wall. Built-in cupboards can be formed by placing a cupboard front in the form of a frame across a recess and then hanging suitable doors to the frame. Another method of forming built-in cupboards is to use a recessed partition wall to serve as cupboard walls and room divider, and attach to this partition suitable cupboard fronts and doors.

Shelving

Shelves can be part of a cupboard fitting or can be fixed to wall brackets or bearers which have been plugged and screwed to the wall. Timber is the usual material for shelving, this can be faced with a large variety of modern plastic finishes. Shelves are classed as solid or slat, the latter being made of 45 x 20 mm slats, spaced about 20 mm apart, and are used mainly in airing and drying cupboards; typical shelf details are shown in Fig. II.31.

15
Ironmongery

Ironmongery is a general term which is applied to builder's hardware and includes such items as nails, screws, bolts, hinges, locks, catches, window and door fittings.

NAILS

A nail is a fixing device which relies on the grip around its shank and the shear strength of its cross-section to fulfil its function. It is therefore important to select the right type and size of nail for any particular situation. Nails are specified by their type, length and diameter range given in millimetres. The diameter range is comparable to the old British Standard Wire Gauge. The complete range of nails is given in BS 1202. Steel is the main material used in the manufacture of nails, other metals used are copper and aluminium alloy.

Nails in common use are:

Cut clasp nails: made from black rolled steel and used for general carcassing work.

Cut floor brads: made from black rolled steel and used mainly for fixing floor boards, because their rectangular section reduces the tendency of thin boards splitting.

Round plain head: also known as round wire nails and made in a wide variety of lengths, used mainly for general carpentry work but have a tendency to split thin members.

120

Oval brad head: made with an oval cross section to lessen the risk of splitting the timber members, used for the same purpose as round wire nails but have the advantage of being able to be driven below the surface of the timber. A similar nail with a smaller head is also produced and is called an oval lost head nail.

Clout nails: also called slate nails, they have a large flat head and are used for fixing tiles and slates. The felt nail is similar but has a larger head and is only available in lengths up to 38 mm.

Panel pins: fine wire nails with a small head which can be driven below the surface, used mainly for fixing plywood and hardboard.

Plasterboard nails: the holding power of these nails with their countersunk head and jagged shank makes them suitable for fixing ceiling and similar boards.

WOOD SCREWS

A wood screw is a fixing device used mainly in joinery and relies upon its length and thread for holding power and resistance to direct extraction. For a screw to function properly it must be inserted by rotation and not be driven in with a hammer. It is usually necessary to drill pilot holes for the shank and/or core of the screw.

Wood screws are manufactured from cold drawn wire, steel, brass, stainless steel, aluminium alloy, silica bronze and nickel-copper alloy. In addition to the many different materials a wide range of painted and plated finishes are available such as an enamelled finish known as black japanned. Plated screws are used mainly to match the fitting which they are being used to fix and include such finishes as galvanised steel, copper plated, nickel plated and bronze metal antique.

Screws are specified by their material, type, length and gauge. The screw gauge is the diameter of the shank and is designated by a number; but, unlike the gauge used for nails, the larger the screw gauge number the greater the diameter of the shank. Various head designs are available for all types of wood screws, each having a specific purpose:

Countersunk head: the most common form of screw head and is used for a flush finish, the receiving component being countersunk to receive the screw head.

Raised head: used mainly with good quality fixtures, the rounded portion of the head with its mill slot remains above the surface of the fixture ensuring that the driving tool does not come into contact with the surface causing damage to the finish.

121

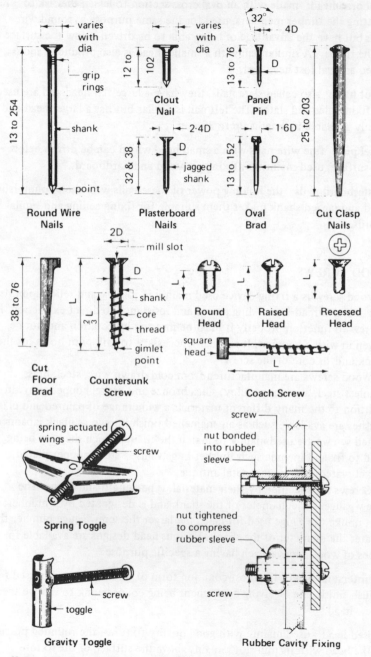

Fig. II.32 Nails, screws and cavity fixings

Round head: the head being fully exposed makes these screws suitable for fittings of material which is too thin to be countersunk.

Recessed head: screws with a countersunk head and a recessed cruciform slot giving a positive drive with a specially shaped screwdriver.

Coach screws: made of mild steel with a square head for driving in with the aid of a spanner and used mainly for heavy carpentry work.

CAVITY FIXINGS

Various fixing devices are available for fixing components to thin materials of low structural strength such as plasterboard and hardboard. Cavity fixings are designed to spread the load over a wide area of the board, typical examples are:

Steel spring toggles: spring actuated wings open out when the toggle fixing has been inserted through a hole in the board and spread out on the reverse side of the board. Spring toggles are specially suited to suspend fixtures from a ceiling.

Steel gravity toggles: when inserted horizontally into a hole in the board the long end of the toggle drops and is pulled against the reverse side of the board when the screw is tightened.

Rubber cavity fixings: a rubber or neoprene sleeve, in which a nut is embedded, is inserted horizontally through a hole in the board, the tightening of the screw causing the sleeve to compress and grip the reverse side of the board. This fixing device forms an airtight, waterproof and vibration resistant fixing.

Typical examples of nails, screws and cavity fixings are shown in Fig. II.32.

HINGES

Hinges are devices used to attach doors, windows and gates to a frame, lining or post so that they are able to pivot about one edge. It is of the utmost importance to specify and use the correct number and type of hinge in any particular situation to ensure correct operation of the door, window or gate. Hinges are classified by their function, length of flap, material used and sometimes by the method of manufacture. Materials used for hinges are steel, brass, cast iron, aluminium and nylon with metal pins. Typical examples of hinges in common use are:

Steel butt hinge: most common type in general use and are made from steel strip which is cut to form the flaps and is pressed around a steel pin.

Steel double flap butt hinge: similar to the steel butt hinge but is made from two steel strips to give extra strength.

Rising butt hinge: used to make the door level rise as it is opened to clear carpets and similar floor coverings. The door will also act as a gravity self closing door when fitted with these butts which are sometimes called skew butt hinges.

Parliament hinge: a form of butt hinge with a projecting knuckle and pin enabling the door to swing through 180° to clear architraves and narrow reveals.

Tee hinge: sometimes called a cross garnet, these hinges are used mainly for hanging matchboarded doors where the weight is distributed over a large area.

Band and hook: a stronger type of tee hinge made from wrought steel and is used for heavy doors and gates. A similar hinge is produced with a pin which projects from the top and bottom of the band and is secured with two retaining cups screwed to the post, these are called reversible hinges.

Typical examples of common hinges are shown in Fig. II.33.

LOCKS AND LATCHES

Any device used to keep a door in the closed position can be classed as a lock or latch. A lock is activated by means of a key whereas a latch is operated by a lever or bar. Latches used on lightweight cupboard doors are usually referred to as catches. Locks can be obtained with a latch bolt so that the door can be kept in the closed position without using a key, these are known as deadlocks.

Locks and latches are either fixed to the face of the door with a staple or keep fixed to the frame when they are termed rim locks or latches. If they are fixed within the body of the door they are called mortice locks or latches. When this form of lock or latch is used the bolts are retained in mortices cut behind the striking plate fixed to the frame (see Fig. II.34).

Cylindrical night latches are fitted to the stile of a door and a connecting bar withdraws the latch when the key is turned. Most night latches have an internal device to stop the bolt being activated from outside by the use of a key.

Door handles, cover plates and axles used to complete lock or latch fittings are collectively called door furniture and are supplied in a wide range of patterns and materials.

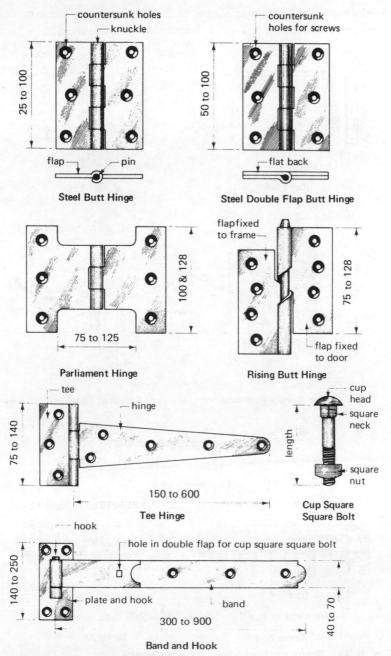

Fig. II.33 Typical hinges

125

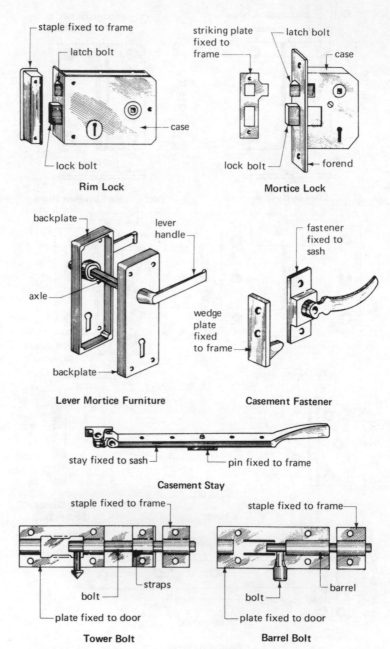

Fig. II.34 Door and window ironmongery

DOOR BOLTS

Door bolts are security devices fixed to the inside faces of doors and consist of a slide or bolt operated by hand to locate in a keep fixed to the frame. Two general patterns are produced: the tower bolt, which is the cheapest form; and the stronger, but dearer, barrel bolt. The bolt of a tower bolt is retained with staples or straps along its length, whereas in a barrel bolt it is completely enclosed along its length (see Fig. II.34).

CASEMENT WINDOW FURNITURE

Two fittings are required for opening sashes, the fastener, which is the security device, and the stay, which holds the sash in the opened position. Fasteners operate by the blade being secured in a mortice cut into the frame or by the blade locating over a projecting wedge or pin fixed to the frame (see Fig. II.34). Casement stays can be obtained to hold the sash open in a number of set positions by using a pin fixed to the frame and having a series of locating holes in the stay or they can be fully adjustable by the stay sliding through a screw down stop fixed to the frame (see Fig. II.34).

LETTER PLATES

These are the hinged covers attached to the outside of a door, which covers the opening made to enable letters to be delivered through the door. The minimum opening size for letter plates recommended by the Post Office is 200 x 45 mm; the bottom of the opening should be sited not lower than 750 mm from the bottom edge of the door and not higher than 1 450 mm to the upper edge of the opening. A wide range of designs are available in steel, aluminium alloy and plastic, some of which have a postal knocker incorporated in the face design.

BS 3287 covers builder's hardware for housing and gives recommendations for materials, finishes and dimensions to a wide range of ironmongery items not covered by a specific standard. These include such fittings as finger plates, cabin hooks, gate latches, cupboard catches and drawer pulls.

16
Painting and decorating

The application of coats of paint to the elements, components, trims and fittings of a building has two functions. The paint will impart colour and, at the same time, provide a protective coating which will increase the durability of the member to which it has been applied. The covering of wall and ceiling surfaces with paper or fabric is basically to provide colour, contrast and atmosphere. To achieve a good durable finish with any form of decoration the preparation of the surface and the correct application of the paint or paper is of the utmost importance.

Paint

Paint is a mixture of a liquid or medium and a colouring or pigment. Mediums used in paint manufacture range from thin liquids to stiff jellies and can be composed of linseed oil, drying oils, synthetic resins and water. The various combinations of these materials forms the type of class of paint. The medium's function is to provide the means of spreading and binding the pigment over the surface to be painted. The pigment provides the body, colour and durability of the paint. White lead is a pigment which gives good durability and moisture resistance but it is poisonous, therefore its use is confined mainly to priming and undercoating paints. Paints containing a lead pigment are required by law to state this fact on the can. The general pigment used for finishing paint is titanium dioxide which gives good obliteration of the undercoating but is not poisonous.

OIL BASED PAINTS

Priming paints: these are first coat paints used to seal the surface, protect the surface against damp air, act as a barrier to prevent any chemical action between the surface and the finishing coats and to give a smooth surface for the subsequent coats. Priming paints are produced for application to wood, metal and plastered surfaces.

Undercoating paints: these are used to build up the protective coating and to provide the correct surface for the finishing coat(s). Undercoat paints contain a greater percentage of pigment than finishing paints and as a result have a matt or flat finish. To obtain a good finishing colour it is essential to use an undercoat of the type and colour recommended by the manufacturer.

Finishing paints: a wide range of colours and finishes including matt, semi-matt, eggshell, satin, gloss and enamel are available. These paints usually contain a synthetic resin which enables them to be easily applied, quick drying and have good adhesive properties. Gloss paints have less pigment than the matt finishes and consequently less obliterating power.

POLYURETHANE PAINTS

These are quick drying paints based on polyurethane resins giving a hard heat resisting surface. They can be used on timber surfaces as a primer and undercoat but metal surfaces will require a base coat of metal primer, the matt finish with its higher pigment content is best for this 'one paint for all coats' treatment. Other finishes available are gloss and eggshell.

WATER BASED PAINTS

Most of the water based paints in general use come under a general classification of emulsion paints: they are quick drying and can be obtained in matt, eggshell, semi-gloss and gloss finishes. The water medium has additives such as polyvinyl acetate and alkyd resin to produce the various finishes. Except for application to iron work, which must be primed with a metal primer, emulsion paints can be used for priming, undercoating and as a finishing application. Their general use is for large flat areas such as ceilings and walls.

VARNISHES AND STAINS

Varnishes form a clear, glossy or matt, tough film over a surface and are a solution of resin and oil, their application being similar to oil based paints. The type of resin used, together with the correct ratio of oil content, forms the various durabilities and finishes available.

Stains can be used to colour or tone the surface of timber before applying a clear coat of varnish; they are basically a dye in a spirit and are therefore quick drying.

Paint supply
Paints are supplied in metal containers of 5 litres, 2·5 litres, 1 litre, 500 millilitres and 250 millilitres capacity and are usually in one of the 88 colours recommended for building purposes in BS 4800. BS 381C gives 99 colours for specific purposes such as standard identification colours used by HM services.

Knotting
Knots or streaks in softwood timber may exude resins which may soften and discolour paint finishes; generally an effective barrier is provided by two coats of knotting applied before the priming coats of paint. Knotting is a uniform dispersion of shellac in a natural or synthetic resin in a suitable solvent. It should be noted that the higher the grade of timber specified, with its lower proportion of knots, the lower will be the risk of resin disfigurement of paint finishes.

Wallpapers

Most wallpapers consist of a base paper of 80% mechanical wood pulp and 20% unbleached sulphite pulp printed on one side with a colour and/or design. Papers with vinyl plastic coatings making them washable are also available, together with a wide range of fabrics suitably coated with vinyl to give various textures and finishes for the decoration of walls and ceilings.

The preparation of the surface to receive wallpaper is very important, ideally a smooth clean and consistent surface is required. Walls which are poor can be lined with a light-weight lining paper for traditional wallpaper and a heavier esparto lining paper for the heavier classes of wallpaper. Lining papers should be applied in the opposite direction to the direction of the final paper covering.

Wallpapers are attached to the surface by means of an adhesive such as starch/flour paste and cellulose pastes which are mixed with water to the manufacturer's recommendations. Heavy washable papers and woven fabrics should always be hung with an adhesive recommended by the paper manufacturer. New plaster and lined surfaces should be treated to provide the necessary 'slip' required for successful paper hanging. A glue size is usually suitable for a starch/flour paste, whereas a diluted cellulose paste should always be used when a cellulose paste is used as the adhesive.

Standard wallpapers are supplied in rolls with a printed width of 533 mm and a length of 10 m giving an approximate coverage of 4·5 m² — the actual coverage will be governed by the 'drop' of the pattern. Decorative borders and motifs are also available for use in conjunction with standard wallpapers.

17

Internal finishes and decorations

Internal finishes which are normally associated with domestic dwellings such as brick walls, lightweight block walls, plastering, dry linings, floor finishes and coverings, fixed partitions and the various trims should have already been covered in the first two years of study. Advance level construction technology therefore usually concentrates on the finishes found in buildings such as offices, commercial and educational establishments. These finishes would include partitions, sliding doors and suspended ceilings.

PARTITIONS

A partition is similar to a wall in that it is a vertical construction dividing the internal space of a building but partitions are generally considered to be internal walls which are lightweight, non-load bearing, demountable or movable. They are used in buildings such as offices where it is desirable to have a system of internal division which can be altered to suit changes in usage without unacceptable costs, minimum of interference to services and ceilings. It should be noted that any non-load-bearing partition could if necessary be taken down and moved but in most cases moving partitions such as timber studwork with plasterboard linings will necessitate the replacement or repair of some of the materials and finishes involved. A true demountable partition can usually be taken down, moved and re-erected without any notable damage to the materials, components, finishes and surrounding parts of the building. Movable partitions usually take the form of a series of doors or door leaves hung to slide or slide and fold and these are described later under a separate heading.

132

Many demountable partition systems are used in conjunction with a suspended ceiling and it is important that both systems are considered together in the context of their respective main functions since one system may cancel out the benefits achieved by the other.

There are many patent demountable partition systems from which the architect, designer or builder can select a suitable system for any particular case and it is not possible in a text of this nature to analyse or list them all but merely to consider the general requirements of these types of partition. The composition of the types available range from glazed screens with timber, steel or aluminium alloy frames to the panel construction with concealed or exposed jointing members. Low level screens and toilet cubicles can also be considered in this context and these can be attached to posts fixed at floor level or alternatively suspended from the structural floor above.

When selecting or specifying a demountable partition the following points should be taken into account:

1. Fixing and stability — points to be considered are bottom fixing, top fixing and joints between sections. The two common methods of bottom fixing are the horizontal base unit which is very often hollow to receive services and the screw jack fixing, both methods are intended to be fixed above the finished floor level which should have a tolerance not exceeding 5 mm. The top fixing can be of a similar nature with a ceiling tolerance of the same magnitude but problems can arise when used in conjunction with a suspended ceiling since little or no pressure can be applied to the underside of the ceiling. A brace or panel could be fixed above the partition in the void over the ceiling to give the required stability or alternatively the partition could pass through the ceiling but this would reduce the flexibility of the two systems should a rearrangement be required at a later date. The joints between consecutive panels do not normally present any problems since they are an integral part of the design but unless they are adequately sealed the sound insulation and/or fire resistance properties of the partition could be seriously impaired.

2. Sound insulation — the degree of insulation required will depend largely upon the usage of rooms created by the partitions. The level of sound insulation which can be obtained will depend upon three factors: the density of the partition construction, degree of demountability and the continuity of the partition with the floor and ceiling. Generally, the less demountable a partition is the easier it will be to achieve an acceptable sound insulation level. Partitions

133

fixed between the structural floor and the structural ceiling usually result in good sound insulation whereas partitions erected between the floor and a suspended ceiling give poor sound insulation properties due mainly to the flanking sound path over the head of the partition. In the latter case two remedies are possible; firstly the partition could pass through the suspended ceiling, or alternatively a sound insulating panel could be inserted in the ceiling void directly over the partition below.

3. Fire resistance — the major restrictions to the choice of partition lie in the requirements of the Building Regulations Part B with regard to fire resistant properties, spread of flame, fire stopping and providing a suitable means of escape in case of fire. The weakest points in any system will be the openings and the seals at the foot and head. Provisions at openings are a matter of detail and adequate construction together with a suitable fire resistant door or fire resistant glazing. Fire stopping at the head of a partition used in conjunction with a suspended ceiling usually takes the form of a fire break panel fixed in the ceiling void directly above the partition below. Most proprietary demountable systems will give a half-hour or one hour fire resistance with a class 1 or class 0 spread of flame classification.

Typical demountable partition details are shown in Figs. II.35 and II.36.

SLIDING DOORS

Sliding doors may be used in all forms of buildings from the small garage to the large industrial structures. They may be incorporated into a design for any of the following reasons:

1. As an alternative to a swing door to conserve space or where it is not possible to install a swing door due to space restrictions.
2. Where heavy doors or doors in more than two leaves are to be used and where conventional hinges would be inadequate.
3. As a movable partition used in preference to a demountable partition because of the frequency with which it would be moved.

In most cases there is a choice of bottom or top sliding door gear which in the case of very heavy doors may have to be mechanically operated. Top gear can only be used if there is a suitable soffit, beam or lintel over the proposed opening which is strong enough to take the load of the gear, track and doors. In the case of bottom gear all the loads are transmitted to the floor. Top gear has the disadvantage of generally being noisier than its bottom gear counterpart but bottom gear either has an upstanding track which can be a hazard in terms of tripping or alternatively it can have a

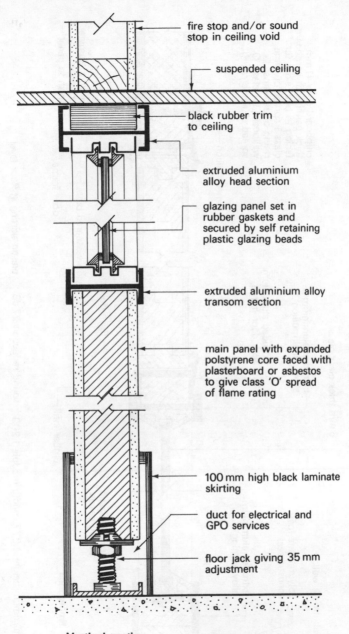

fire stop and/or sound stop in ceiling void

suspended ceiling

black rubber trim to ceiling

extruded aluminium alloy head section

glazing panel set in rubber gaskets and secured by self retaining plastic glazing beads

extruded aluminium alloy transom section

main panel with expanded polstyrene core faced with plasterboard or asbestos to give class 'O' spread of flame rating

100 mm high black laminate skirting

duct for electrical and GPO services

floor jack giving 35 mm adjustment

Vertical section

maximum panel height 3.657
panel thickness 54 mm overall
horizontal module 1.190

Fig. II.35 Typical demountable partition details 1 (Tenon Contracts Ltd)

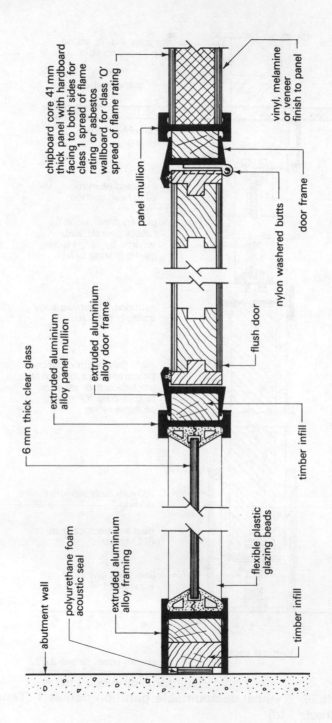

chipboard core 41 mm
thick panel with hardboard
facing to both sides for
class 1 spread of flame
rating or asbestos
wallboard for class 'O'
spread of flame rating

vinyl, melamine
or veneer
finish to panel

panel mullion

door frame

nylon washered butts

extruded aluminium
alloy panel mullion

extruded aluminium
alloy door frame

flush door

6 mm thick clear glass

timber infill

abutment wall

polyurethane foam
acoustic seal

extruded aluminium
alloy framing

flexible plastic
glazing beads

timber infill

maximum height 4.577   width module 1.200   sound reduction 27 dB   plastic skirting at floor level

services can be accommodated within chipboard core and along continuous base ducts.

Fig. II.36 Typical demountable partition details 2 (Venesta International Components Ltd)

sunk channel which can become blocked with dirt and dust unless regularly maintained. In all cases it is essential that the track and guides are perfectly aligned vertically to one another and in the horizontal direction parallel to each other to prevent stiff operation or the binding of the doors whilst being moved. When specifying sliding door gear it is essential that the correct type is chosen to suit the particular door combination and weight range if the partition is to be operated efficiently.

Many types of patent sliding door gear and track are available to suit all needs but these can usually be classified by the way in which the doors operate:

Straight sliding — these can be of a single leaf, double leaf or designed to run on adjacent and parallel tracks to give one parking. Generally this form of sliding door uses top gear — see Fig. II.37 for typical example.

End-folding doors — these are strictly speaking sliding and folding doors which are used for wider openings than the straight doors given above. They usually consist of a series of leaves operating off top gear with a bottom guide track so that the folding leaves can be parked to one or both sides of the opening — see Fig. II.38 for typical details.

Centre-folding doors — like the previous type these doors slide and fold to be parked at one or both ends of the opening and have a top track with a bottom floor guide channel arranged so that the doors will pivot centrally over the channel. With this arrangement the hinged leaf attached to the frame is only approximately a half-leaf — see typical details in Fig. II.39.

Other forms of sliding doors include round the corner sliding doors which use a curved track and folding gear arranged so that the leaves hinged together will slide around the corner and park alongside a side wall, making them suitable for situations where a clear opening is required. The number of leaves in any one hinged sliding set should not be less than three nor more than five. Up and over doors operated by a counterbalance weight or spring are common for domestic garage applications and are available where they form when raised a partial canopy to the opening or are parked entirely within the building. Another application of the folding door technique is the folding screen which is suitable for a limited number of lightweight leaves which can be folded back onto a side or return wall without the use of sliding gear, track or guide channels — see Fig. II.40 for typical details.

SUSPENDED CEILINGS

A suspended ceiling can be defined as a ceiling which is attached to a framework suspended from the main structure thus forming a void between the ceiling and the underside of the

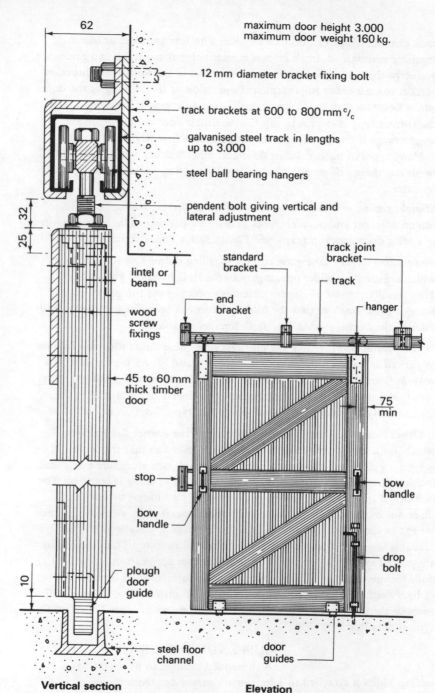

maximum door height 3.000
maximum door weight 160 kg.

12 mm diameter bracket fixing bolt

track brackets at 600 to 800 mm $^c/_c$

galvanised steel track in lengths
up to 3.000

steel ball bearing hangers

pendent bolt giving vertical and
lateral adjustment

lintel or
beam

wood
screw
fixings

45 to 60 mm
thick timber
door

stop

bow
handle

plough
door
guide

steel floor
channel

track joint
bracket

standard
bracket

track

end
bracket

hanger

75
min

bow
handle

drop
bolt

door
guides

Vertical section

Elevation

Fig. II.37 Typical straight sliding door details (Hillaldam Coburn Ltd)

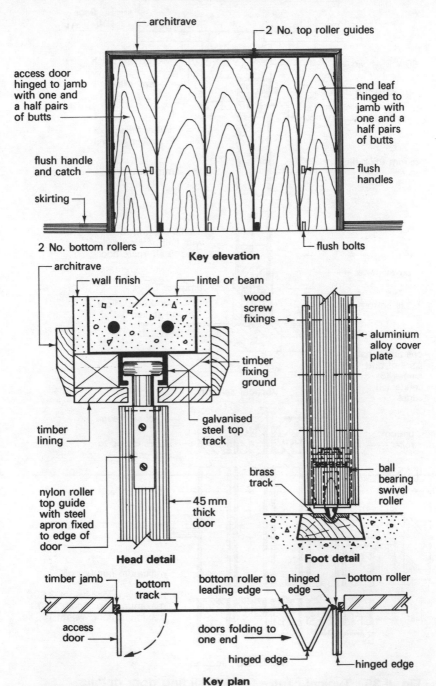

Key elevation

architrave

2 No. top roller guides

access door hinged to jamb with one and a half pairs of butts

end leaf hinged to jamb with one and a half pairs of butts

flush handle and catch

flush handles

skirting

2 No. bottom rollers

flush bolts

Head detail

architrave

wall finish

lintel or beam

wood screw fixings

aluminium alloy cover plate

timber fixing ground

galvanised steel top track

timber lining

nylon roller top guide with steel apron fixed to edge of door

45 mm thick door

brass track

ball bearing swivel roller

Foot detail

Key plan

timber jamb

bottom track

bottom roller to leading edge

hinged edge

bottom roller

access door

doors folding to one end

hinged edge

hinged edge

Fig. II.38 Typical end folding doors detail (Hillaldam Coburn Ltd)

139

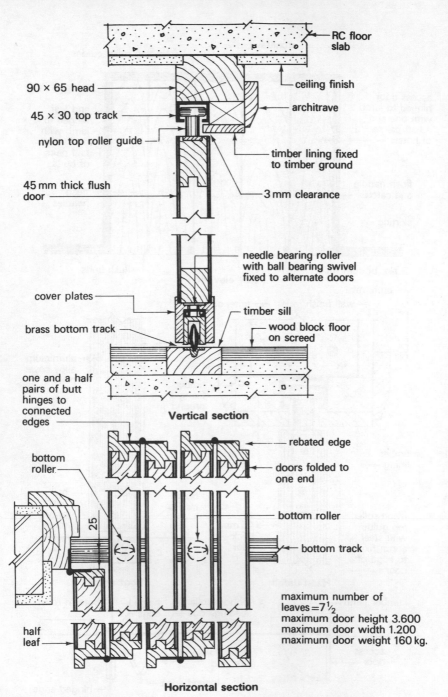

Vertical section

- RC floor slab
- 90 × 65 head
- ceiling finish
- 45 × 30 top track
- architrave
- nylon top roller guide
- timber lining fixed to timber ground
- 45 mm thick flush door
- 3 mm clearance
- needle bearing roller with ball bearing swivel fixed to alternate doors
- cover plates
- timber sill
- brass bottom track
- wood block floor on screed
- one and a half pairs of butt hinges to connected edges

Horizontal section

- rebated edge
- bottom roller
- doors folded to one end
- bottom roller
- 25
- bottom track
- half leaf

maximum number of leaves $= 7\frac{1}{2}$
maximum door height 3.600
maximum door width 1.200
maximum door weight 160 kg.

Fig. II.39 Typical centre folding sliding door details (Hillaldam Coburn Ltd)

140

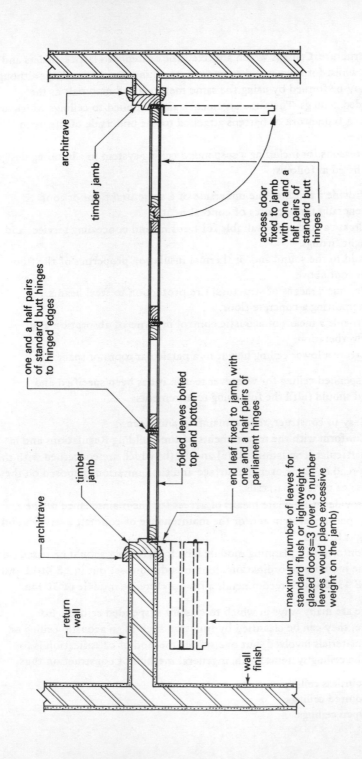

architrave

timber jamb

access door
fixed to jamb with one and a
half pairs of standard butt
hinges

one and a half pairs
of standard butt hinges
to hinged edges

timber jamb

folded leaves bolted
top and bottom

end leaf fixed to jamb with
one and a half pairs of
parliament hinges

maximum number of leaves for
standard flush or lightweight
glazed doors=3 (over 3 number
leaves would place excessive
weight on the jamb)

return wall

architrave

wall finish

Fig. II.40 Typical folding screen details

141

main structure. Ceilings which are fixed for example to lattice girders and trusses whilst forming a void are strictly speaking attached ceilings although they may be formed by using the same methods and materials as the suspended ceilings. The same argument can be applied to ceilings which are fixed to a framework of battens attached to the underside of the main structure.

The reasons for including a suspended ceiling system in a building design can be listed as follows:

1. Provide a finish to the underside of a structural floor or roof generally for purposes of concealment.
2. Create a void space suitable for housing and concealing services and light fittings.
3. Add to the sound and/or thermal insulation properties of the floor or roof above.
4. Provide a means of structural fire protection to steel beams supporting a concrete floor.
5. Provide a means of acoustic control in terms of absorption and reverberation.
6. Create a lower ceiling height to a particular room or space.

A suspended ceiling for whatever reason it has been specified and installed should fulfil the following requirements:

1. Easy to construct, repair, maintain and clean.
2. Conform with the requirements of the Building Regulations and in particular Regulations B2(a) and B2(b) which are concerned with the spread of flame over the surface and the limitations imposed on the use of certain materials.
3. Provide an adequate means of access for the maintenance of the suspension system and/or the maintenance of concealed services and light fittings.
4. Conform to a planning module which preferably should be based on the modular co-ordination recommendations set out in BS 4011 and BS 4330 which recommends a first preference module of 300 m.

There are many ways in which to classify suspended ceilings. For example, they can be classified by function such as an acoustic ceiling or by the materials involved, but one simple method of classification is to group the ceiling systems by their general method of construction thus:

1. Jointless ceilings.
2. Jointed ceilings.
3. Open ceilings.

Jointless ceilings: these are ceilings which, although suspended from the main structure, give the internal appearance of being a conventional ceiling. The final finish is usually of plaster applied in one or two coats to plasterboard or expanded metal lathing. Alternatively a jointless suspended ceiling could be formed by applying sprayed plaster or sprayed vermiculite-cement to an expanded metal background. Typical jointless ceiling details are shown in Fig. II.41.

Jointed ceilings: these suspended ceilings are the most popular and common form because of their ease of assembly, ease of installation and ease of maintenance. They consist basically of a suspended metal framework to which the finish in a board or tile form are attached. The boards or tiles can be located on a series of tee bar supports with the supporting members exposed forming part of the general appearance or by using various spring clip devices or direct fixing the supporting members can be concealed. The common ceiling materials encountered are fibreboards, metal trays, fibre cement materials and plastic tiles or trays — see Fig. II.42 for typical details.

Open ceilings: these suspended ceilings are largely decorative in function but by installing light fittings in the ceiling void they can act as a luminous ceiling. The format of these ceilings can be an open work grid with or without louvres or a series of closely spaced plates of polished steel or any other suitable material. The colour and texture of the sides and soffit of the ceiling void must be carefully designed if an effective system is to be achieved. It is possible to line these surfaces with an acoustic absorption material to provide another function to the arrangement — see typical details in Fig. II.43.

DECORATIONS

The fundamentals of applying decorative finishes in the form of paint and wallpaper should have been covered in the elementary studies of a typical four-year course in construction technology and therefore study at advance level concentrates on deeper aspects of the basic principles particularly in the context of painting timber and metals.

Painting timber

Timber can be painted to prevent decay in the material by forming a barrier to the penetration of moisture thus giving rise to the conditions necessary for fungal attack to begin, or alternatively timber may be painted mainly to impart colour. Timber

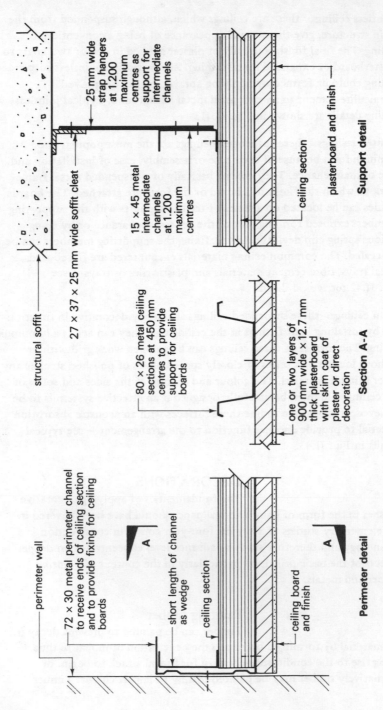

Fig. II.41 Typical jointless suspended ceiling details (Gyproc M/F suspended ceiling system)

structural soffit

25 mm wide strap hangers at 1.200 maximum centres as support for intermediate channels

27 × 37 × 25 mm wide soffit cleat

15 × 45 metal intermediate channels at 1.200 maximum centres

plasterboard and finish

ceiling section

Support detail

80 × 26 metal ceiling sections at 450 mm centres to provide support for ceiling boards

one or two layers of 900 mm wide × 12.7 mm thick plasterboard with skim coat of plaster or direct decoration

Section A-A

perimeter wall

72 × 30 metal perimeter channel to receive ends of ceiling section and to provide fixing for ceiling boards

short length of channel as wedge

ceiling section

ceiling board and finish

Perimeter detail

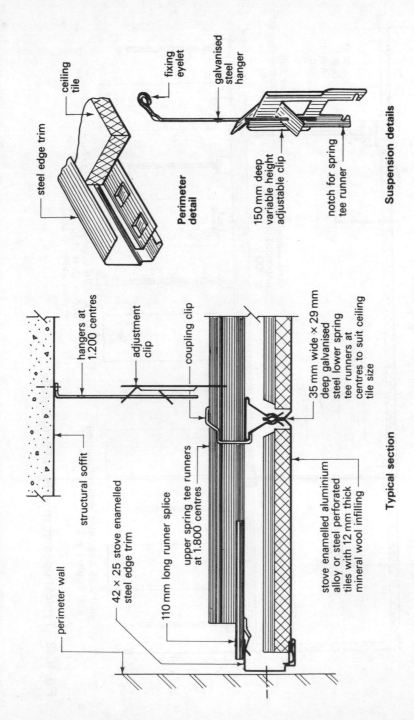

ceiling tile

steel edge trim

fixing eyelet

galvanised steel hanger

Perimeter detail

150 mm deep variable height adjustable clip

notch for spring tee runner

Suspension details

hangers at 1.200 centres

adjustment clip

coupling clip

structural soffit

perimeter wall

42 × 25 stove enamelled steel edge trim

110 mm long runner splice

upper spring tee runners at 1.800 centres

35 mm wide × 29 mm deep galvanised steel lower spring tee runners at centres to suit ceiling tile size

stove enamelled aluminium alloy or steel perforated tiles with 12 mm thick mineral wool infilling

Typical section

Fig. II.42 Typical jointed suspended ceiling details (Dampa (UK) Ltd)

145

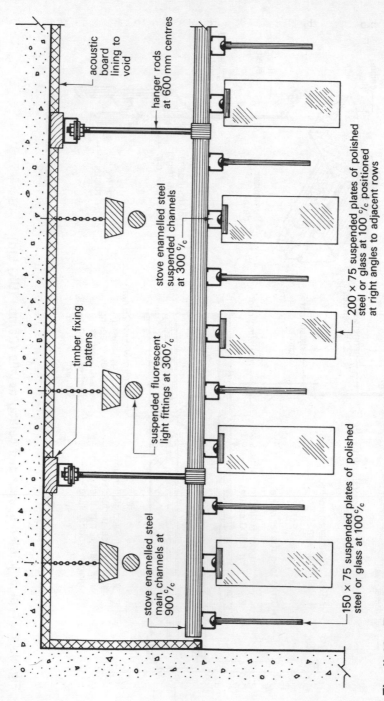

acoustic board lining to void

hanger rods at 600 mm centres

stove enamelled steel suspended channels at 300°/c

200 × 75 suspended plates of polished steel or glass at 100°/c positioned at right angles to adjacent rows

timber fixing battens

suspended fluorescent light fittings at 300°/c

stove enamelled steel main channels at 900°/c

150 × 75 suspended plates of polished steel or glass at 100°/c

Fig. II.43   Typical open suspended ceiling details

which is exposed to the elements is more vulnerable to eventual decay than internal joinery items but internal condensation can also give rise to damp conditions. Timber can also be protected with clear water-repellent preservatives and varnishes to preserve the natural colour and texture of the timber.

The moisture content of the timber to which paint is to be applied should be as near to that at which it will stabilise in its final condition. For internal joinery this would be within an 8 to 12% region depending upon the internal design temperature and for external timber within a 15 to 18% region according to exposure conditions. If the timber is too dry when the paint is applied any subsequent swelling of the base material due to moisture absorption will place unacceptable stresses on the paint film leading to cracking of the paint barrier. Conversely wet timber drying out after the paint application can result in blistering, opening of joints and the consequential breakdown of the paint film.

New work should receive a four-coat application consisting of primer, undercoat and finishing coats. The traditional shellac knotting applied to reduce the risk of resin leaking and staining should be carried out prior to the primer application but in external conditions it may prove to be inadequate. Therefore timber selected for exposed or external conditions should be of a high quality without or with only a small amount of knots. Knotting and priming should preferably be carried out under the ideal conditions prevailing at the place of manufacture. Filling and stopping should take place after priming but before the application of the undercoat and finishing coats. It is a general misconception that a good key is necessary to achieve a satisfactory paint surface. It is not penetration that is required but a good molecular attraction of the paint binder to the timber that is needed to obtain a satisfactory result.

If the protective paint film is breached by moisture, decay can take place under the paint coverings; indeed the coats of paint prevent the drying out of any moisture which has managed to penetrate the timber prior to painting. Any joinery items which in their final situation could be susceptible to moisture penetration should therefore be treated with a paintable preservative. Preservation treatments include diffusion treatment using water-soluble borates, water-borne preservatives and organic solvents. The methods of application and chemical composition of these timber preservatives are usually covered by the science syllabus of most comprehensive courses in building.

Painting metals

The application of paint to provide a protective coat and for decorative purposes is normally confined to iron and steel since most non-ferrous metals are left to oxidise and form their own natural protective coating. Corrosion of ferrous metals is a natural process which can cause disfiguration and possible failure of a metal component. Two aspects of painting these metals must be considered:

1. Initial preparation and paint application.
2. Maintenance of protective paint.

Preparation: the basic requirement is to prepare the metal surface adequately to receive the primer and subsequent coats of paint since the mill scale, rust, oil, grease and dirt which are frequently found on metals are not suitable as a base for the applications of paint. Suitable preparation treatments are:

1. Shot and grit blasting — effective method which can be carried out on site although it is usually considered to be a factory process.
2. Phosphating and pickling — factory process involving immersion of the metal component in hot acid solutions to remove rust and scale.
3. Degreasing — factory process involving washing or immersion using organic solvents, emulsions or hot alkali solutions followed by washing. Very often used as a preliminary treatment to phosphating.
4. Mechanical — site or factory process using hand held or powered tools such as hammers, chisels, brushes and scrapers. To be effective these forms of surface preparation must be thorough.
5. Flame cleaning — an oxy-acetylene flame used in conjunction with hand-held tools for removing existing coats of paint or loose scale and rust.

It is essential that in conjunction with the above preparation processes the correct primer is specified and used to obtain a satisfactory result. As with the painting of timber the types of primers and paints available together with the methods of application are usually contained in the science syllabus.

Maintenance: to protect steel in the long term a rigid schedule of painting maintenance must be worked out and invoked. This is particularly true of the many areas where access is difficult such as pipes fixed close to a wall and adjacent members in a lattice truss. Access for future maintenance is an aspect of building which should be considered during the design and construction stages not only in the context of metal components but to any part of a building which will require future maintenance and/or inspection. To take full advantage of the structural properties of steelwork and at the same time avoid the maintenance problems, weathering steels could be considered for exposed conditions.

148

Weathering steels

These do not rust or corrode as normal steels but interact with the atmosphere to produce a layer of sealing oxides. The colour of this protective layer will vary from a lightish brown to a dark purple grey depending on the degree of exposure, amount and type of pollution in the atmosphere and orientation. The best known weathering steel is called 'Cor-Ten' which is derived from the fact that it is CORrosion resistant with a high TENsile strength. Cor-Ten is not a stainless steel but a low alloy steel with a lower proportion of non-ferrous metals than stainless steel which makes it a dearer material than mild steel but cheaper than traditional stainless steels.

Weathering steels can be used as a substitute for other steels except in wet situations, marine works or in areas of high pollution unless protected with paint or similar protective applications which defeats the main objective of using this material. Jointing can be by welding or friction grip bolts. It must be noted that the protective coating will not form on weathering steels in internal situations since the formation of this coat is a natural process of the wet and dry cycles encountered with ordinary weather conditions.

Part III
Domestic services

18
Water supply

An adequate supply of water is a basic requirement for most buildings for reasons of personal hygiene or for activities such as cooking and manufacturing processes. In most areas a piped supply of water is available from a Public Water Board or Public Utility Company mains supply system.

Water is, in the first instance, produced by condensation in the form of clouds and falls to the ground as rain, snow or hail; it then becomes either surface water in the form of a river, stream or lake, or percolates through the subsoil until it reaches an impervious stratum, or is held in a water bearing subsoil. The water authority by a system of screening, sedimentation, filtration, chlorination, aeration and fluoridation makes the water fit for human consumption before allowing it to enter the mains.

The water company's mains are laid underground at a depth where they will be unaffected by frost or traffic movement. The lay-out of the system is generally a circuit with trunk mains feeding a grid of subsidiary mains for distribution to specific areas or districts. The materials used for main pipes are cast iron and asbestos cement which can be tapped whilst under pressure; a plug cock is inserted into the crown of the mains pipe to provide the means of connecting the communication pipe to supply an individual building.

Terminology
Main: a pipe for the general conveyance of water as distinct from the conveyance to individual premises.

153

Service: a system of pipes and fittings for the supply and distribution of water in any individual premises.

Service pipe: a pipe in a service which is directly subject to pressure from a main, sometimes called the rising main, inside the building.

Communication pipe: that part of the service pipe which is vested in the water undertaking.

Distribution pipe: any pipe in a service conveying water from a storage cistern.

Cistern: a container for water in which the stored water is under atmospheric pressure.

Storage cistern: any cistern other than a flushing cistern.

Tank: a rectangular vessel completely closed and used to store water.

Cylinder: a closed cylindrical tank.

Cold water supply

The water company will provide from their mains tapping plug cock a communication pipe to a stop valve and protection chamber just outside the boundary; this is a chargeable item to the building owner. The goose neck bend is included to relieve any stress likely to be exerted on the mains connection.

A service pipe is taken from this stop valve to an internal stop valve, preferably located just above floor level on an internal wall or at least 600 mm from an external wall. The stop valve should have a drain off valve incorporated in it, or just above it, so that the service pipe or rising main can be drained.

Care must be taken when laying a service pipe that it is not placed in a position where it can be adversely affected by frost, heavy traffic or building loads. A minimum depth of 750 mm is generally recommended for supplies to domestic properties; where the pipe passes under a building it should be housed in a protective duct or pipe suitably insulated within 750 mm of the floor level (see Fig. III.1).

Suitable materials for service pipes are copper, PVC, polythene, lead and galvanised steel. Copper service pipes can be laid on and covered by a layer of sand to prevent direct contact with the earth or alternatively wrapped with a suitable proprietary insulating material. Plastic coated copper pipes are also available for underground pipework. Steel pipes should have a similar protection but plastic pipes are resistant to both frost and corrosion.

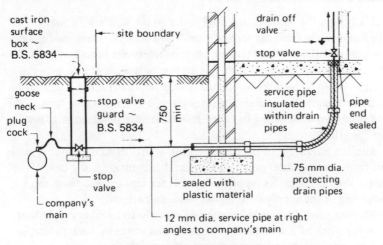

Typical Cold Water Service Layout

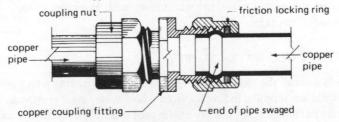

Typical Manipulative Compression Joint

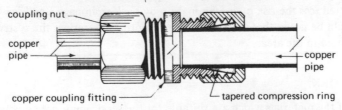

Typical Non-Manipulative Compression Fitting

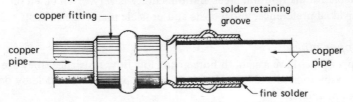

Typical Capillary Joint

Fig. III.1 Supply pipe and copper pipe joint details

DIRECT COLD WATER SUPPLY

In this system the whole of the cold water to the sanitary fittings is supplied directly from the service pipe. The direct system is used mainly in northern districts where large, high level reservoirs provide a good mains supply and pressure. With this system only a small cold water storage cistern to feed the hot water tank is required; this can usually be positioned below the roof ceiling level giving a saving on pipe runs to the roof space and eliminating the need to insulate the pipes against frost (see Fig. III.2).

Another advantage of the direct system is that drinking water is available from several outlet points. The main disadvantage is the lack of reserve should the mains supply be cut off for repairs, also there can be a lowering of the supply during peak demand periods.

When sanitary fittings are connected directly to a mains supply there is always a risk of contamination of the mains water by back siphonage. This can occur if there is a negative pressure on the mains and any of the outlets are submerged below the water level, such as a hand spray connected to the taps.

INDIRECT COLD WATER SUPPLY

In this system all the sanitary fittings, except for a drinking water outlet at the sink, are supplied indirectly from a cold water storage cistern positioned at a high level, usually in the roof space. This system requires more pipework but it gives a reserve supply in case of mains failure and it also reduces the risk of contamination by back siphonage (see Fig. III.2). It should be noted that the local water authority determines the system to be used in the area.

PIPEWORK

Any of the materials which are suitable for the service pipe are equally suitable for distribution pipes and the choice is very often based on individual preference, initial costs and possible maintenance costs.

Copper pipes

Copper pipes have a smooth bore giving low flow resistance, they are strong and easily jointed and bent. Joints in copper pipes can be made by one of three methods:

Manipulative compression joint: the end of the pipe is manipulated to fit into the coupling fitting by means of a special tool. No jointing material is required and the joint offers great resistance to being withdrawn. It is

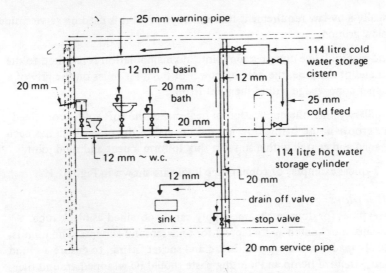

Direct System of Cold Water Supply

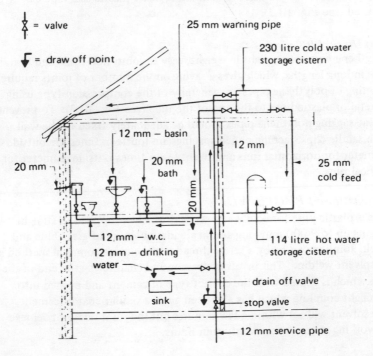

Indirect System of Cold Water Supply

Fig. III.2 Cold water supply systems

157

usually a by-law requirement that this type of joint is used on service pipes below ground.

Non-manipulative compression joint: no manipulation is required to the cut end of the pipe, the holding power of the joint relies on the grip of a copper cone wedge within the joint fitting.

Capillary joint: the application of heat makes the soft solder contained in a groove in the fitting flow around the end of the pipe which has been cleaned and coated with a suitable flux to form a neat and rigid joint.

Typical examples of copper pipe joints are shown in Fig. III.1.

Steel pipes
Steel pipes for domestic water supply can be obtained as black tube, galvanised or coated and wrapped for underground services. The joint is usually made with a tapered thread and socket fitting, to ensure a sound joint, stranded hemp and jointing paste should be wrapped around the thread; alternatively a non-contaminating white plastic seal tape can be used (see Fig. III.3).

Polythene pipe
Polythene pipe is very light in weight, easy to joint, non-toxic and is available in long lengths, which gives a saving on the number of joints required. Jointing of polythene pipes are generally of the compression type using a metal or plastic liner to the end of the tube (see Fig. III.3). To prevent undue sagging polythene pipes should be adequately fixed to the wall with saddle clips, recommended spacings are fourteen times the outside diameter for horizontal runs and twenty-four times outside diameter for vertical runs.

Unplasticised PVC (UPVC)
This is plastic pipe for cold water services which is supplied in straight lengths up to 9 000 mm long and in standard colours of grey, blue and black. Jointing can be by a screw thread but the most common method is by solvent welding. This involves cleaning and chamfering the end of the pipe which is coated with the correct type of cement and pushed into a straight coupling which has also been given a similar coat of cement. The solvent will set within a few minutes but the joint does not achieve its working strength for twenty-four hours.

COLD WATER STORAGE CISTERNS
The size of cold water storage cisterns for dwelling houses will depend upon the reserve required and whether the cistern is intended to feed a hot

water system. Minimum actual capacities recommended in model water by-laws are 115 litres for cold water storage only and 230 litres for cold and hot water services.

Cisterns should be adequately supported and installed in such a position to give reasonable access for maintenance purposes. The cistern must be installed so that its outlets are above the highest discharge point on the sanitary fittings since the flow is by gravity. If the cistern is housed in the roof the pipes and cistern should be insulated against possible freezing of the water; pre-formed casings of suitable materials are available to suit most standard cistern sizes and shapes. The inlet and outlet connections to the cistern should be on opposite sides to prevent stagnation of water—a typical cistern arrangement together with recommended dimensions for outlets are shown in Fig. III.3.

BS 417 defines the sizes of galvanised mild steel cisterns which can be used for cold water storage. They have a limited life of 15-20 years due to the breakdown of the protective zinc coating, and their anticipated life can be extended by coating internally with two coats of black bitumen solution.

Plastic cisterns have many advantages over the traditional mild steel cisterns; they are non-corrosive, rot proof, frost resistant and have good resistance to mechanical damage. Materials used are polythene, polypropylene and glass fibre: these cisterns are made with a wall thickness to withstand the water pressure and have an indefinite life. Some forms of polythene cisterns can be distorted to enable them to be passed through an opening of 600 x 600 mm which is a great advantage when planning access to a roof space.

Ball valves

Every pipe supplying a cold water storage cistern must be fitted with a ball valve to prevent an overflow. The ball valve must be fitted at a higher level than the overflow to prevent it becoming submerged and creating the conditions where back siphonage is possible. A ball valve is designed to automatically regulate the supply of water by a floating ball closing the valve when the water reaches a predetermined level.

Two valves are in common use for domestic work, namely the Portsmouth valve and the Garston or BRS valve. The Portsmouth valve has a horizontal piston or plunger which closes over the orifice of a diameter to suit the pressure; high, medium and low pressure valves are available (see Fig. III.3). The BRS valve is a diaphragm valve which closes over an interchangeable nylon nozzle orifice. This type of valve is quieter in operation, easily adjustable and less susceptible to the corrosion trouble caused by a sticking piston—this is one of the problems that can be encountered with the Portsmouth valve (see Fig. III.3).

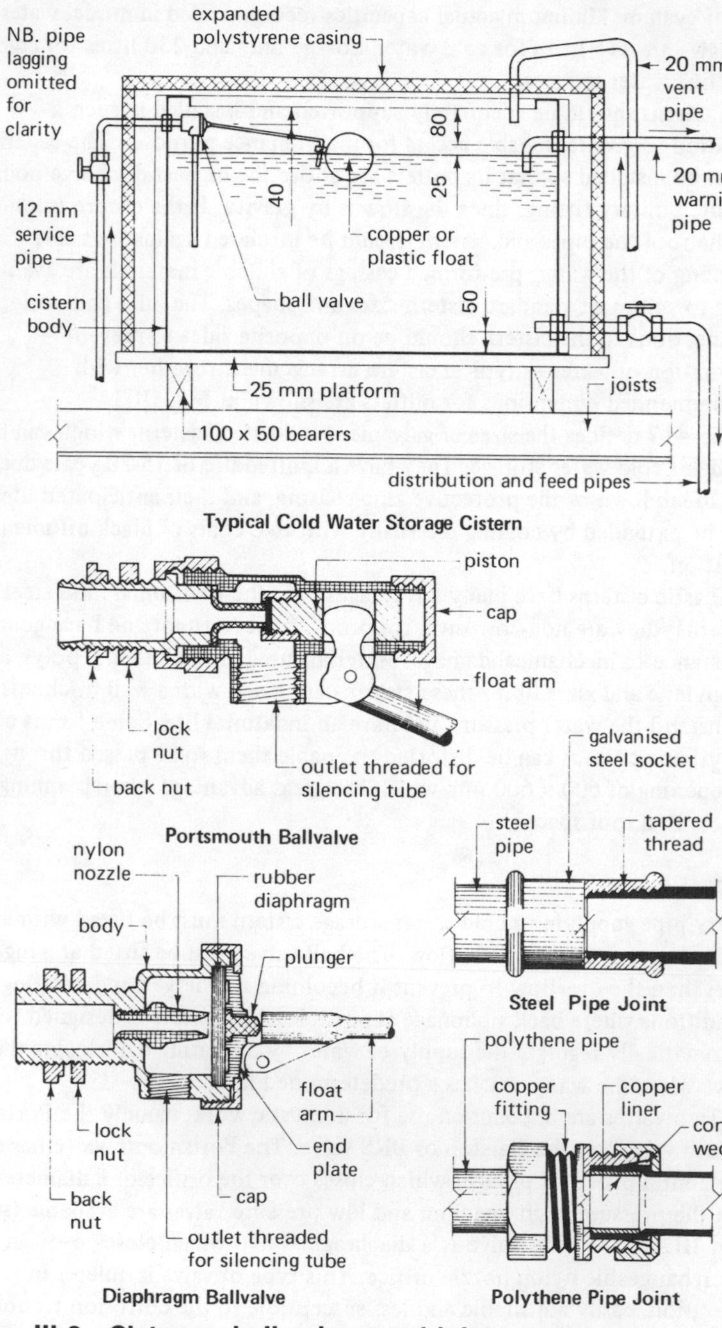
NB. pipe lagging omitted for clarity
expanded polystyrene casing
20 mm vent pipe
80
25
40
20 mm warning pipe
12 mm service pipe
copper or plastic float
ball valve
50
cistern body
25 mm platform
joists
100 x 50 bearers
distribution and feed pipes
Typical Cold Water Storage Cistern
piston
cap
float arm
lock nut
back nut
outlet threaded for silencing tube
Portsmouth Ballvalve
galvanised steel socket
steel pipe
tapered thread
Steel Pipe Joint
nylon nozzle
rubber diaphragm
body
plunger
float arm
lock nut
end plate
back nut
cap
outlet threaded for silencing tube
Diaphragm Ballvalve
polythene pipe
copper fitting
copper liner
cone wedge
Polythene Pipe Joint

Fig. III.3 Cisterns, ball-valves and joints

Hot water supply

The supply of hot water to domestic sanitary fittings is usually taken from a hot water tank or cylinder. The source of heat is usually in the form of a gas fired, oil fired or solid fuel boiler; alternatives are a back boiler to an open fire or an electric immersion heater fixed into the hot water storage tank. When a quantity of hot water is drawn from the storage tank it is immediately replaced by cold water from the cold water storage cistern. Two main systems are used to heat the water in the tank—these are called the direct and indirect systems. For any hot water system copper or steel pipes are generally used, and care must be taken when connecting copper to steel because of the risk of electrolytic corrosion between dissimilar materials.

DIRECT HOT WATER SYSTEM

This is the simplest and cheapest system; the cold water flows through the water jacket in the boiler where its temperature is raised and convection currents are induced which causes the water to rise and circulate. The hot water leaving the boiler is replaced by colder water descending from the hot water cylinder or tank by gravity thus setting up the circulation. The hot water supply is drawn off from the top of the cylinder by a horizontal pipe at least 450 mm long to prevent 'one pipe' circulation being set up in the vent or expansion pipe. This pipe is run vertically from the hot water distribution pipe to a discharge position over the cold water storage cistern (see Fig. III.4).

The direct system is not suitable for supplying a central heating circuit or for hard water areas because the pipes and cylinders will become furred with lime deposits. This precipitation of lime occurs when hard water is heated to temperatures of between 50 and 70°C, which is the ideal temperature range for domestic hot water supply.

INDIRECT HOT WATER SYSTEM

This system is designed to overcome the problems of furring which occurs with the direct hot water system. The basic difference is in the cylinder design which now becomes a heat exchanger. The cylinder contains a coil or annulus which is connected to the flow and return pipes from the boiler. A transfer of heat takes place within the cylinder and therefore, after the initial precipitation of lime within the primary circuit and boiler, there is no further furring since fresh cold water is not being constantly introduced into the boiler circuit.

The supply circuit from the cylinder follows the same pattern as the direct hot water system, but a separate feed and expansion system is required for the boiler and primary circuit for initial supply, also for any necessary topping up due to evaporation. The feed cistern is similar to a cold water storage cistern but of a much smaller capacity. The water levels in the two cisterns should be equal so that equal pressures act on the indirect cylinder.

A gravity heating circuit can be taken from the boiler, its distribution being governed by the boiler capacity (see Fig. III.4). Alternatively a small bore forced system of central heating may be installed.

Hot water cylinders and tanks

Galvanised steel tanks, which are rectangular, can be used for any hot water system where space is restricted and the required storage capacity is less than 155 litres; these storage vessels are usually made to the recommendations of BS 417. Cylinders of galvanised mild steel or copper are produced to the recommendations of BS 1565 and BS 1566 respectively. The standard recommends sizes, capacities and positions for screwed holes for pipe connections.

To overcome the disadvantage of the extra pipework involved when using an indirect cylinder, a single feed indirect or 'Primatic' cylinder can be used. This form of cylinder is entirely self contained and is installed in the same manner as a direct cylinder but functions as an indirect cylinder. It works on the principle of the buoyancy of air which is used to form seals between the primary and secondary water systems. When the system is first filled with water the cylinder commences to fill and fully charges the primary circuit to the boiler with water. When the cylinder water capacity has been reached two air seals will have formed, the first being in the upper chamber of the primatic unit and the second in the air vent pipe. These volumes of air are used to separate the primary and secondary water. When the water is heated in the primary system expansion displaces some of the air in the upper chamber to the lower chamber, this is a reciprocating action; the seals transfer from chamber to chamber as the temperature rises and falls.

Any excess air in the primary system is vented into the secondary system, which will also automatically replenish the primary system should this be necessary. As with indirect systems careful control over the heat output of the boiler is advisable to prevent boiling and consequent furring of the pipework. Typical examples of cylinders are shown in Fig. III.5.

Faults in hot water systems

Unless a hot water system is correctly designed and installed a number of faults may occur such as air locks and noises. Air locks are pockets of trapped air in the system which will stop or slow down the circulation.

162

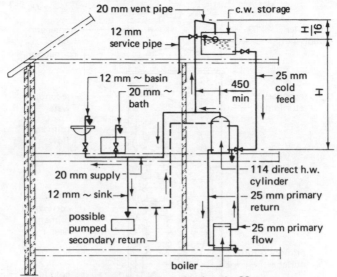

20 mm vent pipe — ┌ c.w. storage

12 mm service pipe →

H/16

12 mm ~ basin
20 mm ~ bath

25 mm cold feed

450 min

H

20 mm supply →

114 direct h.w. cylinder

12 mm ~ sink →

25 mm primary return

possible pumped secondary return

25 mm primary flow

boiler

in hard water areas primary circuit to be 32 mm

Direct Hot Water System

⊠ = valve

▼ = draw off point

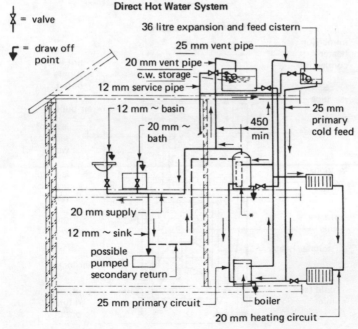

36 litre expansion and feed cistern

25 mm vent pipe

20 mm vent pipe
c.w. storage
12 mm service pipe →

12 mm ~ basin

20 mm ~ bath

25 mm primary cold feed

450 min

20 mm supply →

12 mm ~ sink →

possible pumped secondary return

25 mm primary circuit

boiler

20 mm heating circuit

*114 litre indirect hot water cylinder

Indirect Hot Water System

Fig. III.4   Hot water systems

163

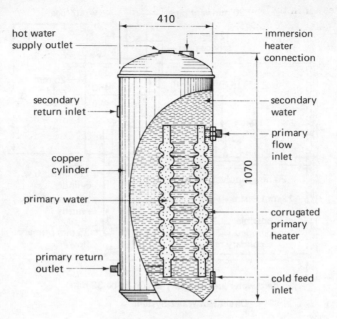

414 Litre Indirect Cylinder

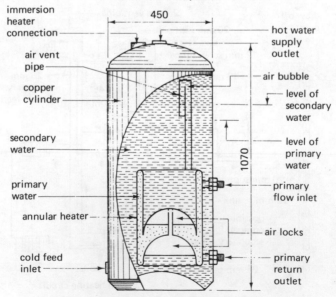

135 Litre Single Feed or 'Primatic' Cylinder

Fig. III.5 Typical hot water cylinders

Suspended air in the water will be released when the water is heated, and rise to the highest point. In a good installation the pipes are designed to rise 25 mm in 3 000 mm towards the vent where the air is released through the vent pipe. The most common positions for air locks are sharp bends and the upper rail of a towel rail, the only cure for the latter position is for the towel rail to be vented.

Noises from the hot water system usually indicate a blocked pipe caused by excessive furring or corrosion. The noise is caused by the imprisoned expanded water and the faulty pipe must be descaled or removed, or an explosion may occur.

19
Sanitary fittings and pipework

Sanitary fittings or appliances can be considered under two headings:

Soil fitments: those which are used to remove soil water and human excreta such as water closets and urinals.

Waste water fitments: those which are used to remove the waste water from washing and the preparation of food including appliances such as wash basins, baths, showers and sinks.

All sanitary appliances should be made from impervious materials, be quiet in operation, easy to clean and be of a convenient shape fixed at a suitable height. A number of materials are available for most domestic sanitary fittings including:

Vitreous china: a white clay body which is vitried and permanently fused with a vitreous glazed surface when fired at a very high temperature generally to the recommendations of BS 3402. Appliances made from this material are non-corrosive, hygienic and easily cleaned with a mild detergent or soap solution.

Glazed fireclay: consists of a porous ceramic body glazed in a similar manner to vitreous china; they are exceptionally strong and resistant to impact damage but will allow water penetration of the body if the protective glazing is damaged. Like vitreous china, these appliances are non-corrosive, hygienic and easily cleaned.

Vitreous enamel: this is a form of glass which can be melted and used to

166

give a glazed protective coating over a steel or cast iron base. Used mainly for baths, sinks and draining boards, it produces a fitment which is lighter than those produced from a ceramic material, is hygienic, easy to clean and has a long life. The finish, however, can be chipped and is subject to staining especially from copper compounds from hot water systems.

Plastic materials: acrylic plastics, glass reinforced polyester resins and polypropylene sanitary fittings made from the above plastics require no protective coatings, are very strong, light in weight, chip resistant but generally cost more than ceramic or vitreous enamel products. Care must be taken with fitments made of acrylic plastics since these become soft when heated, therefore they should be used for cold water fitments or have thermostatically controlled mixing taps. Plastic appliances can be easily cleaned using warm soapy water and any dullness can be restored by polishing with ordinary domestic polishes.

Stainless steel: made from steel containing approximately 18% chromium and 8% nickle which gives the metal a natural resistance to corrosion. Stainless steel appliances are very durable and relatively light in weight; for domestic situations the main application is for sinks and draining boards. Two finishes are available: polished or 'mirror' finish and the 'satin' finish; the latter has a greater resistance to scratching.

The factors to be considered when selecting or specifying sanitary fitments can be enumerated thus:
1. Cost: outlay, fixing and maintenance.
2. Hygiene: inherent and ease of cleaning.
3. Appearance: size, colour and shape.
4. Function: suitability, speed of operation and reliability.
5. Weight: support required from wall and/or floor.
6. Design: ease with which it can be included into the general services installation.

WATER CLOSETS
Building Regulation G4 gives requirements for the receptacle and the flushing apparatus. Most water closets are made from a ceramic base to the requirements of BS 5503 with a horizontal outlet. The complete water closet arrangement consists of the pan, seat, flush pipe and flushing cistern. The cistern can be fixed as a high level, low level or closed coupled; the latter arrangement dispenses with the need for a flush pipe. A typical arrangement is shown in Fig. III.6. The BS 5503 water closet is termed a wash down type and relies on the flush of water to wash the contents of the bowl round the trap and into the soil pipe. An

167

alternative form is the siphonic water closet which is more efficient and quieter in operation but has a greater risk of blockage if misused. Two types are produced — the single trap and the double trap.

The single trap siphonic water closet has a restricted outlet which serves to retard the flow, when flushed, so that the bore of the outlet connected to the bowl becomes full and sets up a siphonic flushing action, completely emptying the contents of the bowl (see Fig. III.6). With the double trap siphonic pan the air is drawn from the pocket between the two traps; when the flushing operation is started this causes atmospheric pressure to expel the complete contents of the bowl through both traps into the soil pipe (see Fig. III.6).

The pan should be fixed to the floor with brass screws and bedded on a suitable compressible material; the connection to the soil pipe socket can be made with cement mortar or preferably a mastic to allow for any differential movement between the fitment and the structure. Connections to PVC soil pipes are usually made with compression rings. The flush pipe is invariably connected to the pan with a special plastic or rubber one-piece connector.

Flushing cisterns together with the flush pipes are usually constructed to the recommendations of BS 1125 and can be made from enamelled cast iron, enamelled pressed steel, ceramic ware or of plastic materials. Two basic types are produced, namely the bell or cone and the piston. The former is activated by pulling a chain which raises and lowers the bell or cone and in so doing raises the water level above the open end of the flush pipe thus setting up a siphonic action. These cisterns are efficient and durable but are noisy in operation (see Fig. III.6). The piston type cistern is the one in general use and is activated by a lever or button. When activated the disc or flap valve piston is raised and with it the water level which commences the siphonage (see Fig. III.6). The level of the water in the cistern is controlled by a ball valve and an overflow or warning pipe of a larger diameter than the inlet and is fitted to discharge so that it gives a visual warning, usually in an external position. The capacity of the cistern will be determined by local water board requirements, the most common being 9, 11.5 and 13.6 litres.

There is a wide range of designs, colours and patterns available for water closet suites but all can be classified as one of the types described above.

WASH BASINS

Wash basins for domestic work are usually made from a ceramic material but metal basins complying with BS 1329 are also available. A wide variety of shapes, sizes, types and colours are

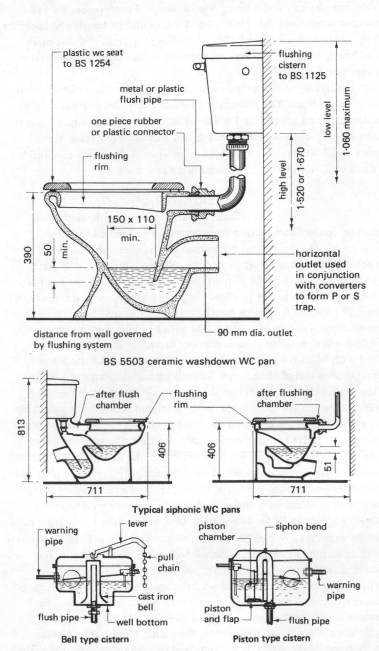

plastic wc seat
to BS 1254

metal or plastic
flush pipe

one piece rubber
or plastic connector

flushing
rim

flushing
cistern
to BS 1125

low level
1·060 maximum

high level
1·520 or 1·670

150 x 110
min.

390

50
min.

horizontal
outlet used
in conjunction
with converters
to form P or S
trap.

distance from wall governed
by flushing system

90 mm dia. outlet

BS 5503 ceramic washdown WC pan

after flush
chamber

flushing
rim

after flushing
chamber

813

406

406

51

711

711

Typical siphonic WC pans

warning
pipe

lever

pull
chain

cast iron
bell

flush pipe

well bottom

Bell type cistern

piston
chamber

siphon bend

warning
pipe

piston
and flap

flush pipe

Piston type cistern

Fig. III.6   WC pans and cisterns

available, the choice usually being one of personal preference. BS 1188 gives recommendations for ceramic wash basins and pedestals and specifies two basic sizes. 635 x 457 and 559 x 406. These basins are a one-piece fitment having an integral overflow, separate waste outlet and generally pillar taps (see Fig. III.7).

Wash basins can be supported on wall-mounted cantilever brackets, leg supports or pedestals. The pedestals are made from identical material to the wash basin and are recessed at the back to receive the supply pipes to the taps and the waste pipe from the bowl. Although pedestals are designed to fully support the wash basin most manufacturers recommend that small wall mounted safety brackets are also used.

BATHS AND SHOWERS

Baths are available in a wide variety of designs and colours made either from porcelain-enamelled cast iron, vitreous enamelled sheet steel, 8 mm cast acrylic sheet or 3 mm cast acrylic sheet reinforced with a polyester resin/glass fibre laminate. Most bath designs today are rectangular in plan and made as flat bottomed as practicable with just sufficient fall to allow for gravity emptying and resealing of the trap. The British Standards for the materials quoted above recommend a co-ordinating plan size of 1 700 x 700 with a height within the range of n x 50 mm where n is any natural number including unity. Baths are supplied with holes for pillar taps or mixer fittings and for the waste outlets. Options include handgrips, built in soap and sponge recesses and overflow outlets. It is advisable to always specify overflow outlets as a precautionary measure to limit the water level and to minimise splashing; most overflow pipes are designed to connect with the waste trap beneath the bath (see Fig. III.8). Support for baths is usually by adjustable feet for cast iron and steel and by a strong cradle for the acrylic baths. Panels of enamelled hardboard or moulded high impact polystyrene or glass fibre are available for enclosing the bath. These panels can be fixed by using stainless steel or aluminium angles or direct to a timber stud framework.

Shower sprays can be used in conjunction with a bath by fitting a rigid plastic shower screen or flexible curtain to one end of the bath. A separate shower fitment, however, is considered preferable. Such fitments require less space than the conventional bath, use less hot water and are considered to be more hygienic since the used water is being continuously discharged. A shower fitment consists of the shower tray with a waste outlet, the impervious cubicle and a door or curtain (see Fig. III.8). Materials available are similar to those described for baths. The spray outlet is normally fixed to the wall and is connected to a mixing valve so that the water temperature can be controlled.

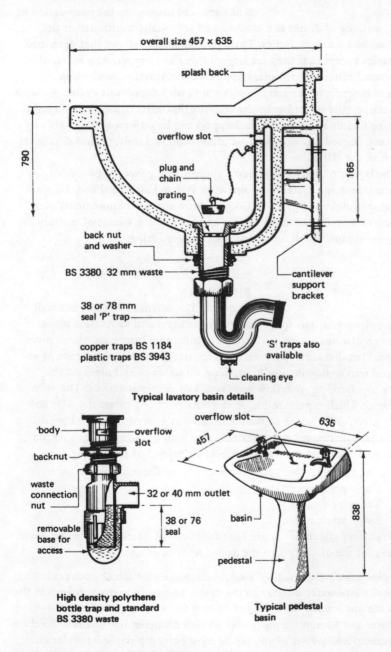

overall size 457 x 635

splash back

overflow slot

plug and chain

grating

back nut and washer

BS 3380 32 mm waste

38 or 78 mm seal 'P' trap

copper traps BS 1184
plastic traps BS 3943

cantilever support bracket

'S' traps also available

cleaning eye

790

165

Typical lavatory basin details

body

overflow slot

backnut

waste connection nut

removable base for access

32 or 40 mm outlet

38 or 76 seal

overflow slot

635

457

basin

pedestal

838

High density polythene bottle trap and standard BS 3380 waste

Typical pedestal basin

Fig. III.7   Basins, traps and wastes

SINKS

Sinks are used mainly for the preparation of food, washing of dishes and clothes, and are usually positioned at the drinking water supply outlet. Their general design follows that described for basins except that they are larger in area and deeper. Any material considered suitable for sanitary appliance construction can be used. Designs range from the simple belfast sink with detachable draining boards of metal, plastic or timber to the combination units consisting of integral draining boards and twin bowls. Support can be wall-mounted cantilever brackets, framed legs or a purpose made cupboard unit; typical details are shown in Fig. III.9.

The layout of domestic sanitary appliances is governed by size of fitments, personal preference, pipework system being used and the space available. Building Regulation G4 lays down specific requirements as to the interconnection of food storage and preparation rooms of sanitary accommodation which contains a water closet fitting.

PIPEWORK

Approved Document H sets out in detail the recommendations for soil pipes, waste pipes and ventilating pipes. These regulations govern such things as minimum diameters of soil pipes, material requirements, provision of adequate water seals by means of an integral trap or non-integral trap, the positioning of soil pipes on the inside of a building, overflow pipework and ventilating pipes. The only pipework which is permissible on the outside of the external wall is any waste pipe from a waste appliance situated at ground floor level providing such a pipe discharges into a suitable trap with a grating and the discharge is above the level of the water but below the level of the grating.

Three basic pipework systems are in use for domestic work, namely:
1. One-pipe system.
2. Two-pipe system.
3. Single stack system.

Whichever system is adopted the functions of quick, reliable and quiet removal of the discharges to the drains remains constant.

One-pipe system: consists of a single discharge pipe which conveys both soil and waste water directly to the drain. To ensure that water seals in the traps are not broken deep seals of 75 mm for waste pipes up to 65 mm diameter and 50 mm for pipes over 75 mm diameter are required. To allow for unrestricted layout of appliances most branch pipes will require an anti-siphon arrangement (see Fig. III.10). The advantage of this sytem is

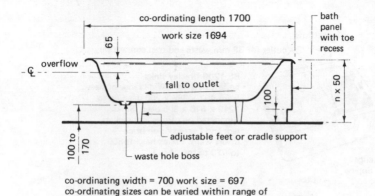

co-ordinating length 1700
work size 1694
65
overflow
bath panel with toe recess
fall to outlet
100
n x 50
adjustable feet or cradle support
100 to 170
waste hole boss

co-ordinating width = 700 work size = 697
co-ordinating sizes can be varied within range of
n x 100 mm where n = any natural number including unity

BS 1189 (cast iron) and BS 4305 (cast acrylic) baths

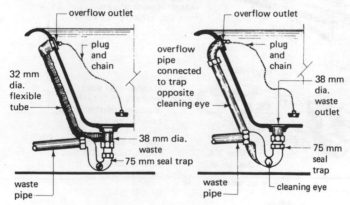

overflow outlet

plug and chain

32 mm dia. flexible tube

38 mm dia. waste
75 mm seal trap

waste pipe

overflow pipe connected to trap opposite cleaning eye

overflow outlet

plug and chain

38 mm dia. waste outlet

75 mm seal trap

waste pipe
cleaning eye

Alternative overflow connections

Typical Sizes:-
600 x 600 x 175 deep
760 x 760 x 175 deep
900 x 900 x 175 deep
also available in
enamelled steel
and perspex

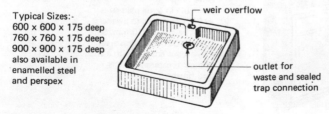

weir overflow

outlet for waste and sealed trap connection

Typical fireclay shower tray

Fig. III.8   Baths and shower trays

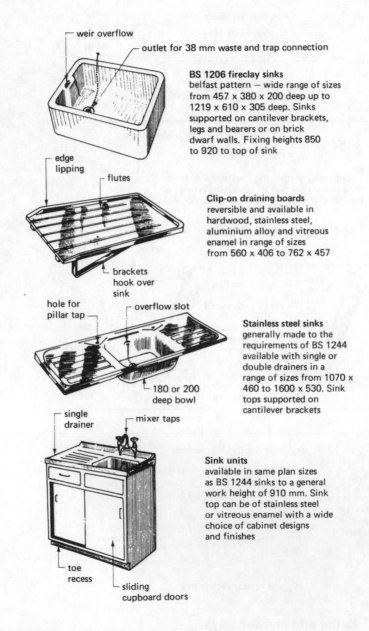

weir overflow

outlet for 38 mm waste and trap connection

BS 1206 fireclay sinks
belfast pattern — wide range of sizes
from 457 x 380 x 200 deep up to
1219 x 610 x 305 deep. Sinks
supported on cantilever brackets,
legs and bearers or on brick
dwarf walls. Fixing heights 850
to 920 to top of sink

edge lipping

flutes

Clip-on draining boards
reversible and available in
hardwood, stainless steel,
aluminium alloy and vitreous
enamel in range of sizes
from 560 x 406 to 762 x 457

brackets
hook over
sink

hole for
pillar tap

overflow slot

Stainless steel sinks
generally made to the
requirements of BS 1244
available with single or
double drainers in a
range of sizes from 1070 x
460 to 1600 x 530. Sink
tops supported on
cantilever brackets

180 or 200
deep bowl

single
drainer

mixer taps

Sink units
available in same plan sizes
as BS 1244 sinks to a general
work height of 910 mm. Sink
top can be of stainless steel
or vitreous enamel with a wide
choice of cabinet designs
and finishes

toe
recess

sliding
cupboard doors

Fig. III.9 Sinks and draining boards

174

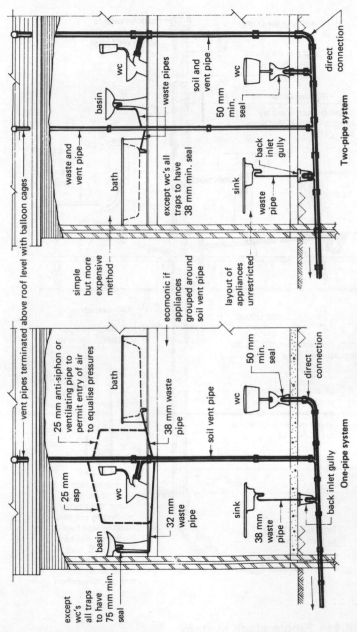

Fig. III.10 Comparison of one-pipe and two-pipe systems

vent pipes terminated above roof level with balloon cages

Two-pipe system

wc

waste pipes

soil and vent pipe

wc

50 mm min. seal

back inlet gully

sink

waste pipe

direct connection

waste and vent pipe

bath

except wc's all traps to have 38 mm min. seal

simple but more expensive method

ecomonic if appliances grouped around soil vent pipe

layout of appliances unrestricted

One-pipe system

25 mm anti-siphon or ventilating pipe to permit entry of air to equalise pressures

bath

38 mm waste pipe

soil vent pipe

wc

50 mm min. seal

direct connection

25 mm asp

wc

32 mm waste pipe

basin

sink

38 mm waste pipe

back inlet gully

except wc's all traps to have 75 mm min. seal

175

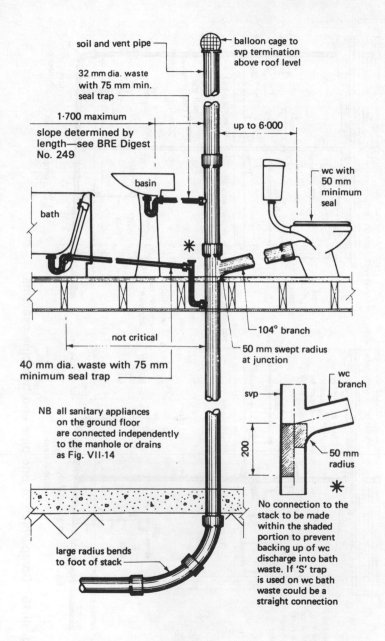

soil and vent pipe

balloon cage to svp termination above roof level

32 mm dia. waste with 75 mm min. seal trap

1·700 maximum

up to 6·000

slope determined by length—see BRE Digest No. 249

wc with 50 mm minimum seal

basin

bath

104° branch

not critical

50 mm swept radius at junction

40 mm dia. waste with 75 mm minimum seal trap

NB all sanitary appliances on the ground floor are connected independently to the manhole or drains as Fig. VII-14

large radius bends to foot of stack

svp

wc branch

200

50 mm radius

No connection to the stack to be made within the shaded portion to prevent backing up of wc discharge into bath waste. If 'S' trap is used on wc bath waste could be a straight connection

Fig. III.11   Single stack system

176

the flexibility of appliance layout; the main disadvantage is cost; and generally the one-pipe system has been superseded by the more restricted but economic single stack system described later.

Two-pipe system: as its name implies, this system consists of two discharge pipes, one conveys soil discharges and the other all the waste discharges. It is a simple, reliable and costly system but has the advantages of complete flexibility in appliance layout and deep seal traps are not usually required. Like the one-pipe system, it has been largely superseded by the single stack system. A comparison of the one- and two-pipe systems is shown in Fig. III.10.

Single stack system: this system was developed by the Building Research Establishment and is fully described in their Digest No. 249. It is a simplification of the one-pipe system by using deep seal traps, relying on venting by the discharge pipe and placing certain restrictions on basin waste pipes which has a higher risk to self siphonage than other appliances. A diagrammatic layout is shown on Fig. III.11.

Materials which can be used for domestic pipework include galvanised steel (BS 3868) with socketed joints caulked with an asbestos material and cement in the form of a cord; cast iron (BS 416) with socketed joints sealed with hemp and caulked with run lead or a cold caulking compound and fixed like galvanised steel pipes by means of holderbolts to the support wall; pitch fibre (BS 2760) with push fit tapered joints or compression ring joints (it should be noted that not all local authorities will permit the use of pitch fibre for soil pipes fixed internally); UPVC (BS 4514), which can be jointed with a ring seal joint or by solvent welding; fixing to the support wall is by holderbolts or clips.

Most manufacturers of soil pipes, ventilating pipes and fittings produce special components for various plumbing arrangements and appliance layouts. These fittings have the water closet socket connections, bosses for branch waste connections and access plates for cleaning and maintenance arranged as one prefabricated assembly to ease site work and ensure reliable and efficient connections to the discharge or soil pipe.

20
Electrical installations

A simple definition of the term electricity is not possible but it can be considered as a form of energy due to the free movement of tiny particles called electrons. If sufficient of these free or loose electrons move an electric current is produced in the material in which they are moving. Materials such as most metals and water which allow an electric current to flow readily are called conductors and are said to have a low resistance. Materials which resist the flow of an electric current such as rubber, glass and most plastics are called insulators.

For an electric current to flow there must be a complete path or circuit from the source of energy through a conductor back to the source. Any interruption of the path will stop the flow of electricity. The pressure which forces or pushes the current around the circuit is called the voltage. The rate at which the current flows is measured in amperes and the resistance offered by the circuit to passage of electrons is measured in ohms. A watt is the unit of power and is equal to the product of volts x amperes; similarly it can be shown that voltage is equal to the product of amperes x ohms.

Another effect of an electric current flowing through a conductor is that it will dissipate wasted energy in the form of heat according to the resistance of the conductor. If a wire of the correct resistance is chosen it will become very hot and this heating effect can be used in appliances such as cookers, irons and fires. The conductor in a filament bulb is a very thin wire of high resistance and becomes white hot thus giving out light as well as heat.

Most domestic premises receive a single phase supply of electricity from an area electricity board at a rating of 240 volts, and a frequency of 50 hertz. The area board's cable, from which the domestic supply is taken, consists of four lines, three lines each carrying a 240 volt supply and the fourth is the common return line or neutral which is connected to earth at the transformer or substation as a safety precaution should a fault occur on the electrical appliance. Each line or phase is tapped in turn together with the neutral to provide the single phase 240 V supply. Electricity is generated and supplied as an alternating current which means that the current flows first one way then the other; the direction change is so rapid that it is hardly discernible in such fittings as lights. The cycle of this reversal of flow is termed frequency.

The conductors used in domestic installations are called cables and consist of a conductor of low resistance such as copper or aluminium surrounded by an insulator of high resistance such as rubber or plastic. Cable sizes are known by the nominal cross sectional area of the conductor and up to 2.5 mm^2 are usually of one strand. Larger cables consist of a number of strands to give them flexibility. All cables are assigned a rating in amperes which is the maximum load the cable can carry without becoming overheated.

For domestic work wiring drawings are not usually required; instead the positions of outlets, switches and lighting points are shown by symbols on the plans. Specification of fittings, fixing heights and cables is given either in a schedule or in a written document (see Fig. III.12).

RING CIRCUITS

Domestic buildings are wired using a ring circuit as opposed to the older method of having a separate fused sub-circuit to each socket outlet. Lighting circuits are carried out by using the 'loop in' method.

The supply or intake cable will enter the building through ducts and be terminated in the area board's fused sealing chamber which should be sited in a dry accessible position. From the sealing chamber the supply passes through the meter, which records the electricity consumed in units of kilowatt/hours, to the consumer unit which has a switch controlling the supply to the circuit fuses or miniature circuit breakers. These fuses or circuit breakers are a protection against excess current or overload of the circuit since should overloading occur the fuse or circuit breaker will isolate the circuit from the supply.

The number of fuseways or miniature circuit breakers contained in the consumer unit will depend upon the size of the building and the equipment to be installed. A separate ring circuit of 30 amp loading should be allowed for every 100 m^2 of floor area and as far as practicable the number

179

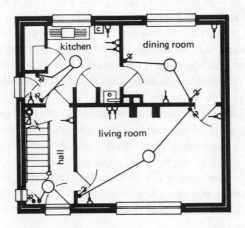

Ground floor plan

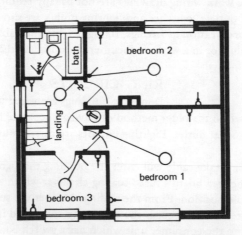

Upper floor plan

Symbols

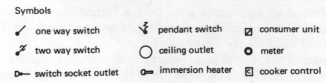

⟋ one way switch	⟍ pendant switch	▨ consumer unit
⟋ two way switch	○ ceiling outlet	● meter
▷— switch socket outlet	○— immersion heater	⊂ cooker control

Fig. III.12 Typical domestic electrical layout

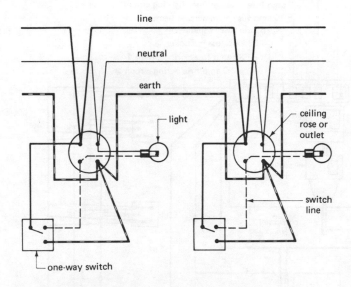

line

neutral

earth

light

ceiling
rose or
outlet

switch
line

one-way switch

'Loop-in' method of wiring using sheathed cable

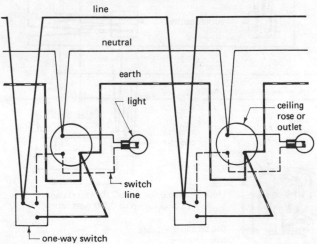

line

neutral

earth

light

ceiling
rose or
outlet

switch
line

one-way switch

Single core cable looped from switch to switch

Fig. III.13 Typical lighting circuits

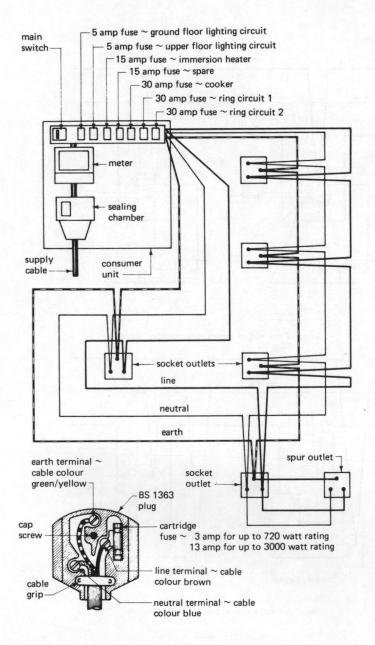

main
switch

5 amp fuse ~ ground floor lighting circuit
5 amp fuse ~ upper floor lighting circuit
15 amp fuse ~ immersion heater
15 amp fuse ~ spare
30 amp fuse ~ cooker
30 amp fuse ~ ring circuit 1
30 amp fuse ~ ring circuit 2

meter

sealing
chamber

supply
cable

consumer
unit

socket outlets
line

neutral

earth

earth terminal ~
cable colour
green/yellow

BS 1363
plug

cap
screw

cartridge
fuse ~   3 amp for up to 720 watt rating
         13 amp for up to 3000 watt rating

line terminal ~ cable
colour brown

cable
grip

neutral terminal ~ cable
colour blue

spur outlet

socket
outlet

Fig. III.14   Ring circuits and plug wiring

182

of outlets should be evenly distributed over the circuits. A typical domestic installation would have the following circuits from the consumer unit:

1. 5 amp: ground floor lighting up to ten fittings or a total load of 5 amps.
2. 5 amp: first floor lighting as above.
3. 30 amp: cooker circuit.
4. 30 amp: ring circuit 1.
5. 30 amp: ring circuit 2.
6. 15 amp: immersion heater.

The complete installation is earthed by connecting the metal consumer unit casing to the sheath of the supply cable or by connection to a separate earth electrode.

For lighting circuits using sheathed wiring a 1.0 mm^2 conductor is required and therefore a twin with earth cable is used. The 'loop-in' method of wiring is shown diagrammatically in Fig. III.13. It is essential that lighting circuits are properly earthed since most domestic fittings and switches contain metal parts or fixings which could become live should a fault occur. Lighting circuits using a conduit installation with single core cables can be looped from switch to switch as shown in Fig. III.13. Conduit installation consists of metal or plastic tubing together with various boxes for forming junctions and housing switches which gives a protected rewireable system. If steel-screwed conduit is used it will also serve as the earth leakage path but plastic conduit, being non-conductive, the circuit must have an insulated earth conductor throughout.

A ring circuit for socket outlets consists of a twin 2.5 mm^2 earthed cable starting from and returning to the consumer unit. The cables are looped into the outlet boxes making sure that the correct cable is connected to the correct terminals (see Fig. III.14). The number of outlets is unlimited if the requirement of 1 ring circuit per 100 m^2 of floor area has been adopted. Spur outlets leading off the main ring circuit are permissible provided the limitation of not more than two outlet sockets on any one spur and not more than half the socket outlets on the circuit are on spurs is not exceeded. Socket outlets can be switched controlled and of single or double outlet; the double outlet is considered the best arrangement since it discourages the use of multiple adaptors. Fixed appliances such as wall heaters should be connected directly to a fused spur outlet to reduce the number of trailing leads. Moveable appliances such as irons, radios and standard lamps should have a fused plug for connection to the switched outlet, conforming to the requirements of BS 1363. The rating of the cartridge fuse should be in accordance with rating of the appliance. Appliances with a rating of not more than 720 watts should be protected by a 3 amp fuse and appliances over this rating up to 3 000 watts should have a 13 amp fuse. As with the circuit, correct wiring of the plug is essential (see Fig. III.14).

The number of outlets is not mandatory but the minimum numbers recommended for various types of accommodation are:

Kitchens: 3 plus cooker control unit with one outlet socket.
Living rooms: 3.
Dining rooms: 2.
Bedrooms: 2.
Halls: 1.
Landings: 1.
Garages: 1.
Stores and workshops: 1.

The outlets should be installed around the perimeter of the rooms in the most convenient and economic positions to give maximum coverage with minimum amount of trailing leads.

Cables sheathed with tough rubber or PVC can be run under suspended floors by drilling small holes on the neutral axis of the joists; where the cables are to be covered by wall finishes or floor screed they should be protected by either oval conduit or by means of small metal cover channels fixed to the wall or floor. Systems using mineral-insulated covered cables follow the same principles. This form of cable consists of single strands of copper or aluminium all encased in a sheath of the same metal which is densely packed with fine magnesium oxide insulation around the strands. This insulating material is unaffected by heat or age and is therefore very durable but it can absorb moisture. The sealing of the ends of this type of cable with special sealing 'pots' is therefore of paramount importance. Cables used in a conduit installation have adequate protection but it is generally necessary to chase the walls of the building to accommodate the conduit, outlet socket boxes and switch boxes below the wall finish level. Surface run conduit is normally secured to the backing by using screwed shaped clips called saddles.

The installation of electric circuits and electrical equipment are not covered by the Building Regulations but the minimum standard required by most authorities are those contained in the 'Regulations for Electrical Equipment of Buildings' issued by the Institution of Electrical Engineers.

21

Gas installations

Gas is a combustible fuel which burns with a luminous flame; it is used mainly in domestic installations as a source of heat in appliances such as room heaters, cookers and water heaters. Gas can also be utilised to provide the power for washing machines and refrigerators; the use of gas as a means of artificial lighting has been superseded by electricity.

Gas is supplied by area boards under the general co-ordination and guidance of the Gas Council. The supply may be in the form of a manufactured gas known as 'town gas' or as a natural gas often referred to as 'North Sea Gas'. Town gas can be processed from coal, oil or imported natural gas and has a high hydrogen content of approximately 50% with a calorific value of about 18.6 MJ/m^3. Natural gas has no hydrogen content but has a very high percentage content of methane of approximately 95% with a calorific value of about 37.3 MJ/m^3. The pressure burning rate and amount of air required for correct combustion varies with the two forms of gas supply and therefore it is essential that the correct type of burner is fitted to the appliance.

The installation of a gas service to a domestic building is usually carried out by the local area board and can be considered in three distinct stages:

Main: this is the board's distribution system and works on the grid principle being laid and maintained by them. For identification purposes gas pipelines are colour coded over their length or in 150 mm wide bands with yellow ochre.

Service pipe: the connection pipe between the main and the consumer control which is positioned just before the governor and meter. In small domestic installations the service pipe diameter is 25—50 mm according to the number and type of appliances being installed. The pipe run should be as short as possible, at right angles to the main, laid at least 760 mm below the ground to avoid frost damage and be laid to a rise of 25 mm in 3 000 to allow for any condensate to drain back to a suitable condensate receiver.

Internal installation: commences at the consumer control and consists of a governor to stabilise the pressure and volume, the meter which records the volume of gas consumed, pipework to convey the gas supply to the appliances.

Pipework can be of mild steel, solid drawn copper pipes and flexible tubing of rubber or metallic pipe for use with portable appliances such as gas pokers. The size of installation pipes will depend upon such factors as gas consumption of appliances, frictional losses due to length of pipe runs and bends. Gas pipes are fixed by means of pipe hooks, clips or ring brackets at approximately 1.500 m centres. All pipes should be protected against condensation, dampness, freezing and corrosion; methods include painting with a red lead or bituminous paint or using plastic-coated copper pipework. Pipes which pass through walls are housed in a sleeve of non-corrodible material surrounded by packing of incombustible material such as asbestos to facilitate easy replacement and to accommodate small differential movements.

Gas appliances fall mainly into two groups:
1. Gas supply only: refrigerators, radiant heaters, gas pokers.
2. Gas supply plus other services: central heating units, water heaters, washing machines.

Gas refrigerators are silent, reliable, requiring little or no maintenance and cheap to run. They work on the absorption principle using ammonia dissolved in water. Free standing, built-in and table models are available; all require a firm level surface, a well ventilated position, clearance for opening of doors and access to the rear to make the fixed connection to the supply. Gas room heaters can be radiant heaters where the heat source is visible, convector heaters or in combination as a radiant-convector heater. Room heaters using gas have high efficiency, rapid heat build-up, easy to clean and low maintenance. Gas fires or room heaters will require a chimney and flue complying with the requirements of Building Regulations J2 and J3 and of the minimum flue size recommended in Approved Document J. Exceptions permitting discharge of gas appliances otherwise than into an open flue are given in the Approved Document. These include cookers in ventilated rooms, and appliances fitted in a bathroom, shower room or a private garage which must be designed and installed as balanced flue appliances. Room sealed or balanced flue heaters are appliances which have the heater body sealed from the room; the heater obtains air for combustion by an inlet connected directly with the external air and return the products of combustion to the external air by a separate outlet but usually to a common grill or guard. The termination of the flues are so designed that the external wind pressure effects are balanced, which obviates the need for a traditional flue.

Gas central heating consists of a boiler, connected to a flue complying with the Building Regulations, which provides the heating source for a fanned warm air system which is flexible in design and has a quick response or a circulated hot water system.

The installation of gas services, like those of electricity, are subjects which the student of building technology will study in detail regarding materials, methods, design and application during a two-year course of advanced work when all aspects of services are covered by a separate syllabus.

Part IV
Design

22
Sound insulation

THE DEFINITION OF SOUND
Anything that can be heard is a sound,
whether it is made by conversation, machinery, or walking on a hard
surface. All sounds are produced by a vibrating object which moves rapidly
to and fro causing movement of the tiny particles of air surrounding the
vibrating source. The displaced air particles collide with adjacent particles
setting them in motion and in unison with the vibrating object. Air
particles move only to and fro but the sound wave produced travels
through the air until at some distance from the source the movement of
the particles is so slight that the sound produced is inaudible.

For a sound to be transmitted over a distance a substance, called the
sound medium, is required. It can be shown by experiments that sound
cannot travel through a vacuum but it can be transmitted through solids
and liquids.

Sounds can differ in two important ways, by loudness and by pitch.
The loudness of a sound depends on the distance through which the
vibrating object moves to and fro as it vibrates; the greater the movement
the louder the sound. The loudness with which a sound is heard depends
upon how far away from the source the receiver or ear is. The unit of
subjective loudness is a phon whilst the objective unit is called a decibel.
Although the loudness of a sound will vary with the frequency of the note
for practical building purposes, the phon and the decibel are considered to
be equal over the range of 0 phons, the threshold of hearing, to 130 phons
the threshold of painful hearing.

The pitch of a sound depends on the rate at which the vibrating object oscillates. The number of vibrations in a second is called the frequency and the higher the frequency the higher the pitch. The lowest pitched note that the human ear can hear has a frequency of approximately 16 hertz whereas the highest pitched note which can be heard by the human ear has a frequency of approximately 20 000 hertz or cycles per second.

When a sound is produced within a building three reactions can occur:

1. The pressure or sound waves can come into contact with the walls, floor and ceiling and be reflected back into the building.
2. Some of the sound can be absorbed by these surfaces and/or the furnishes. It must be noted that sound absorption normally only benefits the occupants of the room in which the sound is generated since its function is to reduce the amount of reflected sound.
3. The sound waves upon reaching the walls, floor and ceiling can set these members vibrating in unison and thus transmit the sound to adjacent rooms.

It must also be noted that sounds can enter a building from external sources such as traffic and low flying aircraft (see Fig. IV.1).

Sounds may be defined as either impact sounds, caused by direct contact with the structure such as footsteps and hammering on walls which will set that part of the structure vibrating, or they can be termed airborne sounds, such as the conversation or radio which sets the structure vibrating only when the sound waves emitted from the source reach the structural enclosure.

A noise can be defined as any undesired sound and may have any one of the following four effects on man:

1. Annoyance.
2. Disturbance of sleep.
3. Interfere with the ability to hold a normal conversation.
4. Damage his hearing.

It is difficult to measure annoyance since it is a subjective attitude and will depend upon the mental and physical well being of the listener, together with the experience of being subjected to such types of noise. Damage to hearing can be caused by a sudden noise such as a loud explosion or by gradual damage resulting from continual noise over a period of years.

The solution to noise or sound problems can only therefore be reasonable to cater for the average person and conditions. The approach to solving a noise problem can be three-fold:

1. Reduce the noise emitted at the source by such devices as mufflers and mounting machinery on resilient pads.
2. Provide a reasonable degree of sound insulation to reduce the amount of sound transmitted.
3. Isolate the source and the receiver.

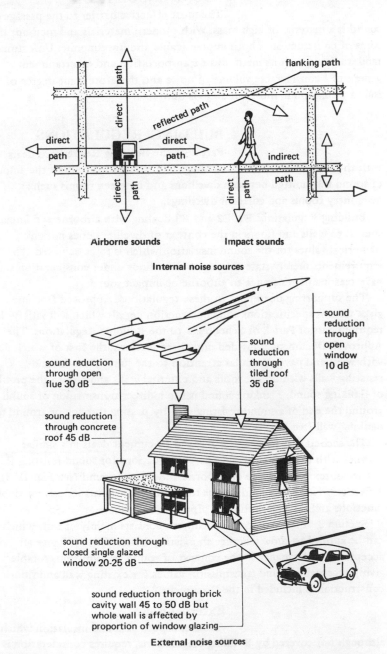

Fig. IV.1 Sources of noise within and around buildings

SOUND INSULATION

The most effective barrier to the passage of sound is a material of high mass. With modern materials and methods this form of construction is both impracticable and uneconomic. Unfortunately modern living with its methods of transportation and entertainment generates a considerable volume of noise and therefore some degree of sound insulation in most buildings is desirable.

BUILDING REGULATIONS

Part E of the Building Regulations deals with the sound insulation of dwellings and is intended to limit the amount of sound transmitted between dwellings and between rooms such as machinery rooms and adjacent dwellings.

Building Regulations E1, E2 and E3 dealing with airborne and impact sounds to walls and floors in the context of dwellings does not give numerical values for the sound insulation which is to be achieved. The requirements merely state that the wall or floor under consideration shall have reasonable resistance to airborne or impact sound.

The supporting document to these regulations, Approved Document E, gives various specifications and construction details which will satisfy the requirements of Part E of Schedule 1 to the Building Regulations. The Approved Document is divided into three sections, the first of which deals with walls and pays particular attention to the junctions of sound-resisting walls with floors, roofs and external walls and also to the problem of flanking sound. Flanking sound is the indirect transmission of sound around the end of a sound-resisting wall by passing through or around the flanking wall (see Fig. IV.2).

The second section of the Approved Document deals in a similar manner with the specifications and constructions for sound-resisting floors in the context of airborne or airborne and impact sound (see Fig. IV.3). This section also gives guidance as to appropriate constructions for floor junctions and the penetration of pipes through floors.

Section 3 of the Approved Document consists mainly of tests which can be applied to show whether an existing wall or floor will give an acceptable performance in the context of sound transmission. A table giving acceptable sound transmission values for existing wall and floor construction is included in the Document.

External noise

Another aspect of sound insulation which, although not covered by Building Regulations, requires consideration is insulation against external noise. The main barrier to external noise is

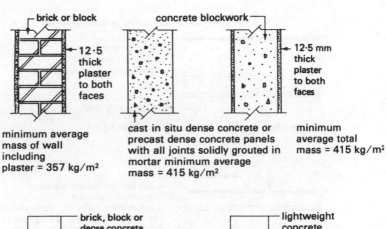

brick or block

concrete blockwork

12·5 thick plaster to both faces

12·5 mm thick plaster to both faces

minimum average mass of wall including plaster = 357 kg/m²

cast in situ dense concrete or precast dense concrete panels with all joints solidly grouted in mortar minimum average mass = 415 kg/m²

minimum average total mass = 415 kg/m²

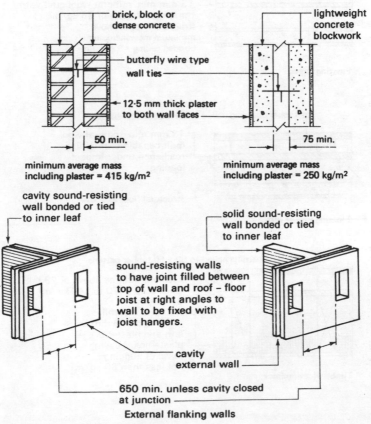

brick, block or dense concrete

lightweight concrete blockwork

butterfly wire type wall ties

12·5 mm thick plaster to both wall faces

50 min.

75 min.

minimum average mass including plaster = 415 kg/m²

minimum average mass including plaster = 250 kg/m²

cavity sound-resisting wall bonded or tied to inner leaf

solid sound-resisting wall bonded or tied to inner leaf

sound-resisting walls to have joint filled between top of wall and roof – floor joist at right angles to wall to be fixed with joist hangers.

cavity external wall

650 min. unless cavity closed at junction

External flanking walls

Fig. IV.2 External flanking walls

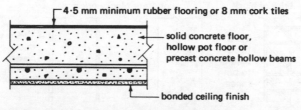

4·5 mm minimum rubber flooring or 8 mm cork tiles

solid concrete floor,
hollow pot floor or
precast concrete hollow beams

bonded ceiling finish

Concrete floors ~ minimum mass of floor = 365 kg/m²

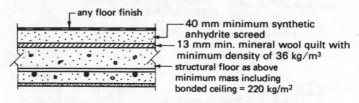

any floor finish

40 mm minimum synthetic
anhydrite screed
13 mm min. mineral wool quilt with
minimum density of 36 kg/m³
structural floor as above
minimum mass including
bonded ceiling = 220 kg/m²

Floating screed

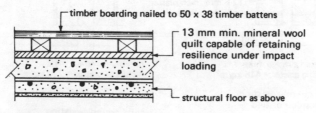

timber boarding nailed to 50 x 38 timber battens

13 mm min. mineral wool
quilt capable of retaining
resilience under impact
loading

structural floor as above

Floating timber raft

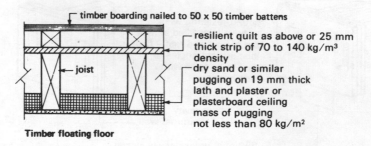

timber boarding nailed to 50 x 50 timber battens

resilient quilt as above or 25 mm
thick strip of 70 to 140 kg/m³
density
dry sand or similar
pugging on 19 mm thick
lath and plaster or
plasterboard ceiling
mass of pugging
not less than 80 kg/m²

joist

Timber floating floor

Fig. IV.3 Sound insulation — floors

provided by the shell or envelope of the building, the three main factors being:

1. The mass of the enclosing structure.
2. The continuity of the structure.
3. Isolation by double leaf construction when using lightweight materials.

Generally the main problem for the insulation against external noise is the windows, particularly if these can be opened for ventilation purposes. Windows cannot provide the dual function of insulation against noise and ventilation, since the admission of air will also admit noise. Any type of window when opened will give a sound reduction of about 10 decibels as opposed to the 45—50 decibel reduction of the traditional cavity wall. A closed window containing single glazing will give a reduction of about 20 decibels or approximately half that of the surrounding wall. It is obvious that the window to wall ratio will affect the overall sound reduction of the enclosing structure.

Double glazing can greatly improve the sound insulation properties of windows provided the following points are observed:

1. Sound insulation increases with the distance between the glazed units; for a reduction of 40 decibels the airspace should be 150—200 mm wide.
2. If the double windows are capable of being opened they should be weather-stripped.
3. Sound insulation increases with glass thickness particularly if the windows are fixed; this may mean the use of special ventilators having specific performances for ventilation and acoustics.
4. Double glazing designed to improve the thermal properties of a window have no real value for sound insulation.

Roofs of traditional construction and of reinforced concrete generally give an acceptable level of sound insulation, but the inclusion of rooflights can affect the resistance provided by the general roof structure. Lightweight roofing such as corrugated asbestos will provide only a 15—20 decibel reduction but is generally acceptable on industrial buildings where noise is generated internally by the manufacturing processes. The inclusion of rooflights in this type of roof generally has no adverse effects since the sound insulation values of the rooflight materials are similar to those of the coverings.

Modern buildings can be designed to give reasonable sound insulation and consequent comfort to the occupiers but the improvement to existing properties can present problems. A useful source of information on the reduction of noise in existing buildings is the Department of Environment advisory leaflet 69 obtainable from Her Majesty's Stationery Office.

23
Thermal insulation

Thermal insulation may be defined as a barrier to the natural flow of heat from an area of high temperature to an area of low temperature. In buildings this flow is generally from the interior to the exterior. Heat is a form of energy consisting of the ceaseless movement of tiny particles of matter called molecules; if these particles are moving fast they collide frequently with one another and the substance becomes hot. Temperature is the measure of hotness and should not be confused with heat.

The transfer of heat can occur in three ways:

Conduction: vibrating molecules come into contact with adjoining molecules and set them vibrating faster and hence they become hotter; this process is carried on throughout the substance without appreciable displacement of the particles.

Convection: transmission of heat within a gas or fluid caused by the movement of particles which become less dense when heated and rise thus setting up a current or circulation.

Radiation: heat is considered to be transmitted by radiation when it passes from one point to another without raising the temperature of the medium through which it travels.

In a building all three methods of heat transfer can take place since the heat will be conducted through the fabric of the building and dissipated on the external surface by convection and/or radiation.

The traditional thick and solid building materials used in the past had a natural resistance to the passage of heat in large quantities, whereas the lighter and thinner materials used today generally have a low resistance to the transfer of heat. Therefore to maintain a comfortable and healthy internal temperature the external fabric of a building must be constructed of a combination of materials which will provide an adequate barrier to the transfer of heat.

Thermal insulation of buildings will give the following advantages:
1. Reduction in the rate of heat loss.
2. Lower capital costs for heating equipment.
3. Lower fuel costs.
4. Reduction in the risk of pattern staining.
5. Reduction of condensation and draughts thus improving the comfort of the occupants.

BUILDING REGULATIONS

Building Regulation L1 states that reasonable provision shall be made for the conservation of fuel and power in buildings. The requirements of this regulation are satisfied by limiting the total aggregate areas of rooflights and windows, and by not exceeding the maximum 'U' values for elements which are given in Approved Document L. The regulations give the maximum thermal transmissions coefficient or 'U' value for various situations. 'U' values are expressed in W/m^2K which is the rate of heat transfer in watts (joules/sec) through 1 m^2 of the structure for 1° Celsius difference between the air on the two sides of the structure.

To calculate a 'U' value the complete constructional detail must be known together with the following thermal properties of the materials and voids involved:

Thermal conductivity: called the 'k' value and is the measure of materials' ability to transmit heat and is expressed as the heat flow in watts per m^2 of surface area for a temperature difference of 1° Celsius per metre thickness and is expressed a W/mK. Values for 'k' can be obtained from tables published by the Institute of Heating and Ventilating Engineers or from manufacturer's catalogues.

Thermal resistivity: this is the ability of a material, regardless of size or thickness, to resist the passage of heat and is the reciprocal of the thermal conductivity and is expressed a $1/k$ or m k/W.

Thermal resistance: this is the product of thermal resistivity and the thickness in metres and is expressed as R or m^2k/W.

Surface resistances: these are given as fixed values in the Building Regulations to provide a standardisation in the calculation of 'U' values.

To calculate the '*U*' value of any combination of materials the total resistance of the structure is found and then the reciprocal of this figure will give the required value as shown in the following example:

Cavity wall of 103 mm brick outer skin, 50 mm wide cavity, 100 mm lightweight block inner skin and 16 mm two-coat plaster internally.

brickwork: $k = 1.150$; $1/k = 0.87$; $R_1\ 0.87 \times 0.103 = 0.089$
cavity: from IHVE guide $R_2 = 0.176$
blockwork: $k = 0.245$; $1/k = 4.08$; $R_3 = 4.08 \times 0.100 = 0.408$
plaster: $k = 0.461$; $1/k = 2.17$; $R_4 = 2.17 \times 0.016 = 0.035$
surface resistances: fixed value $R_5 = 0.18$.

$$'U'\text{ value} = \frac{1}{R_1 + R_2 + R_3 + R_4 + R_5}$$

$$= \frac{1}{0.089 + 0.176 + 0.408 + 0.035 + 0.18}$$

$$= \frac{1}{0.726}$$

$$\simeq 1.4\ \text{W/m}^2\,\text{K}.$$

The maximum '*U*' value requirements of the Building Regulations are shown diagrammatically in Fig. IV.4. Approved Document L of the Building Regulations gives details of deemed to satisfy provisions regarding thermal insulation and specifies various materials and methods.

The thermal insulation of roofs can be carried out at rafter level, beneath the covering or at ceiling level. Generally rafter level insulation will use more material but can be applied as a combined roofing felt and insulation thus saving labour costs. The roof void will be warm and on sheltered sites it should not be necessary to protect the cistern and pipework against frost attack. Applying the insulation at ceiling level will reduce the amount of material required and will also reduce the heat loss into the roof space, but since the void is unheated the plumbing working housed in the roof space will need insulating against freezing temperatures (see Fig. IV.4). Cold roofs will need to be ventilated to comply with Building Regulation F2.

INSULATING MATERIALS
When selecting or specifying thermal insulation materials the following must be taken into consideration:
1. Resistance value of the material.
2. Need for a vapour barrier since insulating materials which become damp or wet, generally due to condensation, rapidly loose their

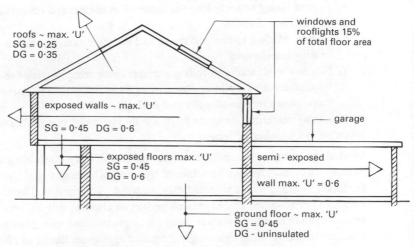

'U' values given in W / m²K ~ SG = single glazing
DG = total double glazing

roofs ~ max. 'U'
SG = 0·25
DG = 0·35

windows and
rooflights 15%
of total floor area

exposed walls ~ max. 'U'

SG = 0·45   DG = 0·6

garage

exposed floors max. 'U'
SG = 0·45
DG = 0·6

semi - exposed

wall max. 'U' = 0·6

ground floor ~ max. 'U'
SG = 0·45
DG - uninsulated

N.B. If calculated rate of heat loss through the solid parts
of exposed elements is less than the maximum 'U' value
trade-off calculations are permitted to ensure total heat
loss of building is no more than permitted had the
maximum 'U' values been used. Approved Document L
gives worked examples of trade-off calculations using
the following 'U' values for rooflights and windows –
single glazing 5·7; double glazing 2·8; triple glazing 2·0.

Maximum Permissible 'U' Values for Dwellings

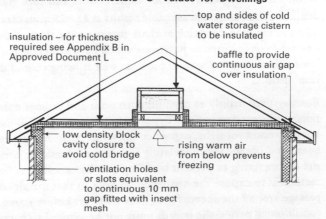

top and sides of cold
water storage cistern
to be insulated

insulation – for thickness
required see Appendix B in
Approved Document L

baffle to provide
continuous air gap
over insulation

low density block
cavity closure to
avoid cold bridge

rising warm air
from below prevents
freezing

ventilation holes
or slots equivalent
to continuous 10 mm
gap fitted with insect
mesh

Fig. IV.4   Building Regulation thermal insulation requirement

insulation properties; therefore if condensation is likely to occur a suitable vapour barrier should be included in the detail. Vapour barriers should always be located on the warm side of the construction.

3. Availability of material chosen.
4. Ease of fixing or including the material in the general construction.
5. Appearance if visible.
6. Cost in relation to the end result and ultimate savings on fuel and/or heating installation.
7. Fire risk — all wall and ceiling surfaces must comply with the requirements of Building Regulation B2 — restriction of spread of flame over surfaces of walls and ceilings.

Insulating materials are made from a wide variety of materials and are available in a number of forms:

Insulating concrete: basically a concrete of low density containing a large number of voids. This can be achieved by using lightweight aggregates such as clinker, foamed slag, expanded clay, sintered pulverised fuel ash, exfoliated vermiculite and expanded perlite, or alternatively an aerated concrete made by the introduction of air or gas into the mix. No fines concrete made by using lightweight or gravel aggregates between 20 and 10 mm size and omitting the fine aggregate is suitable for load bearing walls. Generally lightweight insulating concrete is used in the form of an *in situ* screed to a structural roof or as lightweight concrete blocks for walls.

Loose fills: materials which can be easily poured from a bag and levelled off between the joists with a shaped template. Materials include exfoliated vermiculite, fine glass fibrewool, mineral wool and cork granules. The depth required to give reasonable results is 25–35 mm; care should be taken to indicate, by paint or chalk marks on the sides of the joists, any electrical connections or junctions which have been covered over. Most loose fills are rot and vermin proof as well as being classed as non-combustible.

Boards: used mainly as dry linings to walls and ceilings either for self finish or direct decoration. Types include aluminium foil-backed plaster board, woodwool slabs, expanded polystyrene boards, asbestos insulating board and fibreboards. Insulating fibreboards should be conditioned on site before fixing to prevent buckling and distortion after fixing. A suitable method is to expose the boards on all sides so that the air has a free passage around the sheets for at least 24 hours before fixing. During this conditioning period the boards must not be allowed to become wet or damp.

Quilts: made from glass fibre or mineral wool bonded or stitched between outer paper coverings for easy handling. The quilts are supplied in rolls from 6.000—13.000 m long and cut to suit standard joist spacings. They are laid over the ceiling boards and can be obtained in two thicknesses, 25 mm thick for general use and 50 mm thick for use where a central heating system is installed.

Reflective insulation: used in both ceiling and wall insulation and consists of reinforced aluminium foil which should be used in conjunction with an unventilated cavity of at least 25 mm width.

Insulating plasters: factory produced pre-mixed plasters which have light-weight perlite and vermiculite expanded minerals as aggregates, and require only the addition of clean water before application. They are only one-third the weight of sanded plasters, have three times the thermal insulation value and are highly resistant to fire.

Foamed cavity fill: a method of improving the thermal insulation properties of an external cavity wall by filling the cavity wall with urea-formaldehyde resin foamed on site. The foam is formed using special apparatus by combining urea-formaldehyde resin, a hardener, a foaming agent and warm water. Careful control with the mixing and application is of paramount importance if a successful result is to be achieved; specialist contractors are normally employed. The foam can be introduced into the cavity by means of 25 mm bore holes spaced 1.000 m apart in all directions or by direct introduction into the open end of the cavity. The foam is a white cellular material containing approximately 99% by volume of air with open cells. The foam is considered to be impermeable and therefore unless fissures or cracks have occurred during the application it will not constitute a bridge of the cavity in the practical sense. The insertion of foam must comply with Building Regulation D1. In most cases the foam, upon setting, shrinks away from the inner face of the outer leaf enabling any water penetrating the outer leaf to run down the inside face of the external skin.

The most effective method of improving thermal comfort conditions within a building is to ensure that the inside surface is at a reasonably high temperature and this is best achieved by fixing insulating materials in this position.

Thermal insulation for buildings other than dwellings are covered by separate Building Regulations under Part L in which certain trade off calculations are permitted. The problems, materials and methods involved with these types of buildings are usually studied during the two years advanced technology applicable to most building courses.

24
The problem of fire

Since early times fire has been one of man's greatest aids to his advancement; it gives him a source of both heat and light. Today fire is still of great benefit to man's wellbeing if it is controlled, but if allowed to start and spread without strict control it can be one of the greatest hazards man has to face. Early man considered fire to be a natural element like air and water; later experimenters found that the residue of a burnt fuel (ash) weighed less than the fuel before it was burnt and concluded that some substance was removed during the combustion period; this they called phlogiston after the Greek word phlogistos, meaning inflammable. The doctrine of phlogistics was overthrown by a French chemist Antoine Lavoisier (1743-1794), who became known as the father of modern chemistry.

Lavoisier discovered by his researches and experiments that air consists of $\frac{1}{5}$th oxygen and that the other main gas, nitrogen, accounted for the bulk of the remaining $\frac{4}{5}$ths. He showed that oxygen played an important part in the process of combustion and that nitrogen does not support combustion. This discovery of the true nature of fire led to the conclusion that fire is a chemical reaction whereby atoms of oxygen combined with other atoms such as carbon and hydrogen, releasing water, carbon dioxide and energy in the form of heat. The chemical reaction will only start at a suitable temperature, which varies according to the substance or fuel involved. During combustion gases will be given off, some of which are more inflammable than the fuel itself and therefore ignite and appear as flames, giving light which is due to tiny particles being heated to a point at which they glow. Smoke is an indication of incomplete combustion and can give rise to deposits of solid carbon commonly known as soot.

From the discovery of the true nature of fire and processes of combustion it can be concluded that there are three essentials to all fires:

1. *Fuel* — generally any organic material is suitable.
2. *Heat* — correct temperature to promote combustion of a particular fuel. Heat can be generated deliberately, which is termed ignition, or it can be spontaneous when the fuel itself ignites.
3. *Oxygen* — air is necessary to sustain and support the combustion process.

The above is often referred to as the triangle of fire: remove any one of the three essentials and combustion cannot take place. This fact provides the whole basis for fire prevention, fire protection and fire fighting. If non-combustible materials were used in the construction and furnishing of buildings fires would not develop. This method is far too restrictive on the designer and builder therefore combustible materials are used and protected with layers or coverings of non-combustible materials where necessary. Fire fighters try to remove one side of the fire triangle; to remove the fuel is not generally practicable but by using a cooling agent such as water the heat can be reduced to a safe level, or, alternatively, by using a blanketing agent the supply of oxygen can be cut off and fire extinguished.

The cost to the nation resulting from fires in buildings is very difficult to assess but a figure in excess of £1 000 per minute for every day of the year amounting to an annual cost of over £500 000 000 is not unrealistic The cost to manufacturers and employers in terms of loss of goodwill, loss of production, effect of fatalities and injuries to employees and the delay in returning to full production or working are almost incalculable. Therefore it can be seen that the seriousness of fires within buildings cannot be overstated.

Fire has no respect for persons or places, it can and does break out in all forms of buildings. The common belief that 'it never happens to me, only to others' is one of the major factors. The disregard by people and firms of even elementary precautions to obvious fire hazards is clearly shown by the UK fire and loss statistics published annually by Her Majesty's Stationery Office. These statistics show that private dwellings are most vulnerable, accounting usually for approximately 50% of all fires. Another high risk area is the distributive trades where large quantities of inflammable goods are held in store. One of the main causes of fires is faulty electrical equipment and wiring. This is not an indication that the plant or installation is poor but that maintenance, renewal and routine checks carried out by experienced personnel is in many cases non-existent. In domestic dwellings the same argument can be applied to gas services and installations. Another and indeed frightening statistic is the high number of fires (in excess of 3 000) caused annually in dwellings by children playing with fire, matches and other easily ignitable home gadgets. This could be the result of lack of education as to the dangers or lack of parental control.

Obviously designers and builders alike cannot be held responsible for the actions or non-actions of the occupants of the buildings they create but they can ensure that these structures are designed and constructed in such a manner that they give the best possible resistance to the action of fire should it occur.

The precautions which can be taken within buildings to prevent a fire occurring, or if it should occur of containing it within the region of the outbreak, providing a means of escape for people in the immediate vicinity and fighting the fire can be studied under three headings:

1. Structural fire protection.
2. Means of escape in case of fire.
3. Fire fighting.

The latter, which is generally integrated with the services of a building, is usually considered in that context and therefore apart from passing references no deep study of this aspect is included in this text.

25
Structural fire protection

The purpose of structural fire protection is to ensure that during a fire the temperature of structural members or elements does not increase to a figure at which their strength would be adversely affected. It is not practicable or possible to give an element complete protection in terms of time, therefore elements are given a fire resistance for a certain period of time which it is anticipated will give sufficient delay to the spread of fire, ultimate collapse of the structure, time for persons in danger to escape and to enable fire fighting to be commenced.

Before a fire-resistance period can be determined it is necessary to consider certain factors:

1. Fire load of the building.
2. Behaviour of materials under fire conditions.
3. Behaviour of combinations of materials under fire conditions.
4. Building Regulation requirements as laid down in Part B.

FIRE LOAD

Buildings can be graded as to the amount of overall fire resistance required by taking into account the following:

1. Size of building.
2. Use of building.
3. Fire load.

The fire load is an assessment of the severity of a fire due to the combustible materials within a building. This load is expressed as the amount of heat which would be generated per unit area by the complete combustion of its contents and combustible members and is given in Joules per square metre. It should be noted that the numerical grade is equivalent to the minimum number of hours fire resistance which should be given to the elements of the structure.

Grade 1 — Low fire load, not more than 1 150 MJ/m^2. Typical buildings within this grade are flats, offices, restaurants, hotels, hospitals, schools, museums and public libraries.

Grade 2 — Moderate fire load, 1 150 to 2 300 MJ/m^2. Typical examples are retail shops, factories and workshops.

Grade 4 — High fire load, 2 300 to 4 600 MJ/m^2. Typical examples are certain types of workshops and warehouses.

When deciding the grade no account is taken of the effects of any permanent fire protection installations such as sprinkler systems. The above principles are incorporated into the Building Regulations and in particular Part B.

FIRE RESISTANCE OF MATERIALS

The materials used in buildings can be studied as separate entities as to their behaviour when subjected to the intense heat encountered during a fire and as to their ability to spread fire over their surfaces.

Structural steel is not considered to behave well under fire conditions although its ability to spread fire over its surface is negligible. As the fire progresses and the temperature of steel increases there is an actual gain in the ultimate strength of mild steel. This gain in strength decreases back to normal over the temperature range of 250 to 400°C. The decrease in strength continues and by the time the steel temperature has reached 550°C it will have lost most of its useful strength. Since the rise in temperature during the initial stages of a fire is rapid this figure of 550°C can be reached very quickly. If the decrease in strength results in the collapse of a member the stresses it was designed to resist will be redistributed; this could cause other members to be overstressed and progressive collapse could occur.

Reinforced concrete structural members have good fire resistance properties, and being non-combustible do not contribute to the spread of flame over their surfaces. It is possible however under the intense and prolonged heat of a fire that the bond between the steel reinforcement and the concrete will be broken. This generally results in spalling of the concrete which decreases both the protective cover of the concrete over the steel and the cross sectional area. Like structural steel members, this can result in a redistribution of stresses leading to overloading of certain members, culminating in progressive collapse.

Timber, strange as it may seem, behaves very well structurally under the action of fire. This is due to its slow combustion rate, the strength of its core failure remaining fairly constant. The ignition temperature of timber is low ($250\text{-}300^\circ$C) but during combustion the timber chars at an approximate rate of 0.5 mm per minute, the layer of charcoal so formed slows down the combustion rate of the core. Although its structural properties during a fire are good, timber being an organic material and therefore combustible, will spread fire over its surface which makes it unsuitable in most structural situations without some form of treatment.

From the above brief considerations it is obvious that designers and builders need to have data on the performance, under the conditions of fire, of materials and especially combinations of materials forming elements. Such information is available in BS 476 which is divided into a number of parts which relate to the various fire tests applied to building materials and structures.

FIRE TESTS — BS 476

BS 476 consists of nine parts numbered 3 to 8, 10, 11 and 31. Part 1 has been replaced by part 8 and Part 2 has been incorporated in BS 2782 — Methods of Testing Plastics. Parts 3 to 8 are very significant and worth noting.

Part 3 External Fire Exposure Roof Tests

A series of tests for grading roof structures in terms of time for:

1. Resistance to external penetration by fire.
2. Distance of spread of flame over the external surface under certain conditions.

The tests are applied to a specimen of roof structure 838 mm (33 inches) square which represents the actual roof construction including at least one specimen of any joints used and complete with any lining which is an integral part of the construction.

Three tests are applied:

1. Preliminary ignition test.
2. Fire penetration test.
3. Roof surface spread of flame test.

After testing the specimen or form of roof construction receives a lettered designation thus:

First letter (penetration)

A. No penetration within 1 hour.
B. Specimen penetrated in not less than 1½ hours.
C. Specimen penetrated in less than ½ hour.
D. Specimen penetrated in the preliminary flame test

Second letter (spread of flame)

A. No spread of flame.
B. Not more than 533 mm (21 inches) spread.
C. More than 533 mm spread.
D. Specimens which continue to burn for 5 minutes after withdrawal of the test flame or spread more than 381 mm (15 inches) across the region of burning in the preliminary flame test.

Specimens can be tested as an inclined or flat structure and are prefixed EXT.S or EXT.F accordingly. If during the test any dripping from the underside of the specimen, any mechanical failure and/or development of holes is observed a suffix 'X' is added to the designation thus:

EXT.S.AB—EXT.S.ABX

Part 4 Non-combustibility Test

Generally organic materials are combustible, whereas inorganic materials are non-combustible which can be defined as a material not capable of undergoing combustion. For the purposes of BS 476 materials used in the construction and finishing of buildings or structures are classified as 'non-combustible' or 'combustible' according to their behaviour in the non-combustibility test.

A material is classified by this test as non-combustible if none of the three specimens tested either:

1. Causes the temperature reading from either of the two thermocouples used to rise by 50°C or more above the initial furnace temperature.
2. Observed to flame continuously for 10 seconds or more inside the furnace. Otherwise the material shall be deemed combustible.

It should be noted that mixtures of organic and inorganic materials have a different behaviour pattern to the individual materials, therefore such combinations must be tested and classified accordingly.

210

Part 5   Ignitability Test

This test classifies combustible materials as either 'easily ignitable' or 'not easily ignitable'. The test is intended for rigid or semi-rigid building materials but is not suitable for fabrics for which separate tests are available. It identifies easily ignitable materials of low heat contribution of which the performance in the fire propagation test (Part 6) does not necessarily indicate the full hazard. If the specimen to be tested is of laminated construction or has faces of different materials both faces must be tested and the classification is related to the thickness of the specimen and may not be valid for other thicknesses of similar construction.

A lighted gas jet is applied to the centre of the specimen face to be tested for 10 seconds and after removal any subsequent flaming is noted. If the specimen continues to flame for more than 10 seconds after removal of the test flame or if burning extends to the edge of the specimen within 10 seconds it is classed as easily ignitable and this is denoted by the letter 'X'; alternatively it can be classed as not easily ignitable and lettered 'P'.

Part 6   Fire Propagation Test

The scope of this test is to provide a means of comparing the contribution of combustible materials to the growth of fire. This test is incomplete without the addition of a report on classification carried out under Part 5 — Ignitability Test. The specimen is given an index of performance (I) ranging from 0 (non-combustible) to 100 in a descending order relating to a time/temperature curve which in turn is related to the rise in temperature inside the test apparatus over the ambient temperature. The classification 'X' or 'P' from the ignitability test is also given.

Part 7   Surface Spread of Flame Test

Two tests are covered in Part 7, a large-scale test to determine the tendency of materials to support the spread of flame across their surface and to classify this in relation to exposed surfaces of walls and ceilings. The second is a small-scale test intended for preliminary testing, development and quality control purposes. It must be noted that there is no direct correlation between the two tests.

The sample for testing must have any surfacings or coatings applied in the usual manner. The 230 × 900 mm sample is fixed in the holder of the apparatus and subjected to radiant heat from the test furnace. During the first minute of the test a luminous gas flame is applied to the furnace end of the specimen. Throughout the 10 minutes' duration of the test the distance of flame spread over the surface against the time taken is noted and the sample is placed into one of four classes set out in Table 1 of Part 7.

Classification	Flame spread at 1½ minutes		Final flame spread	
	Limit (mm)	Tolerance for one specimen in sample (mm)	Limit (mm)	Tolerance for one specimen in sample (mm)
Class 1	165	25	165	25
Class 2	215	25	455	45
Class 3	265	25	710	75
Class 4	Exceeding Class 3 Limits			

Approved Document B specifies a higher class than class 1 called class 0 which is defined as a non-combustible material throughout or if the surface material is tested in accordance with BS 476 : Part 6 shall have an index (I) not exceeding 12 and a sub-index (i_1) not exceeding 6.

Part 8   Fire Resistance of Elements

The term 'fire resistance' relates to complete elements of construction and not to the individual materials of which elements are composed. The tests enable elements of construction to be assessed according to their ability to retain their stability, to resist the passage of flame and hot gases and to provide the necessary resistance to heat transmission.

The following elements of construction are covered by the tests laid down in Part 8:

1. Load bearing and non-load bearing walls and partitions.
2. Floors.
3. Flat roofs.
4. Columns.
5. Beams.
6. Suspended ceilings protecting steel beams.
7. Door and shutter assemblies.
8. Glazing.

Wherever possible the specimens used in the tests should be full size and be fully representative of the element including at least one of each type of joint.

During the tests the specimen is heated from one side by a furnace which can produce a positive pressure at standard heating conditions until failure occurs or the test is terminated. During the test the following observations are made and noted:

1. *Stability* — deformation of the specimen, occurrence of collapse or any other factor which could affect its stability. Non-load bearing constructions — failure occurs when collapse of the specimen takes place. Load bearing constructions must support their loads during heating period and for 24 hours after heating period; if collapse occurs stability time is 80% of time taken to collapse.

2. *Integrity* — a 100 × 100 mm cotton wool pad is held over the centre of any crack through which flames and gases can pass. The pad is held 30 mm from and parallel to the crack for a period of 10 seconds to determine if hot gases can cause ignition. The observation is repeated at frequent intervals.

3. *Insulation* — unexposed face of elements having a separating function is observed at intervals of not more than 5 minutes. Failure is deemed to occur if (*a*) mean temperature rises more than 140°C above initial temperature or (*b*) point temperature rises more than 180°C above initial temperature.

The results are given in minutes from the start of the test until failure occurs in one or any of the above observations.

Fire resistance of an element of construction is given in minutes and is the time from the start of the test until failure occurs as given below for each element group.

Walls and Partitions: specimen to be full size or a minimum of 2.500 × 2.500 m and loaded to simulated actual site conditions. Fire resistance — time taken to failure by any one of the three observations.

Floors and flat roofs: specimen to be full size or a minimum of 2.500 m wide × 4.000 m span and loaded to simulate actual site conditions. If ceiling is intended to add to the fire resistance it must be included in the test specimen. Fire resistance — failure time for each observation is noted, specimen is deemed to have failed in stability if deflection exceeds L/30 where L = clear span.

Columns: specimen to be full size or have a minimum length of 3.000 m and loaded to simulate actual site conditions. The specimen is heated on all exposed faces. Fire resistance — time taken for failure in stability only.

Beams: specimen to be full size or have a minimum span of 4.000 m and loaded to simulate actual site conditions. If the beam is exposed to fire on three faces a deck not less than 75 mm thick shall be included in the specimen. Fire resistance — time taken for failure in stability only which is deemed to have occurred if the deflection exceeds L/30 where L = clear span.

Suspended ceilings protecting steel beams: specimen to be full size or a minimum of 2.500 x 4.000 m. The steel beams used to support the specimen have the top flange covered with a lightweight concrete floor at least 130 mm thick. The specimen must be fitted with any light fittings or similar outlets. Fire resistance — limit of effective protection has been deemed to have been reached when:

1. One or more tiles or panels become dislodged or,
2. Loaded beams are unable to support load or mean temperature of beam exceeds 550°C or maximum temperature of beam exceeds 650°C or deflection exceeds L/30 where L = clear span or,
3. Where an unloaded specimen is used the beam temperature at any point is not less than 400°C.

Doors: specimen to be full size or a minimum of 2.500 x 2.500 m and complete with any furniture and fittings. The sample is to be fixed in a wall type similar to that expected on site or in a 100 mm thick brick or concrete wall for up to a 2-hour test or a 200 mm thick brick or concrete wall for over a 2-hour test. Fire resistance — specimen to be given a failure time for all three observations. If the cotton wool pad, used in the integrity observation, cannot be used because of radiant heat from the specimen, failure is deemed to have occurred if an unobstructed gap exceeding 6 mm wide x 150 mm long occurs.

Glazing: specimen to be full size or a minimum of 2.500 x 2.500 m and to include fittings and surrounds. If the specimen is not part of a prefabricated system it is to be housed in a brick or concrete wall. Fire resistance — time taken for failure in both stability and integrity are given. Comments made regarding the use of cotton wool pads for doors are also valid for glazing.

The methods and necessity of testing building materials and components under fire conditions are constantly being reviewed and extended. A typical example is the development for measuring the optical density of smoke produced by small specimens of material. The scope of this test is limited to lining materials used in buildings and the measurement of optical density is measured in terms of the transmittance of a parallel beam of light falling on to a photoelectric cell. The results are recorded, computed and the material given a rating, zero being the best performance.

BUILDING REGULATIONS — PART B

One of the major aims of this part of the Building Regulations is to limit the spread of fire and this is achieved by considering the use of a building, fire resistance of structural elements and surface finishes, size of the building or parts of a building and the degree of isolation between buildings or parts of buildings.

Part B of Schedule 1 to the Building Regulations 1985 contains three regulations which are concerned with fire spread under the headings of:

Internal fire spread (surfaces) — Regulation B2
Internal fire spread (structure) — Regulation B3
External fire spread — Regulation B4

Approved Document B which supports these regulations is comprehensive and gives recommendations and guidance as to meeting the performance requirements set out in the actual regulations. It is not proposed to fully analyse each recommendation but to use the recommendations as illustrations as to how the objectives can be achieved.

A full understanding of the terminology used is important to comprehend the recommendations being made in the Approved Document and these are given in Appendix L under the heading of definitions. Figure IV.5 illustrates some of the general definitions given in this appendix. Other interpretations which must be clearly understood are elements of structure, fire stops, relevant and notional boundaries and unprotected areas. These are illustrated in Figs. IV.6, IV.7, IV.8 and IV.9 respectively.

The use of a building enables it to be classified into one of the nine purpose groups given in Approved Document B. The purpose groups can apply to a whole building, a separated part or a compartment of a building. All buildings covered by Part B of the Building Regulations should be included in one of these purpose groups. The nine purpose groups are set out in two main divisions, namely: residential (those with sleeping accommodation) and; non-residential (those without sleeping accommodation). Each purpose group has a descriptive title thus:

Dwellinghouse — does not include a flat or a building containing flats.

Flat — self-contained and includes a maisonette.

Institutional — hospital, home, school or other similar establishment where persons sleep on the premises.

Other Residential — hotel, boarding house, hostel and any other residential purpose not described above.

215

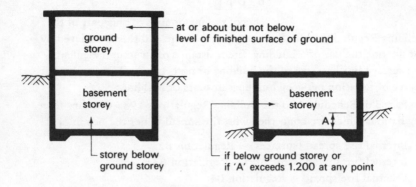

at or about but not below
level of finished surface of ground

ground
storey

basement
storey

storey below
ground storey

basement
storey

A

if below ground storey or
if 'A' exceeds 1.200 at any point

Basement storeys

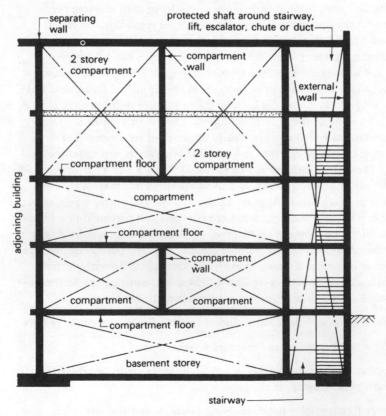

separating
wall

protected shaft around stairway,
lift, escalator, chute or duct

2 storey
compartment

compartment
wall

external
wall

compartment floor

2 storey
compartment

adjoining building

compartment

compartment floor

compartment
wall

compartment

compartment

compartment floor

basement storey

stairway

Fig. IV.5 Approved Document B — general definitions

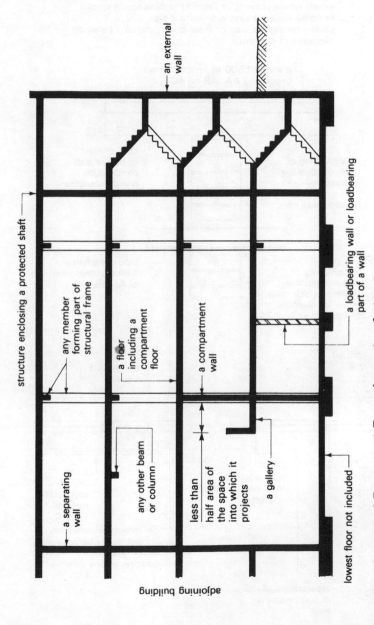

Fig. IV.6 Approved Document B — elements of structure

an external wall

structure enclosing a protected shaft

any member forming part of structural frame

a floor including a compartment floor

a compartment wall

a separating wall

any other beam or column

less than half area of the space into which it projects

a gallery

a loadbearing wall or loadbearing part of a wall

lowest floor not included

adjoining building

217

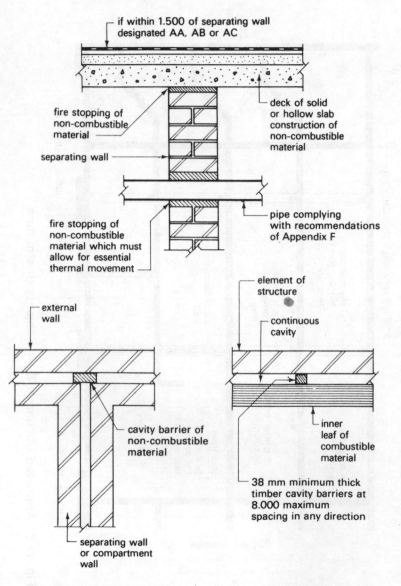

Appendix L — fire stop means a barrier or seal which would prevent or retard the passage of smoke or flame within a cavity, around a pipe where it passes through a wall or floor or at junctions between elements of structure

if within 1.500 of separating wall designated AA, AB or AC

fire stopping of non-combustible material

separating wall

deck of solid or hollow slab construction of non-combustible material

fire stopping of non-combustible material which must allow for essential thermal movement

pipe complying with recommendations of Appendix F

element of structure

continuous cavity

external wall

cavity barrier of non-combustible material

inner leaf of combustible material

separating wall or compartment wall

38 mm minimum thick timber cavity barriers at 8.000 maximum spacing in any direction

Fig. IV.7 Approved Document B — firestopping

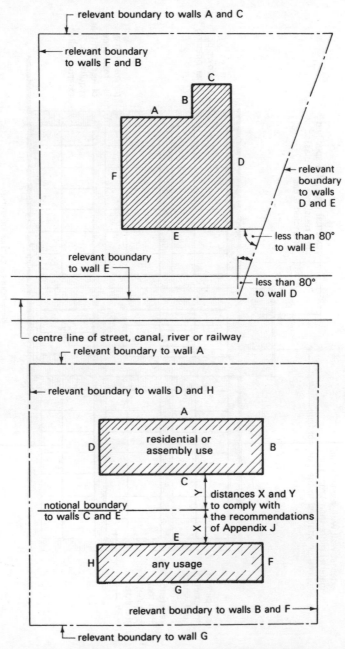

Fig. IV.8 Approved Document B — boundaries

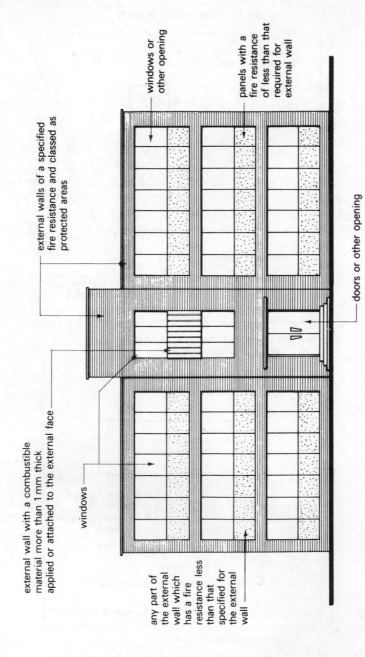

windows or other opening

panels with a fire resistance of less than that required for external wall

external walls of a specified fire resistance and classed as protected areas

doors or other opening

external wall with a combustible material more than 1 mm thick applied or attached to the external face

windows

any part of the external wall which has a fire resistance less than that specified for the external wall

Fig. IV.9 Approved Document B — unprotected areas

Assembly — a public building as defined in Building Regulation 2(2) or a place of assembly of persons for social, recreational or business but not an office, shop or industrial building.

Office — any premises used for office and administration work.

Shop — includes any premises not being a shop but used for any form of retail trade such as a restaurant and hairdressers or where members of the public can enter to deliver goods for repair or treatment.

Industrial — generally as defined in section 175 of the Factories Act 1961.

Other Non-residential — place for storage, deposit or parking of goods and materials (including vehicles) and any other non-residential purpose not described above except for detached garages and carports not exceeding 40 m^2 which are included in the Dwellinghouse purpose group.

The use of fire-resistant cells or compartments within a building (Fig. IV.5) are a means of confining an outbreak of fire to the site of origin for a reasonable time to allow the occupants a chance to escape and the fire-fighters time to tackle, control and extinguish the fire. The Approved Document gives a table for each purpose group setting out the maximum recommended dimensions for buildings or compartments in terms of height of building, floor area and cubic capacity. The tables also give the recommended minimum periods of fire resistance for all elements of structure (see Fig. IV.6). These minimum periods of fire resistance are given in hours according to:

1. Purpose group.
2. Height of building or of separated part in metres.
3. Floor area of each storey or each storey within a compartment in square metres.
4. Cubic capacity of building or cubic capacity of a compartment in cubic metres.
5. Ground or upper storey.
6. Basement storey including the floor over.

The recommended minimum periods of fire resistance given in the tables are of prime concern to the designer and contractor. These tables do not state how these minimum periods are to be achieved but reference is made to the current edition of the BRE report *Guidelines for the construction of fire resisting elements* which gives appropriate and common methods of construction for the various notional periods of fire

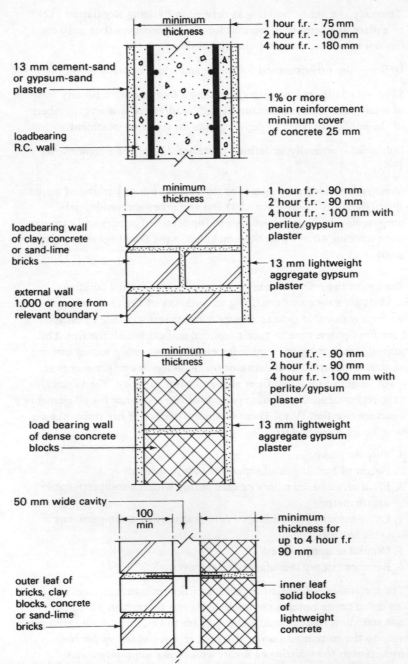

minimum thickness

1 hour f.r. - 75 mm
2 hour f.r. - 100 mm
4 hour f.r. - 180 mm

13 mm cement-sand or gypsum-sand plaster

1% or more main reinforcement minimum cover of concrete 25 mm

loadbearing R.C. wall

minimum thickness

1 hour f.r. - 90 mm
2 hour f.r. - 90 mm
4 hour f.r. - 100 mm with perlite/gypsum plaster

loadbearing wall of clay, concrete or sand-lime bricks

13 mm lightweight aggregate gypsum plaster

external wall 1.000 or more from relevant boundary

minimum thickness

1 hour f.r. - 90 mm
2 hour f.r. - 90 mm
4 hour f.r. - 100 mm with perlite/gypsum plaster

load bearing wall of dense concrete blocks

13 mm lightweight aggregate gypsum plaster

50 mm wide cavity

100 min

minimum thickness for up to 4 hour f.r 90 mm

outer leaf of bricks, clay blocks, concrete or sand-lime bricks

inner leaf solid blocks of lightweight concrete

Fig. IV.10 Fire resistance — walls of masonry construction

222

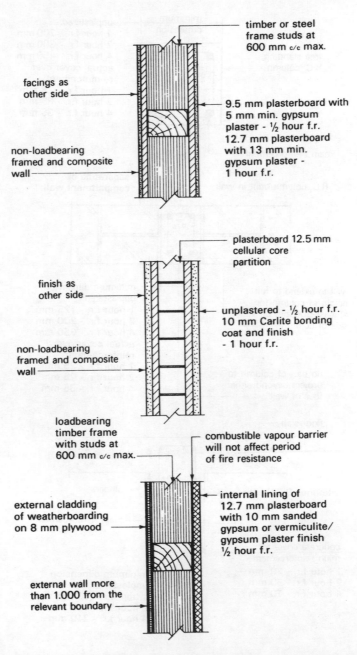

timber or steel frame studs at 600 mm c/c max.

facings as other side

9.5 mm plasterboard with 5 mm min. gypsum plaster - ½ hour f.r. 12.7 mm plasterboard with 13 mm min. gypsum plaster - 1 hour f.r.

non-loadbearing framed and composite wall

plasterboard 12.5 mm cellular core partition

finish as other side

unplastered - ½ hour f.r. 10 mm Carlite bonding coat and finish - 1 hour f.r.

non-loadbearing framed and composite wall

loadbearing timber frame with studs at 600 mm c/c max.

combustible vapour barrier will not affect period of fire resistance

external cladding of weatherboarding on 8 mm plywood

internal lining of 12.7 mm plasterboard with 10 mm sanded gypsum or vermiculite/gypsum plaster finish ½ hour f.r.

external wall more than 1.000 from the relevant boundary

Fig. IV.11   Fire resistance — framed and composite walls

223

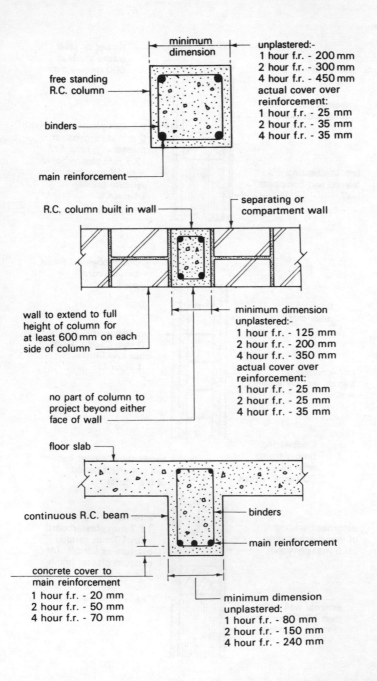

minimum
dimension

free standing
R.C. column

binders

main reinforcement

unplastered:-
1 hour f.r. - 200 mm
2 hour f.r. - 300 mm
4 hour f.r. - 450 mm
actual cover over
reinforcement:
1 hour f.r. - 25 mm
2 hour f.r. - 35 mm
4 hour f.r. - 35 mm

R.C. column built in wall

separating or
compartment wall

wall to extend to full
height of column for
at least 600 mm on each
side of column

no part of column to
project beyond either
face of wall

minimum dimension
unplastered:-
1 hour f.r. - 125 mm
2 hour f.r. - 200 mm
4 hour f.r. - 350 mm
actual cover over
reinforcement:
1 hour f.r. - 25 mm
2 hour f.r. - 25 mm
4 hour f.r. - 35 mm

floor slab

continuous R.C. beam

binders

main reinforcement

concrete cover to
main reinforcement
1 hour f.r. - 20 mm
2 hour f.r. - 50 mm
4 hour f.r. - 70 mm

minimum dimension
unplastered:
1 hour f.r. - 80 mm
2 hour f.r. - 150 mm
4 hour f.r. - 240 mm

Fig. IV.12   Fire resistance — R.C. columns and beams

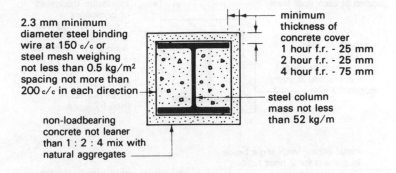

2.3 mm minimum diameter steel binding wire at 150 c/c or steel mesh weighing not less than 0.5 kg/m² spacing not more than 200 c/c in each direction

minimum thickness of concrete cover
1 hour f.r. - 25 mm
2 hour f.r. - 25 mm
4 hour f.r. - 75 mm

steel column mass not less than 52 kg/m

non-loadbearing concrete not leaner than 1 : 2 : 4 mix with natural aggregates

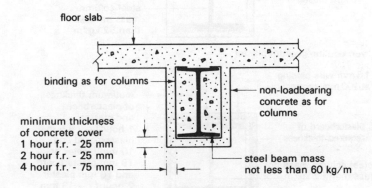

floor slab

binding as for columns

non-loadbearing concrete as for columns

minimum thickness of concrete cover
1 hour f.r. - 25 mm
2 hour f.r. - 25 mm
4 hour f.r. - 75 mm

steel beam mass not less than 60 kg/m

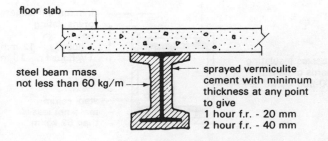

floor slab

steel beam mass not less than 60 kg/m

sprayed vermiculite cement with minimum thickness at any point to give
1 hour f.r. - 20 mm
2 hour f.r. - 40 mm

Fig. IV.13 Fire resistance — steel columns and beams

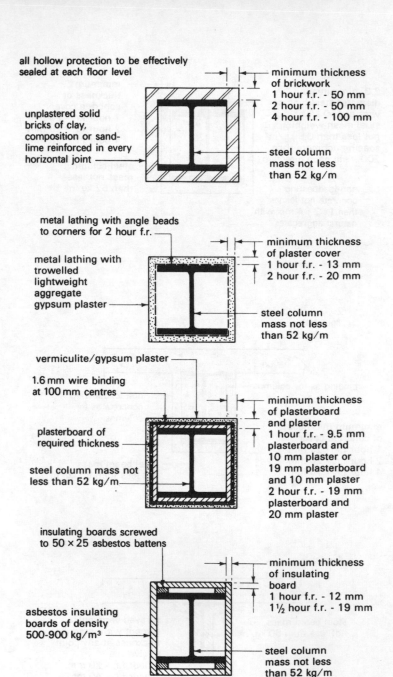

all hollow protection to be effectively sealed at each floor level

minimum thickness of brickwork
1 hour f.r. - 50 mm
2 hour f.r. - 50 mm
4 hour f.r. - 100 mm

unplastered solid bricks of clay, composition or sand-lime reinforced in every horizontal joint

steel column mass not less than 52 kg/m

metal lathing with angle beads to corners for 2 hour f.r.

minimum thickness of plaster cover
1 hour f.r. - 13 mm
2 hour f.r. - 20 mm

metal lathing with trowelled lightweight aggregate gypsum plaster

steel column mass not less than 52 kg/m

vermiculite/gypsum plaster

1.6 mm wire binding at 100 mm centres

plasterboard of required thickness

steel column mass not less than 52 kg/m

minimum thickness of plasterboard and plaster
1 hour f.r. - 9.5 mm plasterboard and 10 mm plaster or 19 mm plasterboard and 10 mm plaster
2 hour f.r. - 19 mm plasterboard and 20 mm plaster

insulating boards screwed to 50 × 25 asbestos battens

minimum thickness of insulating board
1 hour f.r. - 12 mm
1½ hour f.r. - 19 mm

asbestos insulating boards of density 500-900 kg/m³

steel column mass not less than 52 kg/m

Fig. IV.14   Fire resistance — hollow protection to steel columns

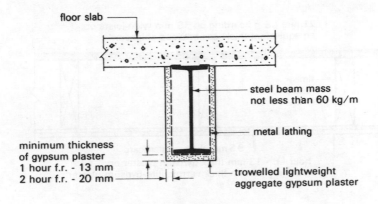

floor slab

steel beam mass not less than 60 kg/m

metal lathing

minimum thickness of gypsum plaster
1 hour f.r. - 13 mm
2 hour f.r. - 20 mm

trowelled lightweight aggregate gypsum plaster

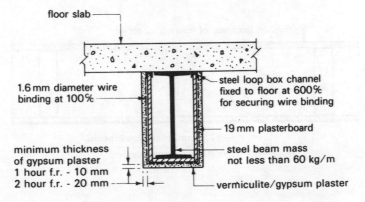

floor slab

1.6 mm diameter wire binding at 100%

steel loop box channel fixed to floor at 600% for securing wire binding

19 mm plasterboard

steel beam mass not less than 60 kg/m

minimum thickness of gypsum plaster
1 hour f.r. - 10 mm
2 hour f.r. - 20 mm

vermiculite/gypsum plaster

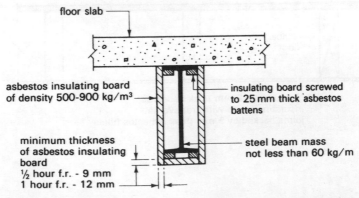

floor slab

asbestos insulating board of density 500-900 kg/m³

insulating board screwed to 25 mm thick asbestos battens

steel beam mass not less than 60 kg/m

minimum thickness of asbestos insulating board
½ hour f.r. - 9 mm
1 hour f.r. - 12 mm

Fig. IV.15 Fire resistance — hollow protection to steel beams

227

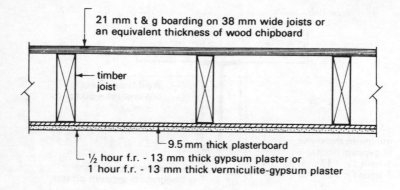

21 mm t & g boarding on 38 mm wide joists or an equivalent thickness of wood chipboard

timber joist

9.5 mm thick plasterboard

½ hour f.r. - 13 mm thick gypsum plaster or
1 hour f.r. - 13 mm thick vermiculite-gypsum plaster

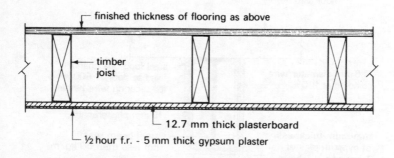

finished thickness of flooring as above

timber joist

12.7 mm thick plasterboard

½ hour f.r. - 5 mm thick gypsum plaster

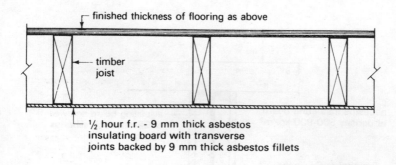

finished thickness of flooring as above

timber joist

½ hour f.r. - 9 mm thick asbestos
insulating board with transverse
joints backed by 9 mm thick asbestos fillets

Fig. IV.16 Fire resistance — timber floors

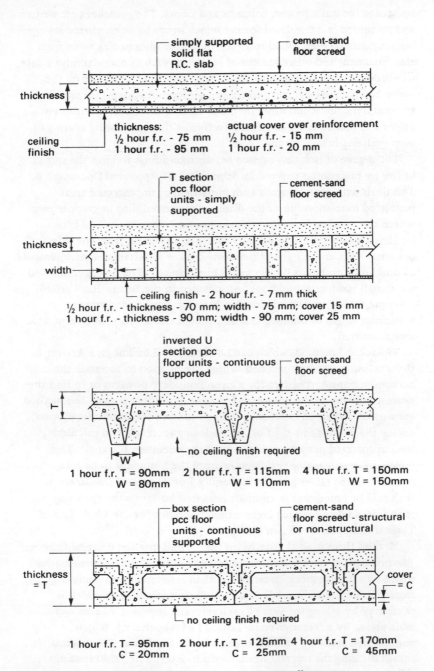

simply supported solid flat R.C. slab

cement-sand floor screed

thickness

ceiling finish

thickness:
½ hour f.r. - 75 mm
1 hour f.r. - 95 mm

actual cover over reinforcement
½ hour f.r. - 15 mm
1 hour f.r. - 20 mm

T section pcc floor units - simply supported

cement-sand floor screed

thickness

width

ceiling finish - 2 hour f.r. - 7 mm thick
½ hour f.r. - thickness - 70 mm; width - 75 mm; cover 15 mm
1 hour f.r. - thickness - 90 mm; width - 90 mm; cover 25 mm

inverted U section pcc floor units - continuous supported

cement-sand floor screed

T

W

no ceiling finish required

1 hour f.r. T = 90mm   2 hour f.r. T = 115mm   4 hour f.r. T = 150mm
W = 80mm   W = 110mm   W = 150mm

box section pcc floor units - continuous supported

cement-sand floor screed - structural or non-structural

thickness = T

cover = C

no ceiling finish required

1 hour f.r. T = 95mm   2 hour f.r. T = 125mm   4 hour f.r. T = 170mm
C = 20mm   C = 25mm   C = 45mm

Fig. IV.17   Fire resistance — concrete floors

229

resistance for walls, beams, columns and floors. The guidelines are written and presented in a tabulated format which needs to be translated into working details. Figs. IV.10 to IV.17 show typical examples taken from this document and other sources of reference such as manufacturer's data.

Students are encouraged to study manufacturers' literature on the many patent ready-cut, easy-to-fix fire protection systems for standard structural members and other methods such as the use of intumescent paints and materials which expand to form a thick insulating coating or strip on being heated by fire.

The degree of isolation needed between buildings to limit the spread of fire by radiation is covered in Appendix J of Approved Document B. This deals with external walls and, in particular, unprotected areas permitted in relationship to the distance of the building or compartment within the building from the relevant boundary and is applicable to buildings which are not less than 1 metre at any point from the relevant boundary. Appendix J gives three methods for satisfying the requirements of Building Regulation B4 (External Fire Spread). The first is concerned with small residential buildings not included in the Institutional group. A simple table gives the relationship between boundary distance, maximum length of building side and the maximum total of unprotected area permitted.

The second method, which can be used for all buildings, is known as the 'enclosing rectangle method' which can be used to ascertain the maximum unprotected area for a given boundary position or to find the nearest position of the boundary for a given building design. The method consists of placing an enclosing rectangle around the unprotected areas, noting the width and height of the enclosing rectangle and calculating the unprotected percentage in terms of the enclosing rectangle. This information will enable the distance from the boundary to be read direct from the tables given in Appendix J of Approved Document B. It should be noted that in compartmentated buildings the enclosing rectangle is taken for each compartment and not for the whole facade. Typical examples are shown in Fig. IV.18.

Method three is an alternative to the second method described above. The principle of isolation is still followed but by a more precise method which will involve more investigation than reference to an enclosing rectangle. Reference is made to an aggregate notional area which is calculated by taking the sum of each relevant unprotected area and multiplying by a factor given in Table J3 of Appendix J. Which unprotected areas are relevant is given in the appendix. The method entails dividing the relevant boundary into a series of 3.000 spacings called vertical datum and projecting from each point a datum line to

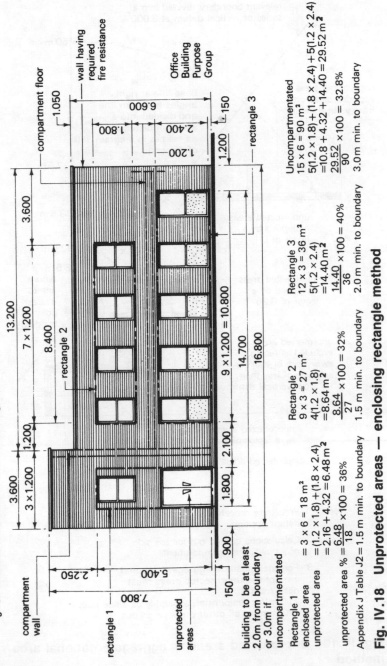

NB. enclosing rectangle figures used are the nearest figures given in tables above actual dimensional figures.

wall having required fire resistance

compartment floor

Office Building Purpose Group

rectangle 3

rectangle 2

compartment wall

rectangle 1

unprotected areas

building to be at least 2.0m from boundary or 3.0m if uncompartmented

Rectangle 1
enclosed area $= 3 \times 6 = 18$ m²
unprotected area $= (1.2 \times 1.8) + (1.8 \times 2.4)$
$= 2.16 + 4.32 = 6.48$ m²
unprotected area % $= \dfrac{6.48}{18} \times 100 = 36\%$
Appendix J Table J2 = 1.5 m min. to boundary

Rectangle 2
$9 \times 3 = 27$ m²
$4(1.2 \times 1.8)$
$= 8.64$ m²
$\dfrac{8.64}{27} \times 100 = 32\%$
1.5 m min. to boundary

Rectangle 3
$12 \times 3 = 36$ m²
$5(1.2 \times 2.4)$
$= 14.40$ m²
$\dfrac{14.40}{36} \times 100 = 40\%$
2.0 m min. to boundary

Uncompartmented
$15 \times 6 = 90$ m²
$5(1.2 \times 1.8) + (1.8 \times 2.4) + 5(1.2 \times 2.4)$
$= 10.8 + 4.32 + 14.40 = 29.52$ m²
$\dfrac{29.52}{90} \times 100 = 32.8\%$
3.0 m min. to boundary

Fig. IV.18 Unprotected areas — enclosing rectangle method

231

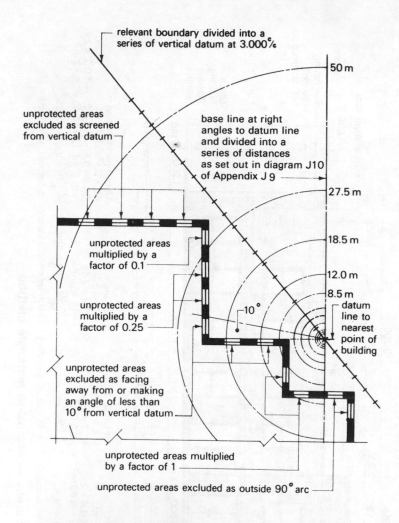

relevant boundary divided into a
series of vertical datum at 3.000%

50 m

unprotected areas
excluded as screened
from vertical datum

base line at right
angles to datum line
and divided into a
series of distances
as set out in diagram J10
of Appendix J 9

27.5 m

18.5 m

unprotected areas
multiplied by a
factor of 0.1

12.0 m

8.5 m

datum
line to
nearest
point of
building

10°

unprotected areas
multiplied by a
factor of 0.25

unprotected areas
excluded as facing
away from or making
an angle of less than
10° from vertical datum

unprotected areas multiplied
by a factor of 1

unprotected areas excluded as outside 90° arc

Notes:- 1. Procedure repeated for each vertical
datum position.

2. Calculations carried out for any side
of a building or compartment.

3. For each position aggregate notional
area of the unprotected areas must
not exceed:
210 m for residential, assembly or office use.
90 mm for all other purpose groups.

Fig. IV.19 Unprotected areas — aggregate notional area method

the nearest point on the building. A base line is drawn through each vertical datum at right angles to the datum line and a series of semicircles of various radii drawn from this point represent the distance and hence the factors for calculating the aggregate notional area (see Fig. IV.19). For buildings or compartments with a residential, assembly or office use the result should not exceed 210 m^2 ; for other purpose groups the result should not exceed 90 m^2 . In practical terms this method would not normally be used unless the situation is critical or the outline of the building was irregular in shape.

The specific recommendations for separating walls, openings in compartment walls, compartment floors, protective shafts, doors, stairways and protecting structure are set out in Approved Document B. Each purpose group is considered separately although many of the recommendations are similar for a number of purpose groups.

26
Means of escape in case of fire

Means of escape in case of fire is concerned with the personal hazard by giving people within a building where an outbreak of fire occurs a reasonable chance to reach an area of safety, taking into account factors such as the risks to human life, unfamiliarity with building layout, problems of smoke and the short space of time available to evacuate the premises before the problems become almost insurmountable.

Fear is a natural response of humans when confronted with uncontrolled fire and in particular fear of smoke, which is justified by the fact that more deaths are caused by smoke and heated gases than by burns. Statistics show that on average approximately 54% of deaths in fires are caused by smoke, 40% by burns and scalds and 6% by other causes. BS 4422 : Part I (Glossary of Terms Associated with Fire) defines smoke as a visible airborne cloud of fine particles, the products of incomplete combustion. Whilst the above statement is indeed true smoke can also be caused by the release into the air of a variety of chemical compounds. The main dangers, contained in smoke, to human life are the carbon dioxide and carbon monoxide gases which are normal products of combustion.

The presence of these gases does not always cause the greatest hazard in human terms since the density of smoke is more likely to create fear than the undetectable gases. Buoyant and mobile dense smoke will spread rapidly within a building or compartment during a fire, masking or even obliterating exit signs and directions. Gases, other than those mentioned previously, are generally irritants which can affect the eyes, causing watering which further impairs the vision, and can also affect the respiratory organs, causing reactions to slow and a loss of directional sense. It is worth remembering that smoke, being less dense than air, rises and that to take up a position as near to the floor as possible will increase the chances of escape.

Carbon dioxide has no smell and is always present in the atmosphere but since it is a product of combustion its volume increases at the expense of oxygen during a fire. The gas is not poisonous but can cause death by asphyxia. The normal amount of oxygen present in the air is approximately 21%; if this is reduced to 12% abnormal fatigue can be experienced; down to about 6% it can cause nausea, vomiting and loss of consciousness; below 6% respiration is difficult, which can result in death. Carbon dioxide will not support combustion and can cause a fire to be extinguished if the content by volume exceeds 14%, a fact used by fire fighters in their efforts to deal with an outbreak of fire.

Carbon monoxide, like carbon dioxide, is odourless but it is very poisonous and, having approximately the same density as air, will spread rapidly. A very small concentration (0.2% by volume) of this colourless gas can cause death in about 40 minutes. The first effects are dizziness and headaches followed in 5 to 10 minutes by loss of consciousness leading to death. As the concentration increases so the time lapse from the initial dizziness to death decreases so that by the time the concentration has reached about 1.3% by volume death can take place within a minute or two.

The heat which is associated with fire and smoke can also be injurious and even fatal. Temperatures in excess of 100°C can cause damage to the windpipe and lungs resulting in death within 30 minutes or sooner as the temperature rises. An interesting fact which emerges from statistics is that females generally have longer survival periods than males, and as would be expected the survival time decreases with age. Injuries caused by heat are generally in the form of burns followed very often by shock which can be fatal in many cases.

The above has been written not to frighten, but to emphasise the necessity for an adequate means of escape to give occupants and visitors a reasonable chance to reach an area of safety should a fire occur. To this end a maze of legislation exists to guide the designer in his task of planning escape routes without being too restrictive on the overall design concept. Scotland has its own regulations and byelaws whilst the rest of the country is covered by Part B of the Building Regulations and various Acts of Parliament.

BUILDING REGULATIONS 1985

Building Regulation B1 requires that in case of fire a means of escape leading from the building to a place of safety outside the building must be capable of being safely and effectively used at all times. The regulation applies only to certain types of buildings, namely: dwellinghouses of three or more storeys; flats of three or more storeys; offices and shops. The regulation is supported by a document entitled *The Building Regulations 1985 — Mandatory rules for means of escape in case of fire* and is the only method of complying with Building Regulation B1 unless the local authority agree upon a relaxation. Most other types of building are covered by designations made under the Fire Precautions Act 1971.

Planning Escape Routes

When escape routes are being planned the type of person likely to be involved must be considered. Occupants of flats will be familiar with the layout of the premises whereas customers in a shop may be completely unfamiliar with their surroundings. In schools the fundamental principle is the provision of an alternative means of escape and in hospitals the main concern is with the adequacy of the means of escape from all parts of the building.

In the context of means of escape in case of fire the building and its contents are of secondary importance. The provision of a safe escape route should, however, allow at the same time an easy access for the fire brigade using the same routes, and since these routes are protected the risk of fire spread is minimised. In practice the provision of an adequate means of escape and structural fire protection of the building and its contents are virtually inseparable. Each building has to be considered as an individual exercise but certain common factors prevail in all cases:

1. An outbreak of fire does not necessarily imply the evacuation of the entire building.
2. Rescue facilities of the local fire brigade should not be considered as part of the planning of means of escape.
3. Persons should be able to reach safety without assistance when using the protected escape routes.
4. All possible sources of an outbreak and the course the fire is likely to take should be examined and the escape routes planned accordingly.

FIRE PRECAUTIONS ACT 1971

This Act received the Royal Assent on 27 May 1971 and is designed to make further provisions for the protection of persons from fire risks. The provisions of this Act do not apply to Northern Ireland and section 11, which deals with means of escape, does not apply to the old Greater London Council area, which has its own byelaws, or to Scotland, which has its own regulations.

A fire certificate is required on any premises designated by the Minister of State at the Home Office within the following classes of use:

1. Sleeping accommodation.
2. Institutions providing treatment or care.
3. Entertainment, recreation or instruction.
4. Teaching, training or research.
5. Any purpose involving access to the premises by members of the public by payment or otherwise.

Certain types of buildings and premises are exempted from the provisions of this Act and these can be listed as follows:

1. Premises covered by the Offices, Shops and Railway Premises Act 1963.
2. Premises covered by the Factories Act.
3. A quarry or mine.
4. Churches, chapels and places of worship.
5. Houses occupied as a single dwelling.

In certain circumstances the fire authority may make it compulsory to have a fire certificate in particular where the premises have a room used as living accommodation which is:

1. Below the ground floor of a building.
2. Two or more floors above the ground.
3. A room of which the floor is 6.000 m or more above the surface of the ground on any side of the building.

The Secretary of State for the Environment has power, by virtue of sections 4 and 6 of the Public Health Act 1961, section 11 of the Fire Precautions Act 1971 and the Building Act 1984 to make building regulations with regard to means of escape in case of fire.

Applications for a fire certificate are made to the Fire Authority on form FP1. The Fire Authority is as defined in the Fire Services Act 1947 and usually the name and address of the relevant Fire Authority can be obtained from the local authority or council offices. It is generally the occupiers' responsibility to make the application and submit any plans, specifications and details required. Penalties for offences under this Act range from £50 to £400 fines plus two years' imprisonment.

The first Designating Order was made on 21 February 1972 and applies to all existing hotels and boarding houses with accommodation for over six people whether guests or staff unless where accommodation is for less than six people and such accommodation is above first floor or below ground floor.

The basic principles embodied in the Act with regards to means of escape in case of fire are:

1. Limitation of travel distances.
2. Escape route considered in 3 stages
   (a)   travel distance within rooms;
   (b)   travel distance from rooms to a stairway or final exit;
   (c)   travel within stairways and to final exit.
3. Provision of a protected route which is defined as a route for persons escaping from fire which is separated from the remainder of the building by fire-resisting doors (except doors to lavatories), fire resistant walls, partitions and floors.

The basic design principles relating to the 3 stages of escape are shown in Figs. IV.20, IV.21 and IV.22.

Flats and Maisonettes

At one time only accommodation over 24.000 m above ground level would have been considered, this being the height over which external rescue by the fire brigade was impracticable. It has become apparent that even with dwellings within reach of fire fighters' ladders external rescue is not always possible. This is because present-day traffic conditions and congestion may prevent the appliance from approaching close to the building or may delay the arrival of the fire brigade.

As with other forms of buildings the only sound basis for planning means of escape from flats and maisonettes is to identify the positions of all possible sources of any outbreak of fire and to predict the likely course the fire, smoke and gases would follow. The planning should be considered in 3 stages:

1. Risk to occupants of the dwelling in which the fire originates.
2. Risk to occupants of adjoining dwellings should the fire or smoke penetrate the horizontal escape route or common corridor.
3. Risk to occupants above the level of the outbreak particularly on the floor immediately above the source of the fire.

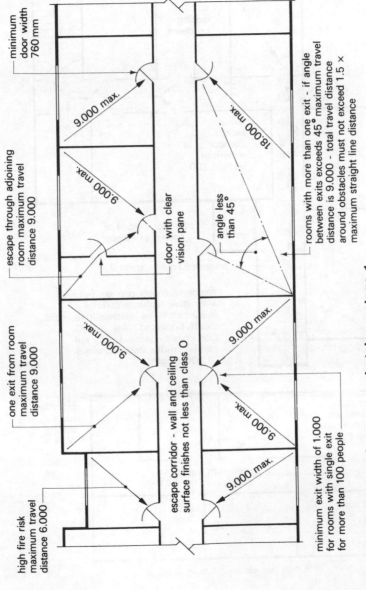

minimum door width 760 mm

9.000 max.

18.000 max.

9.000 max.

escape through adjoining room maximum travel distance 9.000

door with clear vision pane

angle less than 45°

rooms with more than one exit - if angle between exits exceeds 45° maximum travel distance is 9.000 - total travel distance around obstacles must not exceed 1.5 × maximum straight line distance

one exit from room maximum travel distance 9.000

9.000 max.

9.000 max.

9.000 max.

escape corridor - wall and ceiling surface finishes not less than class O

high fire risk maximum travel distance 6.000

9.000 max.

minimum exit width of 1.000 for rooms with single exit for more than 100 people

Fig. IV.20   Means of escape — hotels — stage 1

239

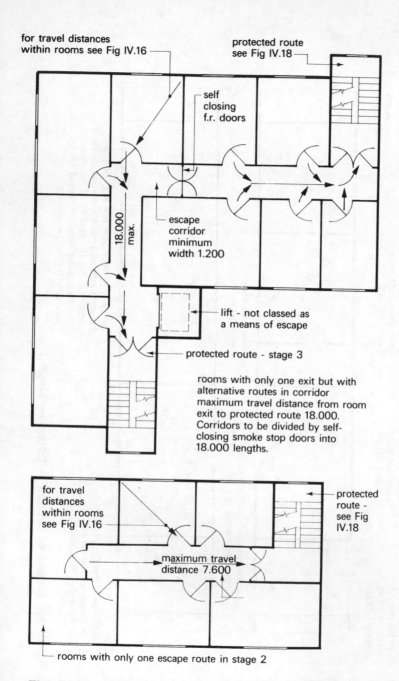

for travel distances
within rooms see Fig IV.16

protected route
see Fig IV.18

self
closing
f.r. doors

18.000
max.

escape
corridor
minimum
width 1.200

lift - not classed as
a means of escape

protected route - stage 3

rooms with only one exit but with
alternative routes in corridor
maximum travel distance from room
exit to protected route 18.000.
Corridors to be divided by self-
closing smoke stop doors into
18.000 lengths.

for travel
distances
within rooms
see Fig IV.16

protected
route -
see Fig
IV.18

maximum travel
distance 7.600

rooms with only one escape route in stage 2

Fig. IV.21   Means of escape — hotels — stage 2

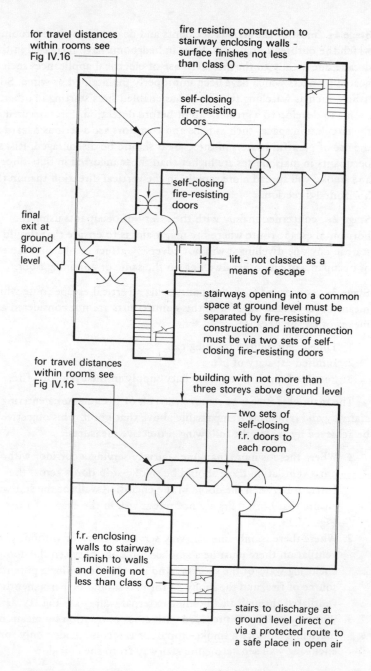

for travel distances within rooms see Fig IV.16

fire resisting construction to stairway enclosing walls - surface finishes not less than class O

self-closing fire-resisting doors

self-closing fire-resisting doors

final exit at ground floor level

lift - not classed as a means of escape

stairways opening into a common space at ground level must be separated by fire-resisting construction and interconnection must be via two sets of self-closing fire-resisting doors

for travel distances within rooms see Fig IV.16

building with not more than three storeys above ground level

two sets of self-closing f.r. doors to each room

f.r. enclosing walls to stairway - finish to walls and ceiling not less than class O

stairs to discharge at ground level direct or via a protected route to a safe place in open air

Fig. IV.22 Means of escape — hotels — stage 3

Stage 1: most of the serious accidents and deaths occur in the room in which the outbreak originates. Fires in bedrooms have increased in the last decade due mainly to the increased use of electrical applicances such as heated blankets which have been improperly maintained or wired. Social habits, such as watching television, has enabled fires starting in other rooms to develop to a greater extent before detection. Fires occurring in the circulation spaces such as halls and corridors are a serious hazard and the use of paraffin heaters in these areas should be discouraged. Risks to occupants in maisonettes are higher than those incurred in flats since fire and smoke will spread more rapidly in the vertical direction than in the horizontal direction.

Stage 2: concerned mainly with the safety of occupants using the horizontal escape route where the major aim is to ensure that should a fire start in any one dwelling it will not adversely affect or obstruct the escape of occupants of any other dwelling on the same or adjoining floor.

Stage 3: concerned with occupants using a vertical escape route which means in fact a stairway, for in this context lifts are not considered as a means of escape because:

1. Time delay in lift answering call.
2. Limited capacity of lift.
3. Possible failure of the electricity supply in the event of a fire.

The main objective is to remove the risk of fire or smoke entering a stairway and rendering it impassable above that point. This objective can be achieved by taking the following protective measures:

1. Where there is more than one stairway serving a corridor without cross ventilation there should be smoke-stop doors across the corridor between the doors in the enclosing walls of the stairways to ensure that both stairs are not put at risk in the event of a fire — see Fig. IV.23.
2. Where there is only one stairway serving a corridor without cross ventilation there must be a smoke-stop door between the door in the enclosing walls of the stairway and any door covering a potential source of fire, and the lobby so formed should be permanently ventilated through an adjoining external wall — see Fig. IV.23.
3. Where corridors are provided with cross ventilation by means of any mechanical device a smoke-stop door is recommended only for the enclosing wall separating the stairway from the corridor.

The basic means of escape requirements for flats can be enumerated thus:

1. Every flat should have a protected entrance hall of half-hour fire resistance.
2. Every living room should have an exit into the protected entrance hall.
3. Bedrooms should be nearer to the entrance door than the living rooms or kitchen.
4. Doors opening on to a protected entrance hall to be type 3 (see section on doors in this chapter).
5. Maximum travel distance from any bedroom exit to entrance door to be 7.500 m; if exceeded an alternative route is to be provided.

A typical flat example is shown in Fig. IV.24.

The basic means of escape requirements for maisonettes can be similarly enumerated:

1. All maisonettes to have a private entrance hall and stairway where there is no fire risk.
2. All living rooms and bedrooms to have direct access to this hall or stairway.
3. Doors opening on to hall or stairway to be type 3.
4. Hall and stairway to have half-hour fire-resistant walls.
5. In most cases alternative means of escape required, an exception being where a half-hour fire-resistant screen is provided at the head of the stairway.

A typical maisonette example is shown in Fig. IV.25.

Students are encouraged to study the many examples of means of escape planning for flats and maisonettes given at the end of CP3 : Chapter IV: Part 1.

Office Buildings

BSS 5588 : Part 3 covers office buildings of all sizes and heights in the context of means of escape in case of fire and is the mandatory code of practice to be used to comply with Building Regulation B1(2).

The planning procedures for means of escape set out in the code are based on attempting to identify the positions of all possible sources of outbreak of fire and to predict the courses that might follow such an outbreak and in particular the passage of the fire and the passage of the smoke and gases ensuing from the fire. The basic planning objectives are to provide protected escape routes in the horizontal and vertical directions which will enable persons within the building confronted by an outbreak of fire to turn away and make a safe escape without outside assistance.

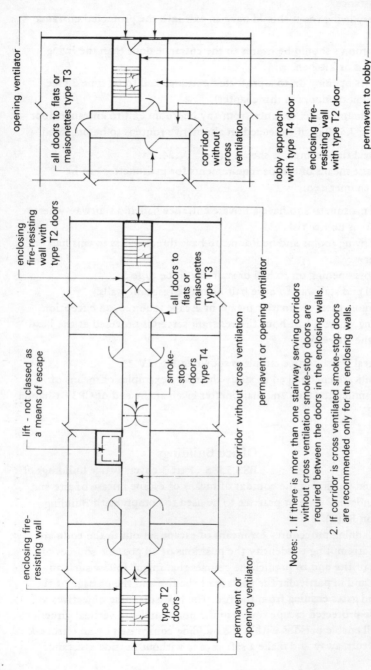

Fig. IV.23 Main stairway protection — flats and maisonettes

opening ventilator

all doors to flats or maisonettes type T3

corridor without cross ventilation

lobby approach with type T4 door

enclosing fire-resisting wall with type T2 door

permavent to lobby

enclosing fire-resisting wall with type T2 doors

lift - not classed as a means of escape

enclosing fire-resisting wall

permavent or opening ventilator

all doors to flats or maisonettes Type T3

smoke-stop doors type T4

corridor without cross ventilation

permavent or opening ventilator

type T2 doors

Notes: 1. If there is more than one stairway serving corridors without cross ventilation smoke-stop doors are required between the doors in the enclosing walls.

2. If corridor is cross ventilated smoke-stop doors are recommended only for the enclosing walls.

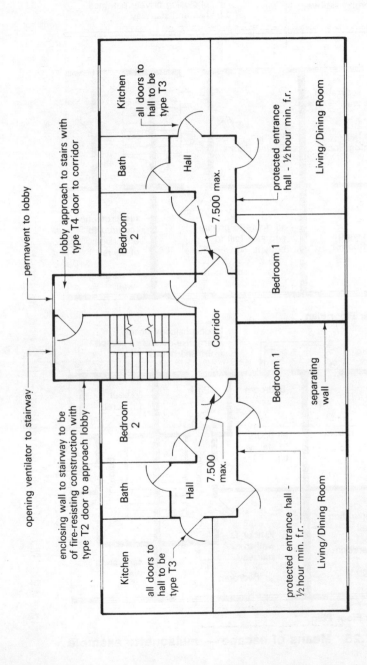

permavent to lobby

opening ventilator to stairway

lobby approach to stairs with type T4 door to corridor

enclosing wall to stairway to be of fire-resisting construction with type T2 door to approach lobby

Kitchen
all doors to hall to be type T3

Bath

Hall

Bedroom 2

Corridor

7.500 max.

protected entrance hall - ½ hour min. f.r.

Living/Dining Room

Bedroom 1

Bedroom 1

separating wall

Kitchen
all doors to hall to be type T3

Bath

Hall

Bedroom 2

7.500 max.

protected entrance hall - ½ hour min. f.r.

Living/Dining Room

Fig. IV.24 Means of escape — example of flats with only one stairway

245

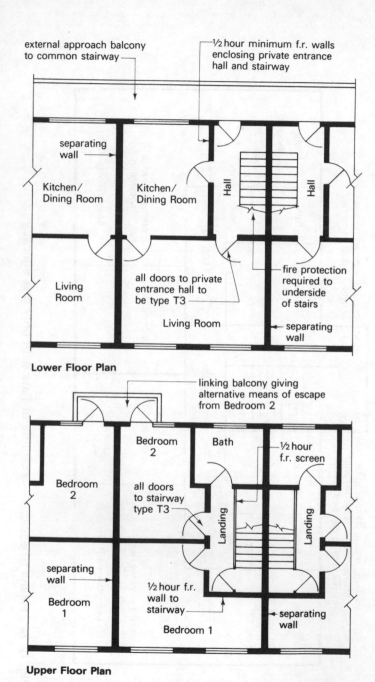

external approach balcony to common stairway

½ hour minimum f.r. walls enclosing private entrance hall and stairway

separating wall

Kitchen/ Dining Room

Kitchen/ Dining Room

Hall

Hall

Living Room

all doors to private entrance hall to be type T3

fire protection required to underside of stairs

Living Room

separating wall

Lower Floor Plan

linking balcony giving alternative means of escape from Bedroom 2

Bedroom 2

Bath

½ hour f.r. screen

Bedroom 2

all doors to stairway type T3

Landing

Landing

separating wall

Bedroom 1

½ hour f.r. wall to stairway

Bedroom 1

separating wall

Upper Floor Plan

Fig. IV.25 Means of escape — maisonette example

To achieve this planning objective there must be sufficient exits to allow the occupants to reach an area of safety without delay. It is not always necessary to plan for the complete evacuation of the building since compartmentation of the building will restrict the fire initially to an area within that compartment.

Two important factors to be considered in planning escape routes are width and travel distance. The width is based upon an evacuation time of 2.5 minutes through a storey exit on the assumption that a unit exit width of 500 mm will allow the flow of 40 persons per minute. The code gives tables for assessing the likely population density and clear widths of escape routes related to the maximum number of persons.

Travel distances are considered under two headings, namely: direct distance and travel distance. A direct distance is the shortest distance from any point within the floor area to the nearest storey exit measured so as to ignore walls, partitions and fittings. Generally the maximum direct distance is 12.000 for escape in one direction or 30.000 for escape in more than one direction. The travel distance is defined as the actual distance travelled from any point within the floor area to the nearest storey exit having regard to the layout of walls, partitions and fittings. Generally the maximum travel distances are 18.000 for escape in one direction and 45.000 for travel in more than one direction. It should be noted that both maximum distances must not be exceeded and that if alternative exits subtend an angle of less than 45° with one another and are not separated by fire-resisting construction they are classified as exits in one direction only.

The horizontal escape routes should be clear gangways with non-slippery even surfaces and if ramps are included these should have an easy gradient of a slope of not more than 1 in 12. The minimum clear headroom should be 2.000 with no projections from walls except for normal handrails. The minimum fire resistance should be not less than half an hour unless a higher resistance is required by the Building Regulations. Limitations on glazing for both escape corridors and doors are given in the text and accompanying tables within the code of practice.

The code recommends that there should not be less than two protected stairways available from any storey unless there are not more than three storeys above the ground storey or the building is of a height of not greater than 11.000 whichever is the lesser. Additional protected stairways should be provided as necessary to meet the requirements for travel distance. Where more than one stairway is provided it is usual to assume that one stairway would be blocked by the fire and therefore the remaining stairways must have sufficient width to cater for the total persons to be evacuated. A typical example of means of escape from an office building is shown in Fig. IV.26.

Shops and Similar Premises

BS 5588 : Part 2 covers all classes of shops and other similar types of premises such as: cafés; restaurants; public houses; and premises where goods are received for treatment, examples being dry cleaners and shoe repairers. The main objective of the code's requirements are to provide safety from fire by means of planning and providing protection of both horizontal and vertical escape routes for any area threatened by fire thus enabling any person confronted by an outbreak of fire to make an unassisted escape. Under the Fire Precautions Act 1971 as amended by the Health and Safety at Work etc., Act 1974 an adequate means of escape is required for all shops and for particular shops a fire certificate will be required.

In planning escape routes there must be sufficient exit facilities, such as protected routes and stairways, to allow the public and staff to reach areas of safety without undue delay. It is not always necessary to plan for complete evacuation immediately an outbreak of fire occurs. Compartmentation of multi-storey shops will limit the rate of fire spread and in such cases a reasonable assumption would be to design for the immediate evacuation of the floor on which the outbreak occurs plus the floor above which is the next portion of the building at risk. Escape widths are based upon an evacuation time of 2.5 minutes and on the assumption that a unit exit width of 500 mm permits the passage of 40 persons per minute. Guidance as to possible population densities is given in the code by means of a table which shows the floor space per person for types of rooms or storeys. Similarly another table gives clear widths for exits related to the total number of persons in a room or storey.

The maximum permitted travel distance is another important factor and can be taken as a maximum distance measured around obstructions such as fixed counters or a direct distance measured over the obstructions. The distances given in a table take into account the number of exits, the relationship of alternative exits and if the floor under consideration is a ground floor or an upper floor. Generally the maximum travel distances in one direction are 18.000 and 45.000 where exits subtend an angle of more than 45°. The maximum direct travel distances being 12.000 and 30.000 for similar conditions.

The vertical escape route via the stairs leading to the final exit leading direct to the open air must also cater for the anticipated number of persons likely to use the stairs for evacuation purposes. A table giving guidance on minimum stair widths related to population density and

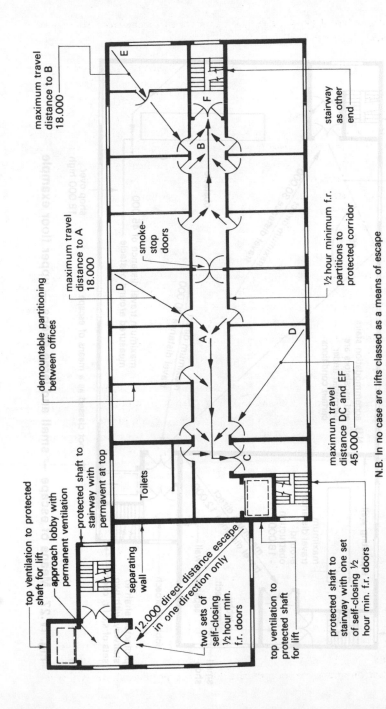

Fig. IV.26 Means of escape — office buildings — upper floor example

top ventilation to protected shaft for lift

approach lobby with permanent ventilation

protected shaft to stairway with permavent at top

demountable partitioning between offices

maximum travel distance to A 18.000

smoke-stop doors

maximum travel distance to B 18.000

E

F

B

A

C

D

D

½ hour minimum f.r. partitions to protected corridor

stairway as other end

maximum travel distance DC and EF 45.000

N.B. In no case are lifts classed as a means of escape

Toilets

separating wall

12.000 direct distance escape in one direction only

two sets of self-closing ½ hour min. f.r. doors

protected shaft to stairway with one set of self-closing ½ hour min. f.r. doors

top ventilation to protected shaft for lift

249

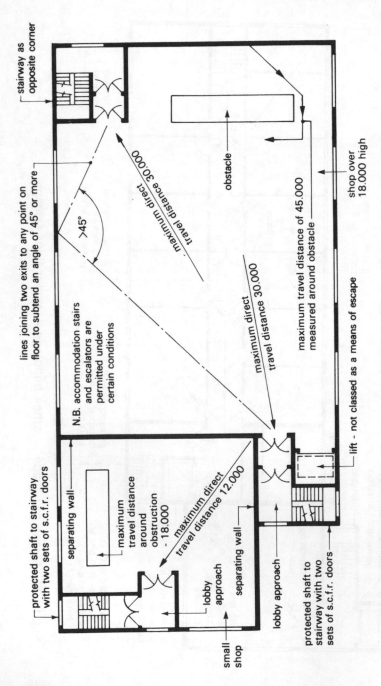

250

Fig. IV.27 Means of escape — small and large shops — upper floor example

stairway as opposite corner

lines joining two exits to any point on floor to subtend an angle of 45° or more

>45°

N.B. accommodation stairs and escalators are permitted under certain conditions

maximum direct travel distance 30.000

obstacle

maximum travel distance of 45.000 measured around obstacle

shop over 18.000 high

lift - not classed as a means of escape

protected shaft to stairway with two sets of s.c.f.r. doors

separating wall

maximum travel distance around obstruction - 18.000

maximum direct travel distance 12.000

lobby approach

separating wall

lobby approach

protected shaft to stairway with two sets of s.c.f.r. doors

small shop

height of building is given in the code. It is recommended that approach lobbies are used for all stairs in buildings over 18.000 high due to the higher risks to occupants in high buildings (see Fig. IV.27). In calculating the number of stairs required it should be assumed that one stair would be inaccessible in the event of a fire if two or more stairs are actually required.

Small shops with floor areas of not more than 280 m^2 in one occupancy and of not more than three storeys high are treated separately. The maximum travel or direct distance being governed by the floor's position within the building. Basement and upper floor distances being 18.000 and 12.000 for single exits with ground-floor distances being 27.000 and 18.000 respectively (see Fig. IV.27).

Staircases: these should be of non-combustible materials and continuous, leading ultimately to the final exit door to the place of safety. The recommended dimensions of going, rise, handrails and maximum number of risers per flight are shown in Fig. IV.28. Fire-resistant glazing is permitted but should be restricted to the portion of the wall above the handrails and preferably designed in accordance with the recommendations of CP 153 : Part 4.

Doors: — in the context of fire, doors are usually classified as fire-check, fire-resisting or smoke-stop. CP3 : Chapter IV : Part 1 however defines doors by type numbers thus:—

Type 1 (T1) must satisfy the Building Regulations as to the requirements for a compartment door.

Type 2 (T2) if fitted in a frame with a 25 mm deep rebate it should have a freedom from collapse and resistance to passage of flame of not less than 30 minutes. It should be fitted with a self-closing device (other than a rising butt) and have unrebated meeting stiles. The door may be single or double leaf, swinging in one or both directions. If there is no rebate to the frame the gap must be as small as practicable.

Type 3 (T3) if fitted in a frame with a 25 mm rebate it should have freedom of collapse for a period not less than 30 minutes and a resistance to the passage of flame for not less than 20 minutes. If of a single leaf it must be hung to swing in one direction only and if of double leaf format to be hung so that the swing of each leaf is in the opposite direction and the meeting stiles are rebated. Doors hung to a frame with rebates of not less than 12 mm should be fitted with an automatic self-closing device.

Type 4 (T4) similiar to T3 doors but the swinging can be in one or both directions. These doors should be fitted with a self-closing device (other than a rising butt) and the frame may be constructed without a rebate.

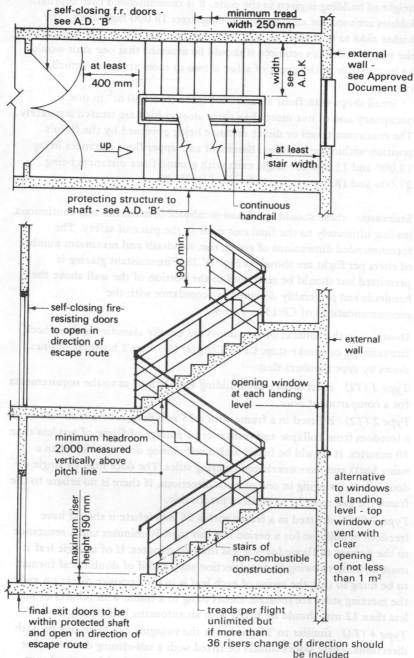

Fig. IV.28 Typical escape stair details

Labels in figure:

- self-closing f.r. doors - see A.D. 'B'
- minimum tread width 250 mm
- at least 400 mm
- width see A.D.K
- external wall - see Approved Document B
- up
- at least stair width
- protecting structure to shaft - see A.D. 'B'
- continuous handrail
- 900 min.
- self-closing fire-resisting doors to open in direction of escape route
- external wall
- opening window at each landing level
- minimum headroom 2.000 measured vertically above pitch line
- alternative to windows at landing level - top window or vent with clear opening of not less than 1 m²
- maximum riser height 190 mm
- stairs of non-combustible construction
- final exit doors to be within protected shaft and open in direction of escape route
- treads per flight unlimited but if more than 36 risers change of direction should be included

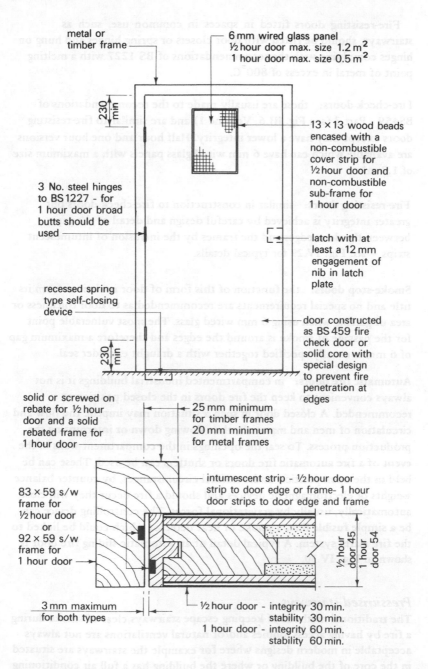

metal or timber frame

6 mm wired glass panel
½ hour door max. size 1.2 m²
1 hour door max. size 0.5 m²

230 min

13 × 13 wood beads encased with a non-combustible cover strip for ½ hour door and non-combustible sub-frame for 1 hour door

3 No. steel hinges to BS 1227 - for 1 hour door broad butts should be used

latch with at least a 12 mm engagement of nib in latch plate

recessed spring type self-closing device

door constructed as BS 459 fire check door or solid core with special design to prevent fire penetration at edges

230 min

solid or screwed on rebate for ½ hour door and a solid rebated frame for 1 hour door

25 mm minimum for timber frames
20 mm minimum for metal frames

intumescent strip - ½ hour door strip to door edge or frame - 1 hour door strips to door edge and frame

83 × 59 s/w frame for ½ hour door
or
92 × 59 s/w frame for 1 hour door

½ hour door 45
1 hour door 54

3 mm maximum for both types

½ hour door - integrity 30 min.
stability 30 min.
1 hour door - integrity 60 min.
stability 60 min.

Fig. IV.29   Fire-resisting doors

Fire-resisting doors fitted in spaces in common use, such as stairways, should be fitted with door closers or spring hinges and hung on hinges complying with the recommendations of BS 1227 with a melting point of metal in excess of 800°C.

Fire-check doors: these are usually made to the recommendations of BS459 : Part 3 (see Fig. III.6, Volume 1) and are similar to fire-resisting doors except they have a lower integrity. Half hour and one hour versions are available which can have 6 mm wired glass panels with a maximum size of 1.2 m^2.

Fire-resisting doors: similar in construction to fire-check doors but greater integrity is achieved by careful design and detail of the gaps between the door edges and the frames by the inclusion of intumescent strips — see Fig. IV.29 for typical details.

Smoke-stop doors: the function of this form of door is obvious from its title and no special requirements are recommended as to door thickness or area of glazing when using 6 mm wired glass. The most vulnerable point for the passage of smoke is around the edges and therefore a maximum gap of 6 mm is usually specified together with a draught excluder seal.

Automatic fire doors: in compartmented industrial buildings it is not always convenient to keep the fire doors in the closed position as recommended. A closed door in such a situation may impede the flow and circulation of men and materials, thus slowing down or interrupting the production process. To seal the openings in the compartment walls in the event of a fire automatic fire doors or shutters can be used. These can be held in the open position under normal circumstances, by counter balance weights or electromagnetic devices and should a fire occur they will close automatically, usually by gravitational forces. The controlling device can be a simple fusible link, a smoke or heat detector which could be linked to the fire alarm system. A typical detail of an automatic sliding fire door is shown in Fig. IV.30.

Pressurised stairways

The traditional methods of keeping escape stairways clear of smoke during a fire by having access lobbies and/or natural ventilations are not always acceptable in modern designs where for example the stairways are situated in the core of the building or where the building has a full air conditioning and ventilation design. Pressurisation is a method devised to prevent smoke

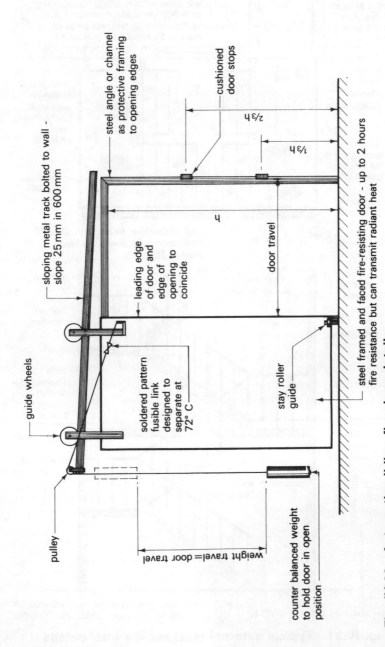

sloping metal track bolted to wall - slope 25 mm in 600 mm

steel angle or channel as protective framing to opening edges

cushioned door stops

$^{2}/_{3}h$

$^{1}/_{3}h$

h

door travel

leading edge of door and edge of opening to coincide

guide wheels

soldered pattern fusible link designed to separate at 72° C

stay roller guide

steel framed and faced fire-resisting door - up to 2 hours fire resistance but can transmit radiant heat

pulley

weight travel = door travel

counter balanced weight to hold door in open position

Fig. IV.30 Automatic sliding fire door details

NB. protective roof and sides omitted for clarity

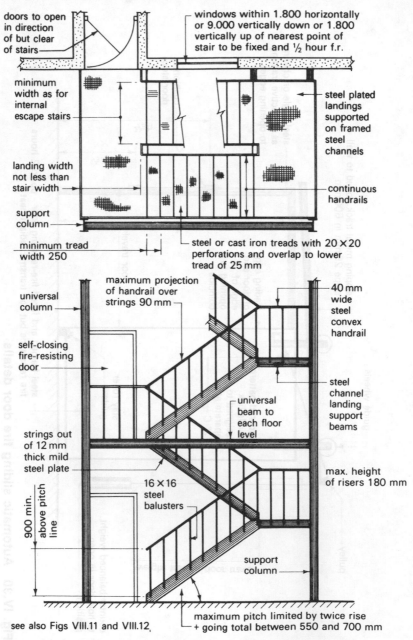

doors to open in direction of but clear of stairs

windows within 1.800 horizontally or 9.000 vertically down or 1.800 vertically up of nearest point of stair to be fixed and ½ hour f.r.

minimum width as for internal escape stairs

steel plated landings supported on framed steel channels

landing width not less than stair width

support column

minimum tread width 250

continuous handrails

steel or cast iron treads with 20 × 20 perforations and overlap to lower tread of 25 mm

universal column

maximum projection of handrail over strings 90 mm

40 mm wide steel convex handrail

self-closing fire-resisting door

steel channel landing support beams

universal beam to each floor level

strings out of 12 mm thick mild steel plate

16 × 16 steel balusters

max. height of risers 180 mm

900 min. above pitch line

support column

maximum pitch limited by twice rise + going total between 550 and 700 mm

see also Figs VIII.11 and VIII.12

Fig. IV.31 Typical external steel escape stair details

256

logging in an unfenestrated stairway by a system of continuous pressurisation which will keep the stairway clear of smoke if the doors remain closed. Only a small fan installation is required to maintain the almost unnoticeable pressure of 8 to 13 N/m^2. In addition to controlling smoke, pressurisation also increases the fire resistance of doors opening into the protected area. It is essential with these installations that the doors are well sealed to prevent pressure loss.

External escape staircases

It is sometimes necessary to provide external escape staircases as an alternative escape route but they can have undesirable features. They can be adversely affected by snow, ice and heat and are generally difficult to design in a manner which can be considered aesthetically pleasing. All such stairs should be constructed throughout in steel, light alloy or concrete and be adequately protected against corrosion. Typical details of a steel external escape staircase are shown in Fig. IV.31.

Having now completed a brief study of fire and the way it affects the design of buildings choice of materials and circulation patterns it must be obvious to the student that this is an important topic which if ignored or treated lightly can have disastrous consequences not only to a structure but also to human life.

27
Wind pressures

Wind can be defined as a movement of air, the full nature of which is not fully understood, but two major contributory factors which can be given are:

1. Convection currents caused by air being warmed at the earth's surface, becoming less dense, rising and being replaced by colder air.
2. Transference of air between high and low pressure areas.

The speed with which the air moves in replacement or transfer is termed its velocity and can be from 0 to 1.5 metres per second, when it is hardly noticeable, to speeds in excess of 24 metres per second, when considerable damage to property and discomfort to persons could be the result.

The physical nature of the ground or topography over which the wind passes will have an effect on local wind speeds since obstructions such as trees and buildings can set up local disturbances by forcing the wind to move around the sides of the obstruction or funnel between adjacent obstacles. Where funnelling occurs the velocity and therefore the pressure can be increased considerably. Experience and research has shown that the major damage to buildings is caused not by a wind blowing at a constant velocity but by the short duration bursts or gusts of wind of greater intensity than the prevailing mean wind speed. The durations of these gusts are usually measured in 3, 5 and 15 second periods and information of the likely maximum gust speeds for specific long term time durations of 50 years or more are available from the Meteorological Office.

When the wind encounters an object in its path such as the face of a building it is usually rebuffed and forced to turn back on itself, this has the effect of setting up a whirling motion or eddy which eventually finds its way around or over the obstruction. The pressure of the wind is normally in the same direction as the path of the wind which tends to push the wall of the building inwards, and indeed will do so if sufficient resistance is not built into the structure. The effect of local eddies however is very often opposite in direction and force to that of the prevailing wind, producing a negative or suction force — see Fig. IV.32.

Many factors must be taken into account before the magnitude and direction of wind pressures can be determined; these include height to width ratio of the building, length to width ratio of the building, plan shape of the building, approach topography, exposure of the building and the proximity of surrounding structures. Account must also be taken of any likely openings in the building, since the entry of wind will exert a positive pressure on any walls or ceilings encountered. These internal pressures must be added to or subtracted from the type of pressure anticipated acting on the external face at the same point. For a detailed study of the effects and assessment of wind loads on buildings students are advised to examine the contents of BRE Digests numbers 119 and 141.

All buildings are at some time subjected to wind pressures but some are more vulnerable than others due to their shape, exposure or method of construction. One method of providing adequate resistance to wind pressures is to use materials of high density; it follows therefore that buildings which are clad with lightweight coverings are more susceptible to wind damage than those using the heavier traditional materials. Factory buildings using lightweight claddings have therefore been taken to serve as an illustration of providing suitable means of resistance to wind pressures.

To overcome the problem of uplift or suction on roofs caused by the negative wind pressures adequate fixing or anchorage of the lightweight coverings to the structural frame is recommended. Generally sufficient resistance to uplift of the frame is inherent in the material used for the structural members, the problem is therefore to stop the covering being pulled away from the supporting member. This can be achieved by the quality or holding power of the fixings used or by the number of fixings employed or by a combination of both. It should be noted that the whole roof considered as a single entity is at risk and not merely individual sheets.

If the supporting member does not have sufficient self dead load to overcome the suction forces, such as a timber plate bedded on to a brick wall, then it will be necessary adequately to anchor the plate to the wall. This can be carried out by means of bolts or straps fixed to the plate and

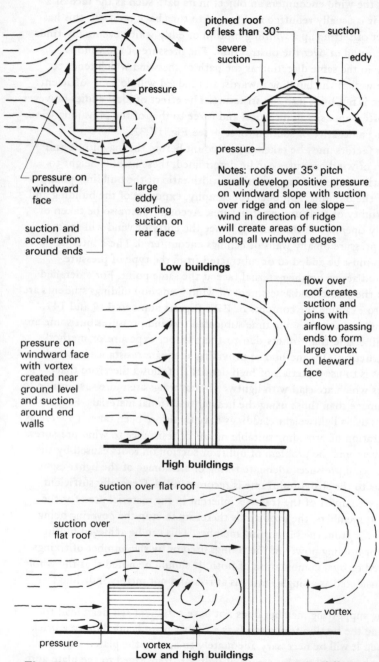

pressure

pitched roof
of less than 30°
severe
suction

suction

eddy

pressure

Notes: roofs over 35° pitch
usually develop positive pressure
on windward slope with suction
over ridge and on lee slope —
wind in direction of ridge
will create areas of suction
along all windward edges

pressure on
windward
face

large
eddy
exerting
suction on
rear face

suction and
acceleration
around ends

Low buildings

pressure on
windward face
with vortex
created near
ground level
and suction
around end
walls

flow over
roof creates
suction and
joins with
airflow passing
ends to form
large vortex
on leeward
face

High buildings

suction over flat roof

suction over
flat roof

vortex

pressure

vortex

Low and high buildings

Fig. IV.32 Typical wind pressures around buildings

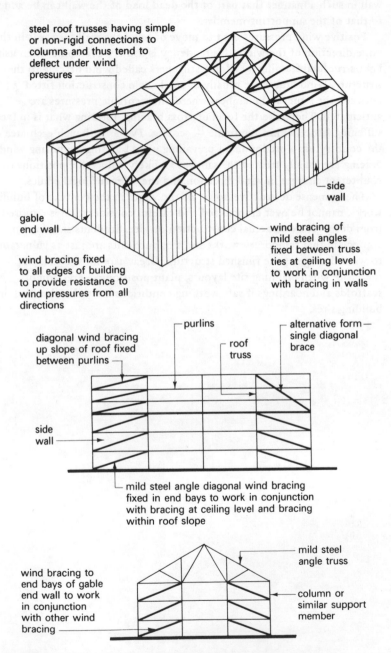

steel roof trusses having simple or non-rigid connections to columns and thus tend to deflect under wind pressures

gable end wall

wind bracing fixed to all edges of building to provide resistance to wind pressures from all directions

side wall

wind bracing of mild steel angles fixed between truss ties at ceiling level to work in conjunction with bracing in walls

diagonal wind bracing up slope of roof fixed between purlins

purlins

roof truss

alternative form— single diagonal brace

side wall

mild steel angle diagonal wind bracing fixed in end bays to work in conjunction with bracing at ceiling level and bracing within roof slope

wind bracing to end bays of gable end wall to work in conjunction with other wind bracing

mild steel angle truss

column or similar support member

Fig. IV.33 Typical wind bracing arrangements

wall in such a manner that part of the dead load of the wall can be added to that of the supporting member.

Positive wind pressures tend to move or bend the wall forwards in the same direction of the wind; this tendency is usually overcome when using light structural framing by adding stiffeners called wind bracing to the structure. Wind braces are usually of steel angle construction fitted between the structural members where unacceptable pressures are anticipated. They take the form of cross bracing, forming what is in fact a stiffening lattice within the frame — see Fig. IV.33. Although each area of the country has a predominant prevailing wind buildings requiring wind bracing are usually treated the same at all likely vulnerable positions to counteract changes in wind direction and the effect of local eddies.

The immense destructive power of the wind, in the context of building works, cannot be over emphasised and careful consideration is required from design stage to actual construction on site. Students should also appreciate that temporary works and site hutments are just as vulnerable to wind damage as the finished structure. Great care must be taken therefore when planning site layouts, plant positioning, erection of scaffolds and hoardings if safe working conditions are to be obtained on building sites.

Bibliography

Relevant BS — British Standards Institution.
Relevant CP — British Standards Institution.
Building Regulations — HMSO.
Relevant BRE Digests — HMSO.
Relevant Advisory Leaflets — DOE.
DOE Construction Issues 1—17 — DOE.
R. Barry. *The Construction of Buildings.* Crosby Lockwood & Sons Ltd.
Mitchells Building Construction Series. B. T. Batsford Ltd.
W. B. McKay. *Building Construction,* Vols. 1 to 4. Longman.
Specification. The Architectural Press.
A. J. Elder. *A. J. Guide to the Building Regulations.* The Architectural
  Press.
R. Llewelyn Davies and D. J. Petty. *Building Elements.* The Architectural
  Press.
Cecil C. Handisyde. *Building Materials.* The Architectural Press.
Drained Joints in Precast Concrete Cladding. The National Buildings Agency.
L. A. Ragsdale and E. A. Raynham. *Building Materials Technology.* Edward
  Arnold Ltd.
The Green Book on Plastering. British Gypsum Ltd.
The Blue Book on Plasterboard. British Gypsum Ltd.
F. Hall. *Plumbing.* Macmillan.
Leslie Wolley. *Drainage Details.* Northwood Publications.
'Sanitation Details by Aquarius', *Building Trades Journal.* Northwood
  Publications.

Fire Protection Series by E. L. Wolley. *Building Trades Journal*, Northwood Publications.

Gas Handbook for Architects and Builders. The Gas Council.

Relevant A. J. Handbooks. The Architectural Press.

Relevant manufacturers' catalogues contained in the Barbour Index and Building Products Index Libraries.

Index

Ring circuits, 179, 182–4
Rolled glass, 75
Rooflights, 86–92
    dormer, 87
    patent glazing, 90–2
    skylight, 88
    translucent sheets, 89
Rough cast glass, 75–6
Rubber tiles, 101

S

Sanitary fittings, 166–77
Screws, 121–3
Scrim, 113–4
Sealants, 31–3
Service pipe, 154–5, 157, 185–6
Shelving, 118–9
Shops – means of escape, 243,
    247–51
Showers, 170, 173
Single stack system, 176–7
Sinks, 172, 174
Skirtings, 116–7
Skylights, 88
Sliding doors, 134, 138–40
Smoke, 205, 234–5
Sound insulation, 191–7
    Building Regulations, 194
    definition of sound, 191–2
    external noise, 194, 197
    floors, 196
    sources of noise, 193
    walls, 195
Steel casements, 71–4
Steel pipes, 158, 160
Storey height cladding panels, 13–4,
    16
Stud partitions, 94–5
Surface resistances, 200
Suspended ceilings, 137, 142–6

T

Thermal insulation, 198–203
    Building Regulations, 199, 201
    conduction, 198
    convection, 198
    insulating materials, 200, 202–3
    radiation, 198
    roofs, 201
    surface resistances, 200
    thermal conductivity, 199
    thermal resistance, 199
    thermal resistivity, 199
    'U' values, 200–1
Thermoplastic tiles, 100–1
Tile hanging, 3–6
Timber infill panel, 20
Timber boards, 103
Timber claddings, 4, 7
Timber sheet flooring, 105
Timber strip, 105–6
Translucent roofing sheets, 89
Triangle of fire, 205
Two pipe system, 175, 177

U

'U' values, 200–1
Undersill cladding panel, 13, 15
Unprotected areas, 220, 230–3
Unprotected zone, 247
UPVC pipes, 158

V

Ventilation, 67
Ventilation of rooms, 68, 78–9
Ventilator, 69–70, 72
Vent pipes, 175–6
Vortex, 260

W

Wallpaper, 130–1
Wash basins, 168, 170–1
Water closets, 167–9
Water cylinders, 154, 157, 162–4
Water main, 153–5
Water service, 153–5
Water tanks, 162
Weathering steels, 149
Wind bracing, 261–2
Wind pressures, 258–62
Windows, 67–85
    bay, 79, 81–2
    Building Regulations, 67–8,
      78–80
    cleaning, 47–8
    double hung sash, 83–5
    furniture, 126–7
    modified casement, 70
    pivot, 85
    standard casement, 68, 71
    steel casement, 71–4
    traditional casement, 68–9
Wood blocks, 105–6
Wood screws, 121–3